BRITAIN TODAY AND TOMORROW

Trevor Beeson, a canon of Westminster, has become one of the most experienced and widely read commentators on religious affairs in Britain and Europe. From 1963 to 1965 he was editor of *Parish and People*, the journal of the Anglican renewal movement, and from 1965 to 1970 editor of the ecumenical fortnightly *New Christian*. Since 1970 he has been the European correspondent of the Chicago-based weekly *The Christian Century*, and has travelled widely in Europe and the United States. He is a frequent broadcaster and writes regularly for *The Guardian*.

Canon Beeson is the author of *Discretion and Valour*, a survey of religious conditions in Russia and Eastern Europe published for the British Council of Churches in 1974, and his other books include *New Area Mission*, *Worship in a United Church*, *An Eye for an Ear*, and *The Church of England in Crisis*.

TREVOR BEESON

BRITAIN
TODAY AND TOMORROW

COLLINS

Fount Paperbacks

First published in Fount Paperbacks in 1978

© The British Council of Churches 1978

Made and printed in Great Britain by
William Collins Sons and Co. Ltd, Glasgow

CONTENTS

PREFACE

This book is the work of many hands. Although the British Council of Churches' 'Britain Today and Tomorrow' project started uncertainly, and always lacked adequate resources, it eventually attracted the collaboration of a considerable number of Christians and others, who gave generously of their time and expertise to the study of the major issues included in the project.

The result of their efforts, extending over eighteen months, eventually appeared as a daunting mountain of reports and documents, the altitude of which was increased further by the addition of a number of reports on related subjects published by the BCC before and during the project itself. It soon became clear to all concerned that the scale and form of this material was quite unsuitable for sharing with the wider Christian community, and with the British public at large. Thus, in a moment of uncharacteristic bravery (or was it weakness?), I accepted the BCC's invitation to turn their mountain into a molehill of a book.

It would be much less than honest to pretend that this was an easy task. But I was allowed complete freedom to select, order, edit and comment upon the material as I considered appropriate. Those who had sight of the original mountain will be aware that I have been ruthless in its reduction, and that much valuable material has been lost in the process. I hope, however, that they will recognize its original contours and may conceivably see its form a little more clearly.

Inasmuch as the choice and presentation of the material is in itself the expression of a personal viewpoint, responsibility for this book is mine alone. In no sense does it represent the official views of the British Council of Churches. But it is the result of a great corporate effort by people of varied backgrounds and skills, who have associated themselves with the BCC, and it is offered in this form in the hope, and with the prayer, that it may stimulate further thought—and much action—as the 'Britain Today and Tomorrow' project moves into its next phase.

Westminster Abbey
25 February 1978   TREVOR BEESON

INTRODUCTION

Have the British churches anything of significance to say
to the British people in their present predicament? This
question presupposes a number of beliefs and evaluations
which are open to debate, but it can hardly be disputed
that British society is now in considerable disarray, and
that the nations comprising the United Kingdom are at
some kind of turning point in their long and varied history.

The symptoms of disorder and change were evident long
before the economic crises of the 1970s gave them dramatic
form, and some of their causes can be traced to the early
years of the present century. But the effects of the Second
World War were decisive. It was indeed a great victory for
British courage and a mighty deliverance for which to be
profoundly thankful. Yet that war could not have been won
by British arms alone, and the end result was not entirely
different from defeat. The nation was left exhausted, lum-
bered with an industrial and economic system too inflexible
to meet new challenges, bound by a social order based on
outmoded concepts of society, deprived of the empire which
had previously given it a leading position in world affairs
as well as cheap supplies of primary products, and—perhaps
most serious of all—reduced to grave uncertainty concerning its future role in the changed international order.

Seen against this background, the social reforms which
led to the creation of the Welfare State in the immediate
post-war years now seem to be little more than the valiant
attempt of desperate people to scratch the surface of a
massive and unprecedented problem, political, economic
and psychological. The need to establish a new base for
the creation of wealth went unrecognized for another
quarter of a century. Until the Suez débâcle, few British
people were aware that their country had ceased to be a
major world power and needed to make appropriate ad-

justments in its relations with the rest of the international community. Within the United Kingdom itself periodic doses of mild socialism created the illusion that great changes were taking place in the distribution of power and wealth, but it was no more than an illusion since political power remained concentrated in few—even if different—hands and was in any case subject to a capitalist economic order that acknowledged no accountability to society as a whole. Most of the poor remained poor, and most of the rich remained rich. In the key area of education, the raising of the school-leaving age and the expansion of higher education concealed the fact that both private and public sectors were continuing to produce a highly privileged élite at the expense of the great mass of young people whose educational facilities were inadequate for their personal needs and for the requirements of an advanced twentieth-century society.

So the sad story is largely one of unwillingness—or inability—to change direction in a rapidly changing world. The area where change has been felt with considerable force has been in the breakdown of traditional patterns of morality and culture—creating much personal and social disorder. And the arrival in Britain of immigrants from New Commonwealth countries, invited here in the 1950s and 1960s to meet the acute labour shortage of that time, has exposed a deep racial prejudice which is divisive and dehumanizing. All of which constitutes a serious national malaise and is the cause of a good deal of depression—and some fear.

Yet Britain remains a country which many people still find agreeable to inhabit, and which millions of tourists regard as the most attractive and friendly among all nations. While industry and commerce have declined, music and the theatre have flourished; and no other broadcasting system in the world excels the B.B.C. Society exhibits an openness and integrity which seems more healthy than the 'respectable' conventions of former times. Minority groups are more widely tolerated. The chances of living and dying in abject poverty have been much reduced.

Women, though not yet fully emancipated, have secured some rights outside the kitchen.

The truth seems to be that there is in British society an instability which has dangerous possibilities—witness the revival of National Front fascism—as well as considerable potential for good. One Christian diagnosis and prescription is that Britain's present condition is due to a deep spiritual disorder and that the task of the churches is to convert individuals to that Christ-like way of life which is the cure for every ill. But, without denying the existence of an underlying spiritual disorder, the mainstream British churches now affirm that the spiritual cannot be separated from the material, and that it is impossible to influence individuals apart from their social setting. In the memorable words of Archbishop William Temple at the end of his influential wartime paperback *Christianity and Social Order*, 'If we have to choose between making men Christian and making the social order more Christian, we must choose the former. But there is no such antithesis.'

It was one of Temple's successors, Michael Ramsey, who, near the end of his tenure of the Archbishopric of Canterbury, and in his final presidential address to the British Council of Churches, challenged the British churches to take a more serious interest in the life of the nation as a whole. Acknowledging that the churches were quite proficient at dealing with personal ethics and matters of pastoral concern, Dr. Ramsey expressed his belief that the time had come for the Christian community to examine and evaluate the wider social, political and economic issues of the time. And his words fell on fertile soil, not simply because of the respect accorded to a distinguished Christian leader, but because of a growing feeling that if the churches had nothing to contribute to the discussions of Britain's future then the validity of the Christian Gospel itself would, not unreasonably, be called into question.

What, then, had the churches to say about a multiplicity of problems, the roots of which lay deep in the character of British society as it had evolved over the greater part of the twentieth century, and which had defied solution by some of the nation's most able statesmen, economists and social thinkers?

Some two-thirds of Temple's *Christianity and Social Order* was taken up with arguing the case for the Church's involvement in social and political questions—still a necessary task in 1942. Only the final thirty pages contained any specific proposals. Most of these were of a somewhat sweeping character, such as the nationalization of land, and state administration of the banks. The problems of what is now known as the Third World were not on Temple's agenda, nor indeed did he feel constrained to show any appreciation of the complex inter-relationship of his own proposals with many other elements in society.

The British churches no longer need to spend a great deal of their time arguing publicly for the right to speak about the principles of social and political affairs. As Temple was at pains to point out, it is the task of the churches not to find the solution to technical problems in these fields, but rather to enunciate the principles which ought to guide the thought and action of the experts. It is possible for legitimate differences of opinion to arise concerning the application of Christian principles, so it is never possible to speak of a 'Christian answer'. On the other hand, the churches are nowadays required—if they are to gain a hearing—to exhibit a reasonable amount of technical expertise concerning possible contemporary applications of the principles they enunciate—and to be aware that particular proposals almost always have repercussions elsewhere in the life of the nation, and often enough in other parts of the world as well. So it has not been easy to take up Temple's task in the 1970s.

As a result of the enthusiastic efforts of the Rev. Harry Morton, who had become General Secretary of the British Council of Churches a year before Archbishop Ramsey's influential presidential address, a scheme was put to the Executive Committee of the BCC at the end of 1974. The idea was for the churches to examine the British political, economic and social situation under the general theme of 'A Christian Hope for our Time'. This was presented to the

BCC Assembly in the spring of 1975 and appeared as an ambitious project. A two-pronged approach was proposed. Individuals and groups with the appropriate technical skills would examine the broad issues connected with a variety of national and international issues, while a considerable number of local groups would examine the problems on their own doorsteps. It was anticipated that the findings of the national and local groups would be conflated and prove to be significant in illuminating points of inter-dependence and tension. Additional staff would be recruited by the BCC to direct the project.

These proposals were, however, rejected by the Assembly on the grounds that they were too broad, too ambitious and too expensive. Something more modest was recommended, and with this in mind the members of the Assembly were each asked to consult three responsible lay Christians during the course of the summer, about the issues which seemed to them to be of primary concern to the future well-being of Britain. Fifty members carried out this assignment, so that by the time of the autumn Assembly a somewhat complicated catalogue of the opinions of 150 people had been assembled. These opinions were reported as presenting a picture of 'insecurity and anxiety verging on fear, disillusionment and tiredness bordering on hopelessness, perplexity and bewilderment leading to a sense of power-lessness'.

At this point the idea of tackling a number of national issues received an unexpected fillip from the action of Dr. Donald Coggan (Michael Ramsey's successor at Canterbury) and Dr. Stuart Blanch (the recently appointed Archbishop of York), who had a week earlier issued a 'Call to the Nation'. This 'call' invited the British people to consider the questions: 'What sort of a society do we want?' and 'What sort of people do we need to be in order to achieve it?' These questions were certainly apposite but their context was somewhat vague, and this prompted the BCC to go ahead with a project that would, among other things, help the churches and their members to think seriously about the kind of issues at which the archbishops seemed to be hinting. Thus the 'Britain Today and To-morrow' project was born.

No additional resources were voted to celebrate the birth or to encourage its growth. The Executive Committee selected what seemed to them to be the ten most important subjects brought to light by the summer survey. The various Divisions of the BCC undertook responsibility for some of them, the rest were farmed out to the social responsibility boards of member churches and other interested church bodies. Gradually, and with varying degrees of enthusiasm, the different groups set to work on their subjects. The lack of a full-time director to oversee what turned out to be a large and complicated operation soon appeared as a serious weakness. The Rev. Andrew Morton, Social Responsibility Secretary, served throughout as project co-ordinator in addition to his normal duties. This arrangement worked, but only just. Moreover, there was tension between those who believed in the traditional approach of intellectual analysis and discussion, and those who felt that the best way forward was through involvement in specific problems and experiments in particular localities.

In the event, the traditional method won most support and the consequences became apparent in the autumn of 1977 when the delegates attending a special BCC Assembly, arranged for the end of November at the Swanwick Conference Centre in Derbyshire, received a large parcel of paper—the reports of the Working Parties. It was clear that a very considerable amount of work had been under-taken by a large number of people during the previous eighteen months. It was equally clear that the Swanwick Assembly would find it quite impossible to digest and seriously debate such a formidable amount of material.

Of the material itself—which has provided the basis of this book—three things may be said. The first is that the Working Party reports are much stronger on analysis than they are on prescription. This is explicable in terms of lack of time or, more likely, lack of clear insight regarding possible solutions of the difficult problems under con-sideration. The second is that they vary considerably in approach and quality. And, thirdly, the whole project suffers greatly from the lack of a coherent intellectual and theological framework to provide the basis for consistent judgement and an over-arching vision and unity.

None the less, the progress of the project thus far—held together by a shoestring budget—is no mean achievement, and the fact that it has actually been embarked upon is not without significance. At a time when the British churches are themselves caught up in the national malaise and have been driven by economic and identity problems into greater introversion than is customary, it may be regarded as a sign of hope that a fairly considerable number of church leaders—lay and clerical—have given sustained attention to most of the major problems facing the nation as a whole. Moreover, they have insisted on viewing these problems in a world perspective and at all times related them to their insights into the nature of the Christian Gospel.

These insights have driven them firmly in the direction of change, and aligned them with what may, at the risk of misunderstanding, be described as the progressive forces in society. The Working Party reports may not be radical enough for all their readers, but none of them is the work of reactionary backwoodsmen. Change is, wherever possible, welcomed as a friend and never, simply, as an enemy to be resisted. There is consistent concern about the persistence of the old inequalities of power in society and the emergence of some new ones. The relationship between poverty and powerlessness is clearly recognized, and positive steps are proposed for the reduction of both. The current problem of unemployment is seen as an expression of a much wider and deeper problem at the heart of industrial society, raising profound questions about the place of work and leisure in human life. The growth of violence in modern society is seen as a matter for anxiety, but constructive proposals are advanced for dealing with its manifestations and causes. Recent trends in education are welcomed but subjected to critical scrutiny, with particular anxiety about the effects of large schools on the already underprivileged. Racism in all its forms is denounced as a major evil in British society and there is a serious analysis of its causes and effects. Britain's changed role in the world is discussed, and the limitations and possibilities inherent in this role are honestly faced. A strong plea is made for support of the New International Economic Order, with its possibilities for redressing the imbalance between the rich and poor nations of the world.

Throughout the analysis of these difficult—often painful —issues the note of hope is never absent. The original title of the project, 'Christian Hope for our Time', has proved the right one. Never is despair allowed to dim the vision of the world as God's world, or weaken the conviction that supernatural resources are available to deal with the most intractable of problems. Where are these resources to be found? Within the corporate and disciplined life of the community of faith, of course; but equally within a disciplined and corporate grappling with the realities of a world which certainly bears the wounds of sin but also reflects the glory of its Creator. The 'Britain Today and Tomorrow' project is never likely to produce any magic remedies for the ills caused by human frailty and folly. But the vision of a new heaven and a new earth remains, and with the vision an imperative to Christian obedience in order that the future may be anticipated in the present.

Herein lies an unresolved tension. The Christian vision projects a new, humane, loving and sacrificial society— far removed in character from the present world order. How are the two to be brought closer together? Through the dramatic, and almost certainly violent, overthrowing of the existing forms of society? Or through the gradual and steady transformation of existing institutions? It should occasion no surprise that a representative group of British church leaders and their advisers should, in the year 1977, opt for the second, gradualist, course. But there are other Christians in Britain, as elsewhere, who believe that a far more impatient approach is now necessary and that it is the task of the churches, in word and deed, to work with prophetic zeal for a new world order which approximates far more closely to the divine vision.

The challenge of this second approach has hardly been heard in the 'Britain Today and Tomorrow' project so far. It is therefore of the greatest importance that its voice should be raised as the project moves into its next phase of practical proposition and local action. Crucial to this next phase will be a high degree of frankness and clarity concerning the kind of society that might be expected to result from the implementation of a significant number of the proposals contained in the Working Party reports. Many of these appear to involve a good deal of state intervention and a level of national planning not previously experienced in Britain. Is this acceptable? How can it be achieved in a democratic society? And at what cost to personal freedom?

Conflict may well result from serious discussion of these and other related questions. But conflict should not be permitted to divide: for the clearest message to be found in the pages that follow is that the different outlooks and opinions and approaches to life which characterize life in Britain today are certain to be there tomorrow. And it may well be the primary task of the British churches to show how this new pluralism can be shared in a single community of love, and through the interaction of a variety of insights and needs help to create a new and more humane —and therefore more Christian—social order.

1. MODESTY IN THE GLOBAL VILLAGE

'New York 3½ hours. Bahrain 3½ hours. Singapore 9½ hours. Small World!' Thus announces the British Airways advertisement for supersonic Concorde; at the same time offering a shorthand outline of the rapidly-changing world in which the British people are struggling to maintain their balance. New York—still the chief city of the most powerful nation the world has ever known. Bahrain—a staging-post for the Middle East, whose oil-rich Arab states have shaken the economies of the Western world. Singapore —the gateway to the Far East where poor, developing nations live under the shadows of an aggressively capitalist Japan and the rumbling giant of Communist China. All of which seems no more than a stone's throw from London Airport: thanks to Concorde—itself a miracle of technological achievement, but at the same time a monument to massive financial miscalculation, a constant threat to the human environment, and, needless to say, available only to the rich minority who can afford to buy its highly-priced tickets.

Faced with such startling evidence of an ever-shrinking world, and of the inter-relatedness of the opportunities and problems that now face humanity as a whole, it is reasonable to suppose that the citizens of the small islands off the north-west coast of Europe are now viewing their own problems and responsibilities in global terms. Dramatic television pictures of President Sadat in Jerusalem, and of rioting in South African townships, bring highly significant developments in world affairs to the fireside.

Yet the British remain as insular as ever, and there is evidence that Little Englanditis is more prevalent today than it was a century ago—long before Concorde and television were dreamt of. There are several reasons for this. The inhabitants of a small group of islands, who have for many centuries been separated, by politics, culture and religion, from even their nearest neighbours, do not find it easy to move into the new 'global village' where the old securities are replaced by unfamiliar boundaries, ideas and neighbours. The liquidation of the former British Empire has undoubtedly reduced the sense of involvement in and responsibility for considerable territories in Africa, Asia, North America and the Pacific. Deplorable though it now seems in this post-colonial era—deplorable as it was, in fact, at the time—the pink patches on maps and globes were regarded as no more than extensions or outposts of the British Isles. Yet the jingoistic celebration of Empire Day provided an older generation of British people with a world view which, regrettably, is not evoked by the more enlightened Commonwealth Day observance.

The social and economic problems which have been a permanent feature of the British landscape throughout the post-World War II era, and have been experienced as a continuation of the dire threat to security posited by that war, have also encouraged a high level of introversion. Those who are struggling to survive—or at least believe they are so struggling—are not easily tempted to look beyond their own barricades, and post-war politicians have quickly discovered that there are few votes in 'foreign affairs'. Another factor militating against a global vision—one frequently overlooked, or at least underestimated—is the sheer complexity of the Concorde world. The appearance of every member of the human race on my own doorstep, and the requirement that we shall all purchase our food from the same supermarket, share the same energy supply, and open a joint account at the same bank, may offer endless scope for good neighbourliness, but it has certainly made life much more complicated for everyone. So complicated, in fact, that even the best brains in this new community are confused to the point of utter impotence when the simplest problems arise. Small wonder, then, that Mr. Average Citizen sometimes succumbs to the temptation to concentrate on tilling his own garden, and when faced with television pictures of disastrous Indian floods responds by uncorking another bottle of whisky.

Any attempt to examine Britain in her world setting must take account of these formidable obstacles in the public mind; otherwise it is bound to fail. But the attempt must be made, since—like it or not—Britain is part of the global village. The attitudes and actions of British people have repercussions throughout the world, and the 1973/74 oil crisis is no more than a dramatic example of the way in which Britain is affected by decisions taken daily in other parts of the world. Hence the decision that the study of 'Britain Today and Tomorrow' could only be conducted in the context of a serious examination of Britain's place in the world as a whole.

The churches are, as it happens, well placed to carry out such an examination. For one thing, their Christian faith is a universalist faith. The Christian God is no local deity, but one who is believed to be the creator and redeemer of the whole human race. The Christian faith is intensely personal, yet what is true for one human being is true for all. The concept of the entire human race as a universal brotherhood lies at the centre of the Gospel. Therefore the churches have a basic framework of belief within which to see the whole world, and also a powerful imperative for avoiding the snares of parochialism—though they do not always manage to do so.

It is also the case that this universalist faith and the missionary endeavours which have flowed from it have given the churches a deep involvement in the life of nations far from the shores of Britain, and an unrivalled network of information and experience concerning the circumstances, outlooks and aspirations of the ordinary people of these nations. The story of the British churches' missionary enterprise is often too close to that of British colonial expansion to be comfortable, and, though the plea from some quarters for a missionary 'moratorium' has not been fully heeded, the reasons for it are well understood in the headquarters of the British missionary societies. Yet it is to the headquarters of these societies, and best of all to their missionaries in the field, that those who wish to know what is really happening in other continents are wise to turn.

Africa: The Re-emerging Continent

It would be perverse to suggest that the colonization of Africa by Britain and other European nations in the nineteenth century did not bring benefits to many African people as well as to their colonial masters—from whom they have yet to be completely liberated. But the price of these benefits has been extremely high: far in excess of the indignities normally suffered by those subjected to foreign rule. And the most costly item on the account has been the destruction, or at least the repression, of African culture in its many different forms.

There remains in Britain a common belief—as widespread inside as outside the churches—that prior to the 'discovery' of the African continent by traders and missionaries a century or so ago, the land was covered by thick darkness and ruled by the violence of the primitive savage. Those brought up on the kind of school textbooks that circulated until comparatively recently may perhaps be forgiven for their ignorance of the fact that the so-called primitive life of an African tribe was an expression of true human community, with an integrity every bit as complete as that of the European nation-state. Likewise, only a small number of British people have been helped to see that, while African music, dancing, painting, customs and family life are very different from those experienced in Europe, yet each has its own authenticity.

Colonial policy involved the imposition on many African people of European methods and manners, and was therefore highly disruptive of the basis of their corporate and personal life. European education, for example —normally regarded as a great gift to Africa—involved, and continues to involve, the destruction of an African's cultural roots: the way in which skills are taught and the attitudes that accompany them are often quite alien to his deepest feelings and needs. There are more ways of brain-washing than those employed on the Gulag Archipelago. And, though it may seem a little hard to include in this category the heroic work of several generations of Christian missionaries, it is impossible to resist the conclusion that the propagation of European forms of Christianity was equally destructive of an authentic way of life, and may well have done more harm than good.

It is from alien forms of culture, as well as from alien rule, that the African continent is now emerging. Hence the note of self-affirmation, 'I am an African', sounded in many keys and increasingly expressed, not simply in protest against the past colonial oppression, but in the flowering of music, poetry, drama and painting in direct continuity with Africa's past. Here is a real liberation, and much from which sensitive European eyes and ears can benefit.

But quite apart from the task of bringing to an end colonial rule in Rhodesia and South Africa, the African people face a number of other serious problems. They are anxious to throw off the alien culture imposed during the colonial era, yet during that era they learned to enjoy many of the products of Western technology—consumer goods, medical techniques and so on. Can African culture and Western technology co-exist? If not, which is the more important to the young African? Again, there are un-resolved problems of African nationalism. The thirty-seven African states that belong to the United Nations Organization form a significant bloc in the world political arena, but the boundaries of many of them are quite artificial. They were created in an arbitrary fashion by white men and often bear little relation to traditional loyalties and community roots. The struggle for independence has helped to give them a new nationalism, but this will almost certainly prove to be too negative a basis for a true national identity, and the authoritarianism of some of the new African states is to be seen as an attempt to hold together groups of people whose roots and loyalties lie elsewhere.

Looming over these post-colonial problems is the ever-present nightmare of poverty and starvation, for most of the new African states are still in the early stages of development and are particularly vulnerable to natural disasters, especially drought. It is also the case that, having noticed European life styles during the colonial era, they have rising expectations and are drawn to the towns, in the vain hope that their streets will be paved with gold. Once more, attempts to meet these expectations tend to clash with traditional African methods of work and organization; and, as in other parts of the world, decisions are needed about appropriate technology and life style.

These are some of the main issues facing Britain's African neighbours. In the small Concorde world, it would be totally unrealistic to suppose that Britain will not be affected by the way in which these issues are resolved. And in view of her past relations with Africa, which have included the wholesale exploitation (some would say theft) of Africa's resources, it cannot be denied that Britain has considerable responsibility for assisting some African states in the solution of their problems—not least in the sphere of development.

Which is not to suggest that the people of Africa are looking North for a further dose of British paternalism. Quite apart from the unpleasant memories of the old colonial era, the more recent attitudes of successive British governments to the white oppressors of Rhodesia, Namibia and South Africa have done nothing to enhance the reputation of Britain in African eyes. Few Africans believe that Britain would have stood idly by had the Rhodesian UDI of 1965 been made by black leaders, or that effective sanctions would not have been applied later, or that white 'freedom fighters' would not have been treated as heroes. Again, Africans ask, why are British people allowed to migrate to South Africa, where they help to bolster white supremacy and take jobs for which African nationals ought to be trained? And why are British companies still allowed to invest in South Africa where they reap large profits from exploited Africans? And why has Britain resisted United Nations attempts to impose a mandatory arms embargo on South Africa? Britain stands under the judgement of these, and related, questions and, though it is too late in the day for her reputation to be redeemed, there still seems to be time for Britain to align herself completely with those who are struggling for justice and liberation.

Asia: Revolutionary and Religious

Most of Africa's contemporary problems are present also in Asia, though it is even more difficult to generalize about a continent that provides a home for more than half the human race and contains cultures and régimes as varied as those of China and the Philippines, Bangladesh and Japan, Indonesia and Singapore. But, with the exception of Japan and her empire, virtually all the Asian nations have, in the post-war era, emerged from prolonged periods of colonialism or semi-colonialism in which they were dominated by Western influence and power. Even China, which escaped military conquest, was under Western domination. As in the case of Africa, the effect was to repress, and therefore interrupt, cultural and political traditions going back through centuries or even millennia of history. Most of the 'new' Asian nations must therefore be regarded as re-emergent rather than emergent. Another effect of Western colonialism was the maintenance of economic power in the hands of the few, which ensured that throughout Asia a basically feudal form of society survived into the middle of the twentieth century. This has presented great problems for new Asian governments seeking to meet the demands of the people for freedom and social justice.

When these governments came to power in the late 1940s they soon recognized that education was one of the most urgent priorities. Apart from Japan and her former empire in Korea and Taiwan, the mass of Asia's people were illiterate. Hence the setting up of massive educational programmes, which have transformed the situation in most countries, especially among the younger generation. Yet the inherited Western methods of education have been ill-suited to the needs of most of the people. The competitive element has produced considerable strain, an ever-increasing pool of educational 'failures', and the reward for those successful enough to gain a university degree is often unemployment or below-capacity employment. In many places attempts are now being made to provide a less academically-orientated form of education, which will equip young people with the rural and agricultural skills which are appropriate for the mainstream of Asian life. Here the influence of Gandhi and his followers, with their emphasis on village crafts and learning, is important, and the most significant and sustained break with Western methods has taken place in China where the emphasis is on social and political, rather than academic, objectives, with a career in rural and frontier areas regarded as more important than a plum job in a city.

Closely related to these problems and attempted solutions is the quest for cultural and national identity. After the years of Western dominance, the new Asian governments have tried to encourage a resurgence of national culture as an expression of the aspirations of the people and also as an aid to national unity. This has taken various forms. In Burma and Pakistan the governments have identified themselves with the dominant religion of the people. India has taken a neutral stance in respect of religion but made a conscious effort to encourage the growth of a distinctive Indian culture. Japan, Singapore and Taiwan had adopted a secular approach, while the Communist governments of China, North Korea and Vietnam have deliberately rejected all religion and all ancient customs in an attempt to create a new cultural pattern. It is too early to judge how successful and permanent any of these developments are likely to be, and it is important to remember that in most Asian countries there are minority groups, as well as large and powerful immigrant communities. Asia is in considerable turmoil and, though the distinctive Eastern approach to life is unlikely to change profoundly, its forms of expression seem certain to become increasingly varied.

But the most serious issue of all, as in Africa, involves the provision of adequate food, clothing and shelter for the mass of the people. Most of the world's poor are located in Asia and, with the exception of certain parts of South East Asia, there is little undeveloped land available for additional food production. Better agricultural methods will improve the output of food in most countries, while the reform of unjust land tenure systems could lead to a fairer distribution of what is produced. Yet the birth-rate in most Asian countries is three or four times higher than in the developed Western world, and it is hard to see how the problems associated with poverty can be solved while the balance between population increase and potential food resources remains so unequal. Some increase in wealth is certainly possible in the industrial and commercial fields but, with the notable exception of Japan, most Asian countries are victims of the protective policies of the rich Western nations who are afraid of the competitive power of cheap-labour production lines. In this respect, the movement of some multi-national corporations into Taiwan and South Korea, in order to exploit cheap labour and syphon increased profits elsewhere, seems unlikely to improve the lot of ordinary workers in either East or West.

It is clear from this necessarily brief outline of the Asian scene that the governments of the Far East are in the main faced with the most appalling problems, and it is not surprising that the difficulties of framing political structures capable of dealing with the challenges of the post-colonial era have proved insuperable. Foreign wars, in Korea and Vietnam, have not helped but there have been many external and civil wars in other parts of Asia, and even in India, where the progress towards parliamentary democracy has been greatest, signs of repression and dictatorship have not been entirely absent. It is reasonable, though obviously regrettable, to believe that Asia will continue to be an area of instability for some time to come, and also necessary to acknowledge that Britain, in the company of other Western nations, bears some responsibility for the inheritance that makes this instability and its consequent suffering inevitable. No one should be surprised that many in Asia are hostile to British policy—present as well as past.

In these circumstances it may well appear that Britain—beset with her own domestic problems and no longer wielding imperial power—can do little to assist the Asian nations as they struggle for survival in the face of tremendous odds. Certainly it would be foolish to over-estimate Britain's ability and influence. But attitudes to Asian immigrants arriving in Britain in search of a new way of life are not unimportant. Neither are decisions about the future of the British textile industry and the activities of multi-national corporations. Above all, a more far-sighted approach to trade and aid issues would contribute something significant to the life and death struggle now taking place in what has, in the past, been one of the most creative areas of human development.

The Middle East: Oil and Instability

The modernization or Westernization of the Arab world, which is now virtually complete, can be traced back to the early years of the nineteenth century, and probably owes more to Arab aspirations than to the deliberate imposition of European values and customs by the British, French and Italian rulers. Indeed, whereas some influential Arab leaders of the nineteenth and early twentieth century sought to introduce their people to the 'benefits' of the Western way of life, British rulers, like Kitchener, were careful to see that the customs and religious feelings of the Arab people were respected and as far as possible maintained. But the powerful European presence in the Middle East soon began to dominate a tired indigenous culture, and today Western values, particularly in the economic sphere and in industrialism, are taken for granted by all but a small minority. This minority, which expresses itself through the Muslim Brotherhood Movement and a number of revolutionary socialist movements, is aware of a serious vacuum in the Arab consciousness, and objects to many of the changes which have taken place as a result of Western influence. But its numbers are small.

Unlike the desperate situation in most of her former colonial or neo-colonial territories, there is of course no question of Britain recognizing an economic obligation to any of the nations of the Middle East. Indeed, the boot is on the other foot, since Britain will for some years remain dependent upon Arab oil, and the massive revenues accumulated by the oil exporting countries since 1974 have given them a dominating position in the world economy. Here it may be noted that these countries have recognized a sense of obligation to the poorer nations of the Third World and are now contributing to their aid a far higher proportion of their Gross National Product than are the industrialized societies of the West. But the oil exporting countries are aware that if the Western world finds itself too dependent on Arab oil, and is asked to pay prices for it that threaten Western economic stability, the Middle East may be subject to economic or even military pressures that could amount to recolonization. There is therefore a mutual interest in maintaining good trading relations between the Western world and the Middle East.

Of more immediate concern is the securing of political stability in the Middle East. The Arab world is itself sharply divided, not least in its approach to the state of Israel, and in spite of the dramatic gesture of President Sadat of Egypt in travelling to Israel in November 1977 to promote peace between Arab and Jew, the path to reconciliation in the Middle East remains narrow and hazardous. This is territory on which the super-powers of West and East need to walk with special delicacy.

Eastern Europe and Human Rights

Although Eastern Europe still appears in Western eyes as

a monolithic bloc, there is a growing awareness in Britain and elsewhere of differences within the Warsaw Pact nations and of changes of policy being initiated from time to time. These should not be exaggerated, but many readers of an earlier report sponsored by the BCC[1] were, it seems, astonished to discover the extent to which religious belief and practice is preserved in countries like Poland and Romania—or even, for that matter, in the Soviet Union itself.

Even so, the denial of human rights—most especially in the expression of political and social dissent—is widespread in all parts of Eastern Europe and .. matter for legitimate concern. At this point the Helsinki Agreement, which included a commitment to the upholding of basic human rights within a document designed to stabilize European frontiers, is highly significant. But there is as yet little sign that it will lead to the wholesale release of dissident prisoners in the U.S.S.R. and, though President Carter's public plea on their behalf was morally admirable, it may well have been diplomatically inopportune. Moreover, Western governments are finding themselves charged with isolating political and religious freedom from economic freedom, and are asked to explain the grounds on which a country like Britain, with $1\frac{1}{2}$ million unemployed, a poor record of racial toleration, and self-confessed use of torture in Northern Ireland, is able to complain about the violation of human rights in, say, the Soviet Union. Like charity, human rights begin—even if they do not end—at home.

Equally important is the need to resist the temptation to use the human rights issue as a stick for beating the Soviet Union and reviving 'cold war' attitudes on both sides. The stabilization of Soviet hegemony over the whole of Eastern Europe is undoubtedly unwelcome to the Western mind, and *détente* has its limitations for those who place a high value on human freedom, but the feasible alternatives are much less attractive, and the importance of maintaining an atmosphere in which SALT talks or their equivalent are possible cannot be over-estimated.

[1] Trevor Beeson, *Discretion and Valour*, Fontana/Fount (1974).

In the West it is more or less taken for granted that NATO could not possibly contemplate launching a war of aggression. This is far from self-evident to governments and peoples in Eastern Europe. In the Soviet Union the non-aggressive nature of Soviet policy is generally accepted as the genuine commitment of the leadership, in contrast to a great deal of ideological propaganda which is not. And if the Soviet leaders were committed to Marxist doctrine they would be content simply to wait for the capitalist nations to collapse one by one, without interference. But they are no longer convinced of the truth of this doctrine and are far more conscious of the fact that traditionally their nation has been attacked from the West. The Swedes, the Poles, the French and the Germans (twice in the present century) have invaded Russia at various times, causing appalling havoc and loss of life. So now, to protect the soil sacred to all Russia, the whole of the rest of the Soviet Union and a cordon of buffer states in Eastern Europe has been created and must be maintained at all costs. Look at a map designed with Moscow at the central point, and Russian feelings of being threatened become understandable. Neither does the growth of so-called Euro-Communism in the West offer the Russians any additional sense of security, since the Communist Parties in Italy and France seem determined to develop an independent identity and ethos.

An attempt to see the situation from the Russian point of view implies no approval for the monstrous totalitarian régime which dominates Eastern Europe. And, while Britain is prepared to enjoy whatever protection the American nuclear umbrella affords, it is difficult to see how any British government can contemplate reneging on its NATO commitments. Opportunities for supporting individual dissidents in the Soviet Union and elsewhere, and for calling attention to their plight, seem likely to remain and at the moment are some way from being fully exploited. But the situation in the Soviet Union and the rest of Eastern Europe is a little more fluid than it has been for some time. It would be utterly unrealistic to anticipate the advent of liberal democracy within the foreseeable future, but anything which promotes the flow of new ideas into the Soviet bloc is worth encouraging. Nor should all the traffic be in one direction. The Jugoslavian experiments in self-management could have something to teach the West about the development of industrial democracy and the East German Protestant Church's attitude of 'critical solidarity' with its Marxist government might well be illuminating for church/state relations in Britain.

Western Europe: What Kind of Community?

Although the founding fathers of the European Economic Community had the vision of a full Western European Union, akin to the United States of America, the main driving force behind the development of the EEC, since the Treaty of Rome was signed in 1957, has been economic. And even though there was much elevated talk about the importance of Britain sharing more fully in the life of an integrated Europe at the time of the 1975 Referendum, the chief bait laid before the British voter consisted of the economic benefits which it was believed would accrue from Britain's access to wider European markets. It is, therefore, not altogether surprising that the serious economic problems which have afflicted Britain in the last few years have led to a certain amount of disenchantment. Superficially, at least, it seems that Britain's membership of the EEC has done no more than open the doors to aggressive German, French and Italian salesmen and, at the same time, raise the price of certain important food items to levels never previously dreamed of in the United Kingdom.

This is how things look to many of those who voted for Britain's entry into the European Community. The reality is somewhat different. By the time Britain joined, the best years of European economic expansion were already over. In any event, the structural problems in Britain's economy —which partly explain why only limited penetration of the wider European markets has proved possible—were far too serious for an overnight cure. And there is little

13

reason to doubt that had Britain remained outside the EEC her present economic position would have been very much worse.

In spite of all the disappointments, Britain is not likely to withdraw from the EEC. All the major political parties are committed to remaining in membership, though the present Labour government has made it clear that the maintenance of national identity is considered to be of fundamental importance—a view shared by France and likely to be reinforced if Portugal, Spain and Greece are admitted to membership. What the EEC amounts to, therefore, is something midway between an alliance of the NATO type and the full Union of the original vision, with many problems unresolved and as many opportunities not yet fully exploited.

A Community in which hoped-for economic advantage has played such a significant part, and which achieved between the early 1950s and the present world recession a rate of economic growth unparalleled in the history of Europe, cannot be indifferent to the current economic disorder in which serious inequalities of growth, inflation rates and values of currency are placing great strain on the Community's systems. Throughout the EEC, unemployment—especially among young people—is at an unacceptably high level, and the migrant workers who provided a reservoir of cheap labour in the 1950s and '60s are suffering very badly.

None of which is likely to bring tears to the eyes of the people of the Third World who still regard the EEC as 'a rich man's club' and one of the major obstacles to the building of a world economic order based on justice. The Lomé Convention was in many ways a remarkable achievement—providing for £1,900 million of financial and technical aid to 46 African, Caribbean and Pacific countries in 1975/80, free access to the Community for most of the products of these countries, and some minimal guarantees that a basic price would be available for a range of their primary products. Agreement was also reached upon some generalized preference for all developing countries. Yet, in spite of all these arrangements, the Third World countries have been left to their own devices within the operation of market forces and now find themselves relatively even poorer than they were before the Lomé Convention was agreed. Moreover it became clear at the UNCTAD IV meeting in Nairobi in 1976 that the EEC members are themselves sharply divided about their responsibilities towards the Third World.

So, although the EEC is in one sense a most potent force for world peace—and presents a remarkable contrast with the divisions in Europe which had such tragic consequences until 1945—its economic power, actual and potential, offers a serious threat to the struggling developing nations; as indeed the development of its political cohesion could easily arouse anxiety in Eastern Europe and lead to a Europe permanently divided into two hostile camps.

Of more immediate concern, however, is the setting up of a directly elected European Parliament. This is—or at least could be—a highly significant development inasmuch as it will call for a much greater concern for Community affairs in every part of EEC territory and will introduce an element of democratic accountability which has hitherto been lacking. For far too long the EEC has been dominated by the Commission and Council of Ministers based in Brussels, but now the members of the European Parliament —of whom 81 out of 410 will be British—will be answerable to the 280 million citizen members of the Community for the broad policy it endeavours to carry out. Precisely how this vast organism will function, and become accountable in practice, remains to be seen. Obviously it has little appeal to those who believe that participation and accountability call for smaller, not larger, political units. And overhanging the entire EEC enterprise there remains the crucial question as to whether there is within the culture and spirituality of Western Europe sufficient interior unity to support institutions based on anything more ambitious than mutual self-interest.

The Christian Contribution

This, then, is part of the global village in which Britain is struggling to find a role and to deal with a number of urgent domestic problems. Only broad impressionistic pictures of the developing situations in Africa, Asia, the Middle East and Europe have been attempted. Not even an outline sketch has been offered of the distinctive societies of the United States of America and explosive Latin America. Britain's loyal and friendly neighbours in Canada and Australasia have been completely ignored. Yet a serious consideration of life in Britain today is bound to take account of the inter-relatedness of all these continents and nations. Many internal problems originate in places far removed from the scene of their chief effects, and are the consequence of decisions made at levels well beyond local influence, much less control. Equally, decisions about local issues in Britain can have far-reaching repercussions elsewhere on the globe. So, although it is impossible to hold in the mind a detailed anatomy of every country and continent, and the likely consequences of this or that local decision, it is absolutely essential to retain a broad perspective. For all but the youngest members of twentieth-century society, this generally calls for a major revolution in thinking, since the world of Concorde has become small very quickly.

For Britain the most difficult part of this revolution lies in recognizing that her influence in the world is now quite small. The possibility of Britain throwing her weight about in the world has gone for good. Modesty is now the order of the day, and in the British churches' consideration of international affairs this is generally recognized. It might also be added that in the allocation of resources for the study of international matters, the British churches are totally committed to the concept of modesty.

None the less, self-confidence has not been so thoroughly destroyed as to remove any idea of British influence in world affairs, or to absolve Britain from discharging certain important responsibilities within the international order. Indeed, a distinguished member of the staff of the World Council of Churches, Dr. Paul Abrecht, has gone so far as to say:

> As an ex-imperial power and also the home of constitutional democracy, as one of the creators of the industrial revolution, and also one of the founders of the modern welfare society, Britain is surely in a unique position to help our world.

The word 'unique' seems questionable here, and the degree to which Britain can help the world must obviously depend on the extent to which the world looks in this direction for assistance, but the need for serious thought about Britain's role in world affairs can hardly be disputed. It is at this point that the British churches are trying to be helpful, and the question immediately arises as to whether they have anything useful to contribute to the discussion.

Martin Conway, Secretary of the BCC's Division of Ecumenical Affairs, has argued that the Christian concern for world affairs has three facets. The first has to do with the quest for truth. Those whose responsibility it is to formulate national policies must obviously take account of the facts of the situations they are handling, and make use of the best available thinking. But in the modern world— and this is especially true of international affairs—there has to be a selection of facts and an evaluation of a mass of data. It is often difficult to see the wood for the trees. Hence any faith (stance, perspective or tradition) which claims a transcendental reference by which to see the full range of facts and opinions more openly and in the longer term, as does the Christian faith, deserves at least a hearing. Which is not to claim that Christians have some kind of 'hot-line' to all the right answers. Christian evidence needs to be evaluated like any other evidence, and in the final resort will be judged by its fruits. But amid the complexities and confusions of the present international scene, the kind of questions which Christians raise about ultimate values are far from being insignificant, and can be pressed without apology.

The second Christian contribution lies within the realm of ethics. Instinct and self-interest play as important a part in government policies as they do in personal decisions, but in civilized societies there is at least some recognition that these motivations must be channelled into some wider and long-term considerations if conflict is to be avoided. Unfortunately, it is normally no clearer to statesmen than it is to ordinary citizens where the channels should be directed, so once again any faith which claims a coherent understanding of what is appropriate for the common good deserves a hearing.

Rather more subtle, but no less important, is the question of mood and attitude. As in ordinary human conversation, the terms and tone of voice in which a government states its viewpoint are often more significant than the actual content of the utterance. Certainly a desire for collaboration or peaceful co-existence is rarely furthered by belligerent, self-justifying and self-aggrandizing postures and, although the realities of power cannot be ignored in a sinful world, the encouragement of honesty, reasonableness and even generosity is become more, not less, important if good relations are to be established and maintained among international neighbours. The Christian faith has always claimed an ability to change and mould human moods and attitudes, corporately as well as individually, and ought therefore to claim a hearing in the affairs of a nation which has Christian roots and whose leaders still claim to be motivated by broadly Christian principles. What has become very much clearer in recent years is that Christians can only make a contribution to the search for an adequate foreign policy if they are prepared to be involved with others in struggling through all the complexities and pressures of today's actual situation, and in imagining and weighing realistically the possibilities for tomorrow. Pious clichés and solemn pronouncements from ivory towers are worse than useless.

Into this involvement and struggle for a foreign policy that will, it is hoped, contribute to a more just and peaceful world, Christians carry a number of basic convictions. The first of these is that God is not only the creator and sustainer of the whole universe, but he has also acted in the life, death and resurrection of Jesus to ensure that his creation will ultimately fulfil the purpose he invested in it: a purpose summed up in the concept and experience of love. This conviction liberates the believer to accept that there is a meaning and purpose behind all human affairs and that the ultimate outcome of human life will be beneficent. Hence an ability to evaluate the transitory events of the present moment in a much broader context, and a confidence in the ultimate victory of good over evil. Since this victory will represent the triumph of love, there is more than a suggestion here that the long-term health of the human race will come more through the surrender of privilege and sovereignty than through seeking to acquire or retain these tempting morsels. There can of course be no general application of this basic conviction to the complex problems of foreign policy, but the introduction of qualities such as hope, purpose and humility into any discussion of human affairs can be liberating and creative.

Inseparable from Christian conviction concerning God's purpose for the world and his ultimate victory, is the belief that his purpose and victory are universal in their scope. They are for all peoples and nations; therefore all boundaries of nation, race, culture, sex and religion are provisional. The Church is meant to be a model and pioneer of what the creator intends for the human community as a whole. This means, among other things, that Christians can never restrict their interest and concern to one local segment of the human race, but must always look out upon the world as a whole and see others in terms of their potential promise as partners, fellow-sufferers and fellow-enrichers. All efforts to encourage human understanding and solidarity are, therefore, to be encouraged —including such modest enterprises as town-twinning, school exchanges, and holiday tours with local people. The

Gospel encourages us to take other people as seriously as we take ourselves, to go and see for ourselves what things are like for them, to enjoy taking on the burdens of solidarity because others are equally taking up solidarity with us.

All of which seems painless enough, until it is recognized that the interests of one people or nation are inherently different from, or even antagonistic to, those of another. International relations are normally closer to the ethos of the jungle than to that of the holiday camp, and in a sinful world the powers and pressures at work in this area of human life cannot be ignored. Christian ethics do not exclude the right kind of toughness in serious negotiation. Yet the universal character of the Christian vision provides an imperative towards collaboration between nations, rather than isolationism, and this not in terms of painful self-denial but in the conviction that individuals and groups become more truly themselves when they are open to others.

Christians have no special insights into the kind of international structures that might provide an adequate expression of the belief that the whole human race is meant to live in unity under God. Indeed, the fragmented character of the Christian Church itself, and the maintenance of ecclesiastical divisions over what appear to be matters of peripheral concern for the future of humanity, might appear to disqualify the churches from expressing any opinion on this matter. Dogmatism would certainly be quite out of place. Yet the experience of individual nations in uniting groups of people of differing backgrounds, interests and cultures, and moulding them into a community far richer than anything they knew when separated, does suggest that some form of world government will one day be essential. A shrinking world, with an interlocking system of dependence in human affairs, requires international supervision.

The problems involved in trying to unite Western Europe, and the thirty years of bickering in the United Nations, offer little encouragement for those whose sights are set on world government. And there is evidence that the development of larger units of government, and the remote control that seems their inevitable concomitant, is actually encouraging the revival of old forms of nationalism in various parts of the world. But these problems, which are to be anticipated when peoples and nations begin to pioneer uncharted territory, are a challenge rather than a deterrent to those who are possessed by the vision of the world as a city of universal justice and peace.

Underlying the Christian belief about the ultimate victory of God's will and purpose for the world, and the universality of his design, is the basic conviction that all human beings are created in the image of God and therefore deserve a dignity, a respect, and room to grow and act such that they can respond equally to him in love. In practical politics this means that Christians are committed to a quest for equality both within nations and between nations. The implications of this occupy a good deal of space in the remainder of this book, but, in the context of Britain's role in the world and decisions in the realm of foreign policy, two particular points need to be emphasized now. The first is that decisions about Britain's relations with the rest of the world ought to be recognized as matters of concern for the whole nation, and not left to a specialist élite. The British diplomatic service has a unique record of skill and devotion to duty and, although Britain's influence in world affairs is now modest, it is generally recognized that a significant British presence in the world's capitals ought to be maintained. Yet diplomats and Foreign Office officials can and do make mistakes, and in any event growth towards a more closely integrated world community calls for more than embassy cocktail parties. The meeting of a wide variety of people from different interest groups (trade unions, professional associations, local authorities, educational institutions and so on), to share insights and on occasion to work out common programmes of work, will play an increasingly important part in the development of international relations. Whether viewed in terms of opportunity or responsibility, the concept of equality is significant.

This is also the case when judgements are called for

concerning the conditions under which particular groups or nations might be expected to live. Within the unity of the human race there will always be wide variety, and it is no part of the Christian understanding of equality to deny this or to work for its reduction. Yet this can never be an excuse for the not-uncommon view that somehow it is natural for, say, Asians and Africans to live on a more restricted level than Europeans and Americans, and that it is right for white people to live more comfortably and wield more influence. Such a view is obviously unacceptable to Asians and Africans gathered around an international conference table; it cannot be expressed or implied by anyone who is working within the framework of the Christian view of the nature and dignity of every human being. There are implications here for race relations in Britain, where the presence of so many people of different colours, races and cultures offers a great opportunity for working out what a multi-racial, multi-cultural world community might look like, but where the mishandling of the situation has negative repercussions throughout the world. No responsible person will suggest that the bringing together of peoples of different races and cultures is simple and straightforward, but it is quite clear that unless decisions are derived from a conviction that human beings are equal, there is no possiblity of avoiding conflict.

Enough has been said to indicate that Christian beliefs are by no means irrelevant to the issues now facing the global village, and to the part that Britain might play in helping to resolve these issues in the best possible way. Which is not to say that religious belief ever offers an easy way forward or an escape from the task of grappling with life's painful realities. All—and it is a great deal—that the Christian believer can claim is that his faith provides a vision and a set of related values and attitudes that enable the struggle with reality to reach a more constructive and humane conclusion.

Not least among the realities which have to be faced is that of failure—individual failure and corporate failure—which not only causes suffering but also tends to destroy hope. It is at this point that Christian belief about forgiveness may be recognized as offering something significant to those involved in international affairs. Down the centuries Christians have known, and lived by the fact, that God's loving forgiveness is permanently available whatever our human failure, sin or guilt, and however half-hearted the repentance in which we ask for it. Hence Martin Conway's assertion: 'We need never feel stuck by the mess the world is in, let alone by a sense of guilt for our part in bringing that about, but can in repentance and forgiveness make a new start along a new way that corresponds more closely to God's will.'

It is not easy for politicians and statesmen to confess failure, nor for those they represent or confront to offer them forgiveness. Yet whenever this happens there arises a new freedom and with it the possibility of new beginnings. All of which calls for a high degree of mutual trust, and it may well be argued that it is precisely this lack of trust that lies behind most of the world's problems at the present moment. Yet if there is to be a real breakthrough in the areas of greatest human conflict some risks will have to be taken—calculated risks, no doubt—and among these risks Christians will want to give priority to an admission of Britain's failings in many areas of international concern, accompanied by a readiness to enter into discussions as to how a more adequate future can be secured for all. Only the readiness to admit failure provides the freedom in which a new start can be made.

God, the creator and sustainer of the universe, has acted through Jesus Christ to ensure that his will and purpose for the world will ultimately be fulfilled. His will and purpose are universal in their scope. Every human being is created in the image of God and therefore deserves dignity and respect. God's loving forgiveness is always available to individuals and groups. Here are some basic Christian beliefs which bear directly on the issues facing the British people as they seek an appropriate role in a rapidly changing world.

Yet these beliefs can be used or developed in a variety of

ways. They can, for instance, inform the minds and wills of those engaged in the work of patient diplomacy and negotiation. As opportunities arise in the various councils of the nations, so modifications can be made here and there to the existing international set-up. The results are unlikely to be dramatic but they may well reflect the conscientious efforts of Christian statesmen working within the existing economic and political structures. On the other hand, the same beliefs can lead to a far more radical approach to world problems. In the face of the acute suffering of some two-thirds of the world's people, who lack the basic necessities of life and are powerless to influence an international order which is loaded against them, the tactics of patient diplomacy may well seem an inappropriate expression of deep Christian convictions about equality, human dignity and the possibility of making a new start. The world situation is critical and calls for urgent and radical action to deal with a manifest evil.

Where do the British churches stand in this matter and how does their stance affect their attempts to influence government policy? In their official statements, the churches have been consistent in pleading the cause of the powerless and poor of the Third World. Their record is on the whole infinitely better than that of the major political parties, the trade unions and most other bodies concerned with world affairs. It is less certain that the main body of church members have identified with the views of their leaders, and to this extent a great deal of educational work still needs to be carried out in local churches.

Such work will become even more important when Christian thinkers begin to work out the implications for life in Britain of a better deal for the underprivileged in other parts of the world. The cost can hardly be small or the effects painless, since the resources of the earth are limited. It could well be that certain of the improvements in British society called for in other parts of this book are—in the short term at least—inconsistent with the churches' championing of the desperate citizens in other parts of the global village. Is this so? If it is, how are the British people to be won over to the sacrifices involved, and what degree of priority is to be accorded to the items in Britain's own social programme? Here is a major piece of work waiting to be tackled, and if the British churches are serious in their plea that the world should be seen whole, then they have a clear responsibility to consider the practical consequences of a widespread acceptance of their own outlook.

Not unrelated to this is the need for far greater emphasis on the fact that, since Britain is no longer a major world power, any creative influence she may have in the world will largely belong to the moral order. Clearly, attitudes and actions concerned with the poor and the oppressed reveal the quality of Britain's moral contribution to world affairs. So also does the way in which Britain orders her own domestic life; it is quite unrealistic to expect the rest of the world to listen attentively to a Britain whose internal affairs display qualities that no one can admire. Reform of Britain's own political, social and economic life is an essential precondition for an effective foreign policy in the world at large.

2. LADY BOUNTIFUL BOWS OUT

Setting Britain firmly in her international context, the 'Britain Today and Tomorrow' project produced a document of unusual cogency and expertise on 'World Justice and Britain's Future'.

It was largely the work of James Mark, for many years a senior Civil Servant in the Ministry of Overseas Development and a lay theologian who now shares in the joint editorship of the magazine *Theology*. But the paper was influenced by discussion with a wide circle of experts and, although the Working Party were unable to reach a consensus on the action demanded by the basic analysis, there was agreement on a few sentences which summed up their attitude to the broad issue and which they regarded as providing the only acceptable basis for the discussion of any of the important issues now facing the British people:

As a consequence of technological developments the interdependence of all parts of the globe has increased to the point where only the welfare of humanity as a whole—including even future generations—can be taken as the goal of the order to be established and the policies to be followed. The only acceptable goal is the welfare of all and as an integral part of it the welfare of the poor masses in the developing countries.

At the subsequent Swanwick 'Hearings' devoted to this document, a good deal of time was spent in preparing a resolution on the subject of a Common Fund, which had been proposed at the fourth United Nations Conference on Trade and Development in 1976 and which was at the time of the Swanwick Assembly under discussion by the official representatives of over a hundred rich and poor nations meeting in Geneva. The resolution, which was passed by the Assembly on 24 November and transmitted to the British government, read:

The Assembly
mindful of the concern about unemployment and inflation in developing and industrial countries alike, and
recalling its previous resolutions on world development, particularly that of April 1976 on UNCTAD IV which supported the proposals for a Common Fund,
urges Her Majesty's Government to accept the substance of the current proposal by the developing countries in the UNCTAD conference now meeting in Geneva in negotiations for a Common Fund for the stabilization of world commodity prices.

The Assembly
believing that the attitude currently identified with Britain, the United States and West Germany is a threat to world development and international co-operation,
calls on Her Majesty's Government to accept:

(a) that the Common Fund should have its own funds subscribed by consumer and producer governments, with the ability to initiate and fund international commodity agreements;

(b) that the government contributions called for from all countries of $1 billion paid in, and $1 billion on call, are small in relation to the rate of creation of international liquidity, and the benefits available to all from price stabilization;

(c) that the Common Fund should have built in facilities (sometimes called a second window) to assist weaker commodity producers to improve their position through diversification, productivity and marketing arrangements.

The Assembly
believing that the proposals by Britain and other countries for a Common Fund which is a minimal pooling of the funds of the independent commodity arrangements and which allows a credit facility to a commodity scheme of only one third of its own subscribed funds are inadequate,
is confident that within the framework proposed by the developing countries it is possible to make progress in world development, safeguarding the financial viability of the Common Fund, the legitimate interests both of the producer and consumer countries, while helping to stabilize commodity prices.

The Assembly
accepting that commodity stabilization and the Common Fund will not solve all the problems of international commodity trade, let

alone the problems of social justice and world development, is nevertheless aware that a failure in the present conference substantially to meet the constructive proposals to which over 100 developing countries are deeply committed will gravely prejudice co-operation in world trade.

Here the British churches were showing themselves concerned, not simply to make general statements about the need for greater justice in the ordering of world affairs, but—having received and considered expert advice—were ready to intervene in a world conference considering a specific topic and to advocate a policy known to be contrary to that of the British government. This intervention was no flash in the pan, for as long ago as 1966 a BCC Working Party had produced a notable report entitled *World Poverty and British Responsibility*, which was devoted to answering the question 'What can the British nation do to help poor countries struggling to develop themselves?' During the following decade the Working Party had kept a close watch on British efforts (or lack of them) in this direction. Moreover, through the work of its own Christian Aid department, which now raises almost £5 million annually for development aid, the BCC has earned the right to have its views on these matters taken seriously.

Even so, the Geneva conference broke up in disarray on 1 December because of a major disagreement between the rich and poor nations, with the representatives of the developing nations complaining bitterly that it was 'utterly futile' to continue the negotiations until the rich nations demonstrated the political will to make them succeed. The disagreement—knowledge of which had prompted the BCC resolution—centred on the unwillingness of the rich nations to allow the proposed Common Fund to become much more than a banking facility, whereas the poor nations hoped that it might be the creative agency for a variety of development projects. After the break-up of the conference, a statement issued by several of the small richer nations, including Norway, Sweden, the Netherlands and Finland, made it clear that they were willing to go much further to meet the requests of the Third World, but they had been unable to convince the hardliners—the United States, Japan, West Germany *and the United Kingdom.*

This sequence of events, all taking place within a matter of days, offers a graphic summary of the issues now facing the British nation as she seeks her own economic salvation in a world where the gap between rich and poor countries is becoming ever wider. During the last decade official development assistance from the Western countries and Japan has fallen from nearly 0.56 per cent of their gross national product to just over 0.3 per cent; in the U.K. the decline has been much the same. There has been a little progress towards making it easier for the poor countries to export their goods to the richer countries, and of course a few of the developing countries have benefited greatly from the increase in the price of oil. A handful of countries (Taiwan, South Korea, Singapore) have been developing strikingly fast for various unusual reasons. But the overall situation is depressing in the extreme for anyone who is concerned with justice, or indeed simply with the sanctity of human life. And church resolutions have so far done nothing to change it.

The Demand for Justice

The statistics of poverty and affluence have been quoted endlessly in recent years, and the television screen has brought the sight of starving men, women and children to those seated at the heavily-laden dining tables of the West. Yet what seems to be a combination of indifference, a feeling of helplessness, and an inability to face more than a certain amount of reality, has stood in the way of the growth of a widespread movement to change the situation. A Food and Agriculture Organization report in 1975 drew attention to the fact that the richer countries are now consuming twice as much (or more) animal protein as is desirable from a nutritional point of view. Thus the people of these countries are falling prey to what is described as 'the nutritional disease of abundance', and this helps to explain why diabetes, hypertension and ischemic heart diseases are responsible for the largest number of deaths and disabilities in developed countries. The same report discussed the close relationship between malnutrition and infant mortality in the poorer countries, and suggested that one half of child deaths (200 million) can be attributed to malnutrition. A UNICEF report, also published in 1975, estimated that over ten million children are in great danger of dying, and even if aid were provided immediately some million children would still die. Another ninety million are in such a frail state of health that they will not be able to withstand serious illness. Against the background of this devastating information, it has to be recorded that in November 1976 Britain's socialist government announced a cut of £50 million a year in its overseas aid programme, while maintaining domestic social benefits at their previous level.

In this situation the poorer nations are in no mood to ask for charity, and the basic question asked by the BCC's 1966 report is therefore no longer appropriate to the debate. The issue is seen by the Third World not in terms of the help they should be given, but of the justice they should claim. For they have discovered, during the last deca e, that the present international trading system is so heavily weighted against them that it is impossible for them to earn from trade the resources needed for development. Only structural changes in the way the international economy is run will meet their needs and offer them justice. Hence the bitterness that attended the breakdown of the Geneva conference—the first time the representatives of the developing countries have walked out of such a conference— because they believed that the rich nations were deliberately procrastinating. Having secured, often at considerable cost, their political independence in the post-World War II era, the developing countries now find themselves held in economic chains.

One of their most able and eloquent spokesmen has listed six ways in which the basic inequality and injustice of the present world economic order is displayed:

1. In the creation of international credit;
2. In the small fraction of the final price of their products that the developing countries receive;
3. In the protective wall which rich countries erect round their economies, restricting movements of goods, capital and people;
4. In the relations of the poor countries with the multi-national corporations, which 'reflect a fairly inequitable sharing of benefits';
5. In the small share of the poor countries in the economic decision-making of the world;
6. In the 'intellectual world and the mass media', especially in their subjection to 'concepts of development and value systems that were largely fashioned abroad'.

Which leads him to this conclusion:

> We must keep stressing, as often as we can, that the basic struggle is for equality of opportunity, not equality of income. We are not chasing the income levels of the rich nations. We do not wish to imitate their lifestyles. We are only suggesting that our societies must have a decent chance to develop, on an equal basis, without systematic discrimination against us, according to our own value systems, and in line with our own cultural traditions. We are not asking for a few more crumbs from the table of the rich. We are asking for a fair chance to make it on our own.[1]

At this point it is important to be clear, not only about possible ways of sharing the world's resources more fairly, but as to the carrying capacity of the earth itself. Given that the earth's surface is finite, what is the potential for increasing production to meet present and future demands? An answer to this question was provided by Radha Sinha, of Glasgow University, in a paper designed to dispel a number of myths about world poverty and development, and to suggest possible ways forward. In his view, which is

[1] Mahbub ul Haq, *The Third World and the International Economic Order*, 1976, Overseas Development Council, Washington, pp. 2f.

the result of considerable research, 'all the evidence suggests that there is not any immediate or imminent risk of complete exhaustion of the earth's capacity to feed its growing population'. Of course, the earth cannot sustain a rapidly rising population indefinitely, but the general opinion of experts is that the maximum food production of the world may be as much as 30—40 times the present cereal production. Some researchers suggest that world population growth will reach a maximum in about 150 years from now and will be stabilized at 12,000 million, by which time the present food production will need to be increased by approximately five times. 'This should not be a difficult target to achieve', says Sinha.

Turning to the question of energy needs and resources, Sinha is of the opinion that, while there are genuine problems of likely shortages of energy and the risk of environmental pollution, many of these arise from mismanagement rather than inherent lack of resources. The agricultural systems of the developed countries are extremely wasteful of energy: whereas the developing countries are able to produce from 5—50 calories for each calorie they invest through their agricultural systems, the richer countries invest ten calories to get one in return. 'Thus even in 1970, with the given acreage under cultivation and without any improvement in technology, the world could have had 14 per cent more calories than were nutritionally required.'

Information of this kind is, of course, no reason for complacency about the highly complex problem of world population growth, and there is bound to be an element of speculation in the assessment of future prospects concerning food production and energy use. But there appear to be reasonably solid grounds for the belief that the problem of finding support for human life is not beyond solution. Essentially, it is a matter of creating the right social and economic organization. And this in turn calls for a proper understanding of the true relationship between individual human beings and between groups of human beings, with their varied needs and aspirations. Christian involvement in attempts to find a solution ought therefore to be characterized by realism—and hope.

Among the most comprehensive schemes to have evolved so far is one put forward by the Third World countries in 1974 as a series of demands, and, after some modification in tone and substance, finally approved unanimously by the United Nations in September 1975. This is now known as the 'New International Economic Order'. It comprises seven 'areas of concern':

(a) *International Trade*, covering the stabilization of markets for primary commodities; measures to improve their marketing; diversification of the trade of developing countries; and the fixing of the prices of their exports in relation to their imports ('indexation').

(b) (i) *Transfer of Resources* (i.e. aid), covering acceptance of 0.7 per cent of GNP by the richer countries, to be provided as an assured flow on easier terms. This should be increasingly through international institutions and therefore insulated from the political pressures and budgetary decisions of individual donor countries.

(ii) *International monetary reform*, covering the substitution of the Special Drawing Rights issued by the International Monetary Fund for national currencies as the vehicle of international credit; the linking of international credit with the financing of development; an increasing use of the resources of the IMF for the benefit of the developing countries; and a larger share for them in its decision-making.

(c) *Science and Technology*, covering help for developing countries to develop the kinds of technology they need; improved access to information about technology and to its availability to the poorer countries.

(d) *Industrialization*, envisaging an increase in the share of developing countries from the present 7 per cent to 25 per cent by the end of the century. It provides for consultations on the changes in the world economy which this will necessitate; the re-deployment of capacity in developed countries to facilitate the production in the poorer countries of the goods which can be produced most cheaply there; and help from richer countries, including investment, to develop the industrial capacity of the poorer ones.

e) *Food and Agriculture*, emphasizing the need for a rapid increase in food production in the poorer countries, the provision of fertilizers and other kinds of help by the richer countries, and improved arrangements for the provision of food to meet emergencies.

f) *Co-operation among developing countries*, which is much less specific, but envisages strengthening of UN institutions which can help, and studies on, for example, the liberalization of trade, the transfer of technology and the promotion of investment.

g) *Reconstruction of the Economic and Social sectors of the UN system*, a series of technical proposals.

This outline of a New International Economic Order, coming as an impatient demand from the Third World, represents a major challenge to the richer nations, and has to be taken very seriously. In general, it makes a powerful claim on Christian support and, in the absence of any comparable policy document, is likely to provide the basis for debate (and, hopefully, action) for years to come. If, therefore, questions are asked about the apparent limitations of the proposals, these should be seen, not as attempts to evade responsibility in the West, or to introduce qualifications that kill both the spirit and the letter of the scheme, but rather as an acceptance of the seriousness of its ideas and as an attempt to improve them by means of suggestion and criticism in the context of debate.

The first question to be raised is whether the proposals are sufficiently comprehensive. Naturally, the Third World nations are specially concerned about their relations with Europe, North America and Japan, but the world has become so small, and its economic systems so interlocked, that any proposals claiming to constitute a New *International Economic Order* might reasonably be expected to take account of the economic relations between *all* countries. At the risk of appearing to be Utopian and thoroughly unrealistic, Christians are—by virtue of their universal vision—obliged to plead for a new order that embraces the whole and is not restricted to part, albeit a large and important part. The statement of the NIEO says nothing about relations between the market economy countries; or between those countries and the Communist countries; and little about those of the Communist countries with the Third World. Many of the Communist countries of Eastern Europe are themselves extremely poor and can be categorized as developing nations, so there is little likelihood of their providing much assistance to the Third World. Yet the demand of the USSR for wheat can, as was recently demonstrated, have a profound effect on its availability and price in many other parts of the world. So the Communist world needs to be involved in the building of the new order, and the wider approach might also have the effect of silencing those who attempt to discredit the proposals on the grounds that they represent no more than another attack on the capitalist nations.

Another notable omission from the proposals is any recognition of the resources likely to be available to it in the short and medium terms, and the effects on the environment of the manner in which they are used. This is perfectly understandable, since the poorer countries are most conscious of the need to obtain as much as they can to enable their people to survive, and in any case they are aware that the problems connected with the depletion of resources and pollution of the environment are largely caused by the rich countries. It will be necessary to return to this issue later, but meanwhile it seems fairly obvious that a New International Economic Order ought to take account of the escalating problems in this particular area of human life. Needless to say, decisions to restrict consumption of primary resources, which might form part of the Order, should be directed towards the richer countries and not affect the relatively modest claims of the poorer ones.

Then there is the extremely delicate, but not unimportant, question of how the available resources in the poorer countries are actually used and distributed. This is hardly a matter for inclusion in a series of proposals designed to regulate international relations, but it would be quite unrealistic to suppose that in any debate of the proposals questions might not be asked about the internal affairs of the countries seeking a better deal. Often enough questions of this kind are raised as part of an attempt to evade responsibility for the plight of the poor, and the motives of those who raise them need to be carefully examined. But there *are* problems related to land tenure and political favouritism in some of the poorer countries (let the Western nations without fault in these areas cast the first stones) and, quite apart from the benefits that would accrue to the majority of the people of these countries, the task of Western advocates of the NIEO would be eased if the problems were known to be about to be tackled.

This is, it needs to be emphasized, no excuse for the richer countries to attempt to interfere in the internal affairs of their poorer neighbours. The Western-based multi-national corporations already call far too many tunes—not all of them edifying or wholesome—in the Third World. Certainly it is of the utmost importance that individual countries should work out their own patterns of development, and not seek slavishly to follow patterns which appear to have been successful elsewhere. This is partly a matter of making the best possible use of the resources available in a particular country or region, but also involves sensitivity to the socio-cultural implications of development processes. Of course the developing countries will continue to need external assistance as they struggle to discover an 'appropriate technology', and no doubt mistakes will be made—as they have frequently been made in the rich West—but the important thing is that the poorer nations should be given the kind of opportunities and the kind of help that will enable them to make choices and in the end make their own efforts effective.

This, then, is the broad strategy necessary for movement in the direction of world justice and the redressing of the present imbalance between the rich and poor nations. The United Nations have committed themselves to this strategy, and various specialist conferences on international trade and aid have considered specific issues within this kind of framework. But very little has happened to implement the strategy, and the breakdown of the Geneva Conference on the Common Fund proposals in December 1977 is hardly encouraging. There can be no doubt that the burden of responsibility for securing greater world justice lies with the rich nations, whose present attitude was accurately, and sadly, summed up by James Mark:

There is a feeling that something ought to be done to redress the imbalances in the division of wealth (though not necessarily to change the economic system) but, broadly speaking, none of the rich countries has been willing to consider action which would involve any sacrifice, however temporary, of its own interest except in the case of a colony or ex-colony or when there have been other political reasons for it. Nor has there been significant public pressure for such action. If politicians are to be blamed it is not for ignoring public opinion but for failing to give a lead to change it. Hence the disparity between their expressions of sympathy and the choices which they feel bound to make. Aid does not win votes.

Equally depressing for the poorer nations were two assessments presented to the Society for International Development in November 1976. Maurice Williams, Chairman of the Development Assistance Committee of the Organization for European Co-operation, thought that 'all the OECD countries have accepted an obligation to respond, in an enlightened manner, to the fundamental development concerns of our time'. But, having identified seven major areas in which action is needed, he could make only modest forecasts. Aid would increase by 25 per cent or more in real terms by 1980, and there would be some improvement in international monetary arrangements following an IMF Conference in Jamaica. 'Everything else remains under discussion.'

David Hopper, President of the International Development Research Centre of Canada, had been invited to speculate on the situation as it might be in 25 years' time. He foresaw no great changes in the economic structure of the world, which would remain based on national economies functioning according to current interpretations of national self-interest. He doubted the power of the international community to conquer major problems. There would be shifts and improvements in food production, but the world food problem would remain unsolved. Unemployment would remain a problem in the poor countries, while hours of work would shorten in the rich ones. There would, he believed, be considerable changes in the relative pace of development both in the rich and poor countries; some gaps would close and many developing countries would join the ranks of the developed. The gap in technology would, however, remain, though the poor countries would be making a greater contribution to knowledge and developing their own resources of technological manpower. The objectives put forward by the poor countries as regards their relations with the richer would be attained, but new problems would have come into existence. Aid would, he thought, continue without radical change.

In the light of these facts and prognostications, it is hard to disagree with James Mark's conclusion:

There does not appear to be anything approaching a consensus among the richer countries that they are compelled to agree to any radical change in the existing order . . . It does not appear, on present evidence, that either deliberate measures of policy or more or less unplanned courses of events can prevent the continuance and probably the increase of deprivation and misery among a large part of the world's population. This, and the increasing gulf between those unfortunates and those who have enough, must clearly generate an atmosphere of increasing frustration and resentment in international affairs.

All of which is extremely discouraging, not least to those Christians who regard the development of a more just world order as a necessary expression of human obedience to the Divine Will. And unless despair, with all its potential for destruction, is to be allowed to dominate the scene, a powerful combination of realism and vision will be needed to redeem the situation. Since the churches are apt to make quite large claims about themselves in both these areas of human experience, it is not unreasonable to suppose that they might have a significant contribution to make, and this undoubtedly lies behind the efforts for world justice made in recent years by both the British Council of Churches and the World Council of Churches. Even greater efforts are evidently going to be needed in the future.

Motives for Action

It may be helpful to pause for a moment to consider the broad context in which the problem of world justice has to be tackled. What follows is not to be interpreted as an excuse for the cruel complacency or naked self-interest of the richer nations when faced with an appalling human catastrophe. It is no more—and no less—than an acknowledgement of reality: in particular the state of mind that needs to be changed.

The twentieth century has witnessed unprecedented changes in the world order and in the opportunities and dangers confronting the human race. The possibilities of creating wealth have been enlarged on a scale that earlier generations would certainly have regarded as miraculous. Hence the mounting expectations that the economic poverty in which most human beings have lived throughout history will be eliminated. Again, the development of modern means of communications has led to a highly developed system of international trade, with larger and larger economic units—interlocked and increasingly complicated in operation. And the post-World War II era has seen the almost universal achievement of political independence by former colonial territories, resulting in considerable shifts of political power and rising expectations among the populations of the newly-independent nations. The exposure of these nations to the technologies and the economic and social systems of the Western world have introduced into their life—often within two decades—elements quite alien to their traditional culture and life-style. It is hardly surprising that some of them have found it difficult to cope with such dramatic changes and have become politically unstable.

Among the richer nations, the changes have in many ways been less acute, yet hardly less traumatic. Dean Acheson's celebrated remark that 'Britain has lost an empire but not found a role' was more unkind than untrue, and it is certainly the case that the older generation of British people, who still constitute the main bulwark of national leadership, find it extremely difficult to accept that Britain is no longer a major world power. Equally, they cannot really believe that Britain's former colonial territories, especially those in Africa and Asia, are now standing on their own political feet, with complete freedom to make their own decisions—not all of which are in Britain's interests. For this same generation, and for some younger people too, the sight of Arabs from the oil-rich nations of the Middle East entering, and in some cases even owning, hotels in London's exclusive Park Lane is quite puzzling. Here is just one indication that the British have yet to recognize the changes that have taken place in their relationships with the rest of the world, especially the Third World.

There is mounting evidence that the speed of these, and other, changes has exceeded the capacity of the leadership of the richer nations to deal with their implications, so that the problem is not simply one of lack of moral responsibility, but also includes lack of appropriate skill. Hence the wide disagreements about the right way forward now to be found among economists and others who share a commitment to world justice. This point was made with some force in a comment on James Mark's paper by T. F. Cripps, a Cambridge economist.

Mr. Cripps noted that, although the New International Economic Order had been extensively discussed, the paper scarcely suggested by what means the New Order, or any other major reform, could be implemented:

Thus the fundamental problem of power is largely ignored, and without collective understanding and a shared exercise of power it is hard for citizens to know what actions they should take to help secure a more just world ... The sense of perplexity may be a major reason why little is done in practice to advance world justice ... I suspect that there may be an increasing awareness in Britain and other rich countries of the needs of poorer countries and a broadening sense of community with people all over the world. But we do not know, and cannot agree because we do not know, what should be done. What some people believe to be clearly justified courses of action may seem to other people not merely unconvincing but positively misleading and potentially destructive. In this state of confusion it may be natural, but it is not necessarily correct, to suspect the goodwill of those with whom we disagree.

Perplexity is particularly difficult to cope with when it concerns structural changes which may affect the lives of people or whole communities very profoundly. It is easy enough for those who do not live in a textile town to advocate entry to Britain for textiles produced by Third World factories paying low wages, even if they are not all that sure about the ultimate consequences of such a policy. But for those who will be directly affected such a policy would be very difficult to accept unless they were certain that it would serve an essential purpose. To reduce perplexity about world justice it may be necessary to try to answer very difficult questions. The concept of a world order itself needs to be examined critically. Can a world order be a good order? Could decisions taken in one part of the globe always be well-informed about their consequences elsewhere? Who controls the world order? Can it be controlled? Is there not already too much inter-dependence?

There is undoubtedly a genuine sense of perplexity among many of the people who are concerned about the injustice of the present world economy. The questions ought not to be dodged, and there needs to be a sensitivity to the bewilderment felt even by highly educated people when they are confronted by some of the major problems in the world justice debate. Yet millions of people are at this moment suffering the effects of malnutrition and something needs to be done immediately to alleviate their suffering and to modify the economic system that is causing it. To retire from the battle because of intellectual 'shell-shock' or to discuss the larger strategic issues is an improper response to the crisis that now exists. Moreover, a certain amount of caution needs to be exercised in respect of what is believed to be the increasing goodwill of the citizens and statesmen of the richer nations. The evidence for such goodwill is not extensive, and, even when signs of it appear, it often seems somewhat fragile: stopping well short of personal or corporate sacrifice. It would be unwise to presume that matters related to motivation can be left to look after themselves while attention is concentrated on discovering the elusive know-how. A more prudent course would seem to be to extend the moral/motivation debate as far as possible, so that expert decisions become politically possible; and it may even be the case that the right technical decisions about development, economic justice and so forth can only emerge in a climate that includes a high degree of moral responsibility and a glad acceptance of interdependence within the human race.

A number of reasons why the richer countries should take action to help the poorer nations are generally advanced. One belongs to the realm of self-protection, and is based on the fear that unless the rich nations are prepared to make economic sacrifices there might be an explosion of violence in the Third World, including even the threat of nuclear attack by a country rendered desperate by poverty. This last possibility is by no means as remote as it may appear by those now sitting comfortably in the West. On the whole it is extremely unlikely that any Third World country suffering acute poverty would be able to muster sufficient strength among its population to embark on conventional warfare in a quest for wealth, or even to make a nuisance of itself. Internal revolutionary movements seem to depend on a country reaching a certain stage of development; after all, physical fitness is an important element in the success of conventional violence.

But if the poor nations are to make any of the technological advances deemed necessary for their economic salvation, and if the development of energy is essential to the growth of a country which has some industrial component, there must be at least the possibility of nuclear proliferation, and with it the capacity to make weapons which, in fanatical hands, could create the most appalling havoc. Dr. Hans Singer called attention to this problem in his Presidential Address to the U.K. Chapter of the Society for International Development in May 1977, and added: 'How can we with any moral justification or credibility withhold nuclear power technology which might cross the thin boundary between peaceful and dangerous uses, how can we impose controls and restrictions upon those [poor] countries, unless we are willing and able, at the same time, to provide other, less dangerous alternatives? We really cannot have it both ways.' And what might these less dangerous alternatives be? Dr. Singer suggested that in the long term these could include solar power, wave power, tidal power, wind power, geothermal power, biogas and so on. But, since these cannot be available for at least another ten or twenty years, the only immediate effective alternative to nuclear proliferation is generous support, both financial and technical, for further exploration and development of oil, coal, hydro-electricity and any other more 'conventional' energy sources, including also the provision of finance to cover energy-related balance-of-payments deficits and measures for energy conservation. The need for non-nuclear energy aid has become urgent. Here it should be emphasized that Dr. Singer does not himself suggest fear as the main motive for the furtherance of world justice, but he is aware of the risks as well as the moral issues involved in doing nothing, and has stated them with authority.

The second motive for action is that of 'enlightened self-interest'. A peaceful world, free from intolerable tensions in international relations, is obviously a better place for everyone to live in, and has certain advantages for those Western nations who prosper from international trade. Moreover there is an influential body of opinion which argues that in the not-so-long run the economies of the richer countries would benefit from an improvement in the lot of the poorer nations.

It could be, for example, that the developing countries concentrated on the production of certain goods, suitable to their own resources and skills, leaving the richer countries to concentrate on items which they are best fitted to produce (and which might conceivably be far more profitable to their manufacturers). Even in the case of something as sensitive as textiles, it might well be in the interests of Britain to close down her textile mills, benefit from the lower consumer prices made possible by the importing of textiles from the poorer countries, and at the same time sell more goods to these countries who would be in a better position to pay for them as a result of their own increased export earnings. Lancashire's textile workers might not be impressed by this reasoning, and could reasonably enquire what benefits they would themselves receive from a change of policy along these lines, but, in general, it remains true that when facilities for international trade are improved the benefits do not flow in only one direction—unless, of course, steps are taken to ensure that they do. These possibilities apart, Mahbub ul Haq (who evidently has few illusions about the character of current Western morality) believes that 'it is essential that whatever proposals we formulate balance the interests of rich and poor nations. If we are to live without major confrontations, we should think of proposals which, while benefiting the Third World, do not hurt the interests of the world as a whole and which can obtain more willing co-operation from the rich nations.'[2]

From the point of view of the poor nations, the motives that may—or may not—drive the richer countries to action for greater world justice are likely to be far less important than the fact of their actually taking significant action to bridge the gap between rich and poor. Those who long to see a united world community based on mutual respect and responsibility naturally hope for action based on something more altruistic than fear or enlightened self-

[2] *The Third World and the International Economic Order*, p. 52.

interest. But when multitudes of p·ople are actually dying of starvation, and all attempts at self-help are frustrated by unfair international rules, the reasons for the appearance of more food and better rules are bound to seem secondary. And if a parallel is drawn with the steps that have proved necessary for bridging the gap between rich and poor *within* the more affluent nations, it will be seen that fear and self-interest have often been powerful factors in the wringing of concessions from the holders of wealth and power. Regrettable though it undoubtedly is, altruism has rarely governed adjustments in economic relations, and it is of the greatest importance that this should be recognized by those for whom moral considerations are paramount.

And what are these moral considerations? Paul Streeten, Warden of Queen Elizabeth House, Oxford, and Director of the Institute of Commonwealth Studies, outlined some of them in an article in *Crucible*, the journal of the Church of England Board for Social Responsibility (July—September 1976):

> In my view, the most fundamental argument for international co-operation in development is that human beings, wherever born, should be able to develop to the fullest extent their capacities, both in order to fulfil themselves and in order to contribute to the common heritage of civilization. The simple argument for making sacrifices in order to assist development is this: we, the rich, are partly (though only partly and arguably) responsible for the poverty of the poor; we can do something about it: it follows that we ought to. The argument rests only partly (and controversially) on our responsibility. Even if we had no share at all in the responsibility, the Christian and humanist belief in the brotherhood of man imposes certain obligations to alleviate misery and to aid in the full development of others where we can.

Streeten goes on to define 'injustice' as 'the unequal treatment of equal people in equal situations' and, following

Aristotle, draws a distinction between a general injustice, resulting from the effects of institutions, organizations and arrangements, whether intended or unintended, and specific forms of injustice resulting from deliberate actions and policies in contravention or disregard of law and custom. Some of the present divisions between rich and poor clearly belong to the first category:

> An international arrangement, by which human beings are organized in nation-states which can enjoy the resources within their boundaries, and an international distribution of wealth, power and opportunity, determined by the ratio of people to resources within the boundaries of each nation-state is, by Christian and humanist standards, an unjust arrangement.

Other divisions are, equally clearly, the result of policies quite deliberately designed 'to give the lion's share to the lion'. Having itemized some of these policies, Streeten comments, 'Unless we start from the thoroughly un-Christian notion that only citizens of our own nation count and foreigners count for nothing, these arrangements are clearly unjust.' He concludes his article with the assertion: 'the basic case for international co-operation rests on the brotherhood of man'.

There is nothing in Streeten's discussion of justice and brotherhood that might not be as acceptable to a humanist as to a Christian. Christians may wish to argue that the concept of human brotherhood is grounded in belief in the fatherhood of God, but that is another issue, and the fact is that both humanists and Christians are deeply concerned for the creation of a more just world order—and for the same moral reasons. Hence the level of co-operation that is possible between bodies like Christian Aid, Oxfam and War on Want, and the belief of the general public that all three are engaged in the same work, which of course they are.

None the less, it is necessary to ask whether Christians have any distinctive insights into the nature of the problems and their possible solution. To which the broad answer must be No. The Bible, which is one of the primary sources of Christian insight, certainly does not address itself directly to the complex issues facing twentieth-century politicians and development economists. The Old Testament emerged from a relatively primitive community, based on a pastoral and agricultural economy, and has a good deal to say about justice in economic and social relationships—including the need for a spirit of mercy and a readiness to help one's neighbours, especially the poor. This is obviously relevant to current concerns, but is hardly distinctive and, in any case, has to be applied to specific twentieth-century situations before it can be said to offer solutions. Again, the New Testament is concerned with broad principles, values, attitudes and commitments; it is governed by the vision of the Kingdom of God. Precisely because these things are *not* tied to any particular political, social or economic theory, Christians in every age have found them illuminating and challenging. But they have to be applied to concrete situations by those who have been gripped by the vision and the challenge, and neither the New Testament nor the Christian tradition as a whole offers infallible guidance at this point.

The most that can be said—and its importance should not be undervalued—is that Christians see secular problems within a particular perspective, and that the insights into the nature of man in community which come to them through their belief in the God who disclosed himself in Jesus of Nazareth provide a powerful imperative for action in the cause of world justice.

An example of this is provided by one of the stories told by Jesus—concerning Dives and Lazarus (Luke 16: 19-31) —which was the subject of special study by a group contributing to the 'Britain Today and Tomorrow' project. Like all the other stories in the gospels, it is a challenge to the individual and this one concerns the situation in which a man is placed by reason of his material possessions. There is a gulf between Dives and Lazarus—created by Dives' wealth and the privilege and power which this gives him.

That gulf makes it impossible for Dives to recognize a relationship with his fellow man; he does not even see him. Lazarus, on his side of the gulf, suffers poverty which deprives him of the right to live, in any meaningful sense. Here is a clear appeal to the kind of social justice which is taught in the Old Testament, though it leads to no specific prescriptions. Dives should work out for himself what responsibility he feels: what a recognition of Lazarus as his fellow man should impel to him do. Both Dives and Lazarus will come to judgement, and the material conditions of their earthly lives will have vanished away, but what they did in those conditions will have determined their destinies. All this happens under the Old Testament dispensation, by the light of what Moses and the prophets knew of God; but the fact that Jesus tells the story implies that, whatever the message of the Gospel, the relationships and responsibilities of the story are not to be set aside. Indeed, the Gospel breaks into this situation with a new force. God is on the side of the poor; and his coming into history in the person of Jesus reverses the sinful order: 'The hungry he has filled with good things and the rich he has sent empty away' (Luke 1: 40f). He comes 'to preach good news to the poor . . . to proclaim release to the captives and recovering of sight to the blind, to set at liberty those who are oppressed, to proclaim the acceptable year of the Lord.' (Luke 4: 18f).

There is material here for Christian reflection on the use of wealth and power, and how this affects human relationships, in situations far removed from that in which the story of Dives and Lazarus was first told. But this reflection is influenced by the individual's wider understanding and experience of the Christian faith, and in meeting the demands of faith in the concrete situations of daily life. Illumination comes through the interaction of the past and the present, the disclosed and the discovered—all of which are, for the Christian, expressions of his relationship with the living God.

Man's place in the created world has been radically changed, not least because of developments during the last two centuries, and more particularly during the last fifty years. Man is still a creature and, however greatly he has developed his capacity to mould the created world to his purposes, it remains a world which he did not create himself. Yet his power to use created things to serve his purposes has been transformed out of all recognition: the notion of man being given dominion over all created things (Genesis 1 : 26) has acquired a quite new dimension of meanings. We do not know what this may mean in practice; the expansion of the the world's population and of its use of known resources, and its capacity to discover new ones, are all too uncertain. But what is clear is that man has been given a power to shape his own destiny that he did not possess before. The material constraints on that power have not, of course, disappeared, but both the power to take decisions and the effects of those decisions have been enormously increased. Now, more than ever before, man can shape his future by responsible decisions taken in relative freedom.

How man defines that notion of responsibility is therefore all-important; and this will depend on his understanding of his own nature, of what he is and what he wants to become. This, in turn, raises the question of what he needs in order to become what he wants to be. Clearly the mere pursuit of increasing material well-being is inadequate; the striking and depressing thing, however, is that the idol of GNP is so commonly worshipped not merely because there are undeniable needs to be met, but because there is nothing better to put in its place. It is the lack of such a vision that is crucial. Notions such as the responsible stewardship of resources are important but secondary, firstly because no one can know what resources we have or can discover; and secondly because the notion acquires much greater force if we have some idea of the ends of life that it serves.

This transformation of man's ability to create wealth affects profoundly the distribution of power in the world. There have always been strong nations and weak ones, but the disparities have now become more acute for several reasons: because of the growing divergence in economic strength; and because communications are all-pervasive in the world of our day, and because communications bring us all so much closer together. The instinct of those who have power is to use it, not necessarily for ends which they would confess to be selfish, but because it seems natural to do so. But however benevolent the intentions of the rich and (therefore) the powerful may be, the situation is unhealthy: first, because of the natural selfishness of human beings and (vastly more) of nations; secondly, because such an imbalance of power makes genuine relationships impossible, as the story of Dives and Lazarus illustrates. Conversely, the creation of genuine relationships must involve a renunciation of power on the part of those who have it: a recognition that they ought not to impose their will; that they should genuinely recognize the rights, because they recognize the individuality, of the weaker. For Christians, the pattern of life displayed by Jesus of Nazareth, and his ultimate surrender of power on the Cross, is particularly significant and, paradoxically, this renunciation of power had the effect of changing the whole course of world history.

In terms of the present day, the renunciation of power, whether by individuals or corporate groups, implies the creation of a community in which rights do not depend solely on power. This may seem unrealistic, in the light of the way in which nations behave, but it must be the basis of any New International Economic Order which gives the poorer countries a fair chance to overcome their poverty and to achieve a healthy pattern of development; it is fundamental to any social ethic derived from either the Old Testament or the New. It is very different from the appeal to charity which has been the main strength of the voluntary fund-raising organizations in Britain and other rich countries. Which is not to undervalue the need to relieve hardship; but what is at issue here is not charity, but justice—and, even more, fellowship; that rich nations should recognize the right of poor ones to help in their efforts to overcome their poverty. Such recognition involves a radical transformation of relationships. It requires, for example, the renunciation of attempts to use aid as a means of exerting political influence, and the substitution of dialogue for prescription by the donor country of the purpose for which aid is to be used; in other words, the substitution for the donor-client relationship of a relationship based on genuine co-operation. It means accepting what poorer countries can best produce and sell and adapting the economies of richer countries to enable them to do so—the ultimate aim being a world community in which each nation contributes what it can and the resources of all are used to the best effect.

The British churches have therefore at their disposal a body of principles which they share with the Church universal and which have a direct bearing on the issue of world justice. They are also aware of the appalling effects in the poorer countries of the present injustice in world economic affairs and, although their advisers are not in complete agreement, they are reasonably well-acquainted with the diagnosis of the problem and the prescription(s) for its solution. What, then, do the churches say to the British people in general, and their political leaders in particular, about Britain's policies in relation to the quest for world justice?

Fighting for the New Order

Commitment to action within the broad framework of the New International Economic Order is basic. And if votes in the United Nations are anything more than international window-dressing, it must be acknowledged that Britain is now committed to this New Order. What is in doubt is whether Britain proposes to do anything to make it a reality, and here James Mark has identified five courses of action that would indicate a positive response to the NIEO challenge.

1. We should be a party to a number of long-term arrangements intended to stabilize supplies and prices of primary

commodities, probably with some increase in prices over a period—at least for countries of the Third World.

2. We should need to reshape our economy further and more systematically in order to accept processed and manufactured goods which countries of the Third World could produce more cheaply. This would mean reductions in employment in, for example, textiles and other industries involving the processing of raw materials from countries of the Third World, and the diversion of the labour force into other forms of work.

3. We should need to increase our aid very substantially (at least to double it within a few years), for a number of objectives in particular:

(i) to provide aid for the poorest countries;
(ii) to help to finance a programme of food production which will relieve hunger in the Third World;
(iii) to finance the development and transfer of appropriate forms of technology;
(iv) to finance industrial development (though this, like other productive investment, would no doubt be financed in part by private capital).

4. We should be required to acquiesce in the final phasing-out of sterling as a reserve currency, as part of a more rational and controlled system of international credit.

5. We should be required to agree to arrangements governing the operations of transnational corporations, some of which have their headquarters wholly or partly in the United Kingdom.

This is, in all conscience, a modest enough programme and, though it might appear to the Third World as a sign of movement in the right direction, it would remain a long way from meeting their urgent demands. Yet, as James Mark himself acknowledges in his paper, a programme along these lines is not one that would be readily accepted by a British government formed from either major party. Here it may be noted that nothing remotely connected with the issue of world justice has so far figured in public discussion of the possible uses to which North Sea oil funds might be put. At a meeting of the TUC—Labour Party liaison committee, convened in November 1977 to discuss a paper (prepared jointly by Mr. Healey, Chancellor of the Exchequer, and Mr. Wedgwood Benn, Secretary of State for Energy) setting out six options for the use of oil revenues, general agreement was reached that the purpose of oil revenue should be 'to raise living standards, reduce inflation and restore full employment in all parts of the United Kingdom'.

Nothing could illustrate more clearly the obsessive concern with her own affairs in which the British nation has become engulfed over the last decade. At the first UNCTAD Conference in 1964 Britain played a prominent role and seemed anxious to share in efforts to create a more just world order. When the Labour government headed by Harold Wilson came to office in 1964 its programme included a commitment to increased aid and the liberalization of trading arrangements with the Third World. But these commitments were not honoured and the Ministry of Overseas Development found itself isolated from the rest of the administration, and always fighting a losing battle when seeking to arouse concern for the poorer nations. The Conservative government of 1970—74 backed private investment rather than aid, arguing that market forces and the prospect of profit would solve the problem, which of course they did not. And since 1974 the Labour government has been struggling with inflation, the oil crisis, economic stagnation, high unemployment, and other related domestic problems which have created an atmosphere in which there is little sympathy for the troubles of the poorer nations; indeed there are those in Britain who believe that their nation is now to be numbered among the poorer nations, rather than among those who have a major responsibility for correcting the imbalance in the distribution of the world's resources.

The truth is that in international terms Britain remains a rich nation. Her income per head is many times that of all but a small handful of Third World countries, the exceptions being those which enjoy large oil revenues. Britain will herself enjoy considerable oil revenues for a time, or at least be spared the cost of purchasing expensive oil elsewhere, and it is generally recognized that this will provide a breathing space in which the country can, if wisely led, put the basis of her economic and social life on a much sounder footing. The excuse, expressed with varying degrees of sophistication, that 'we cannot afford to assist or make concessions to the Third World' must, therefore, be rejected as utterly invalid. As in the case of rich individuals who are not quite wealthy enough to do everything they might wish, it is a matter of listing and choosing priorities. And the choice is as significant in terms of disclosing the character of the decision-maker as it is in terms of the assistance rendered to any beneficiaries. The British churches have a clear responsibility to help the nation as a whole to see the economic situation in a true, international perspective, and to be aware of the moral factors involved in the selection of priorities.

This said, the fact remains that with the best will in the world any British government seeking to re-order its priorities in respect of the Third World will be subject to a number of serious constraints—for the next few years, at least. The economic malaise, which showed itself in the hyper-inflation and sterling crises of the mid-1970s, runs very deep, and certainly cannot be cured overnight. The best (and also the least) that can be hoped for is a gradual improvement. Moreover, it is in the interests of the Third World that Britain should put her own house in order, since London remains an important centre for international trade and finance, and no good purpose is served when such a centre is located within a nation that appears to be demoralized or floundering. Courageous and imaginative leadership, with a clear view of long-term objectives, is called for, and also steps that will help to restore the confidence of the nation as a whole. This means reducing inflation to at least a manageable level, some reduction in unemployment, and probably some increase in consumption—all of which reduce a democratic government's room for manoeuvre when deciding overseas aid and trade policies.

On the other hand, sound policies aimed at furthering world justice and linked to correct domestic policies would almost certainly assist Britain's own economic recovery. According to James Mark, 'the achievement of more orderly and predictable arrangements within the international economy may bring substantial advantages to Britain, which might even outweigh whatever sacrifices we might be called on to make'. He reasons:

Britain, as a major importer of food, has a major interest in ensuring a steady growth of world food supplies and a balanced international trading system. Similarly, Britain depends on imported raw materials more than most other industrialized countries and might find increased stability in supplies well worth some increase in price over a period. The importing of larger quantities of goods from Third World sources under long-term trade agreements can help to reduce inflation, while the diversion of resources from older industries into those in which we can use our potentially higher standards of technology can help to rejuvenate our economy. We have a great deal to gain from the establishment of more efficient financial arrangements. The international role of sterling is now a burden rather than an advantage, and a better planned international monetary system might help us. Moreover the provision of funds through the linking of credit expansion with development, much of which would go to Commonwealth countries, should give us opportunities to earn foreign exchange if we can take advantage of them. We are affected by the operations of the transnational corporations in two different ways: as the home base for some of them we gain from their operations in other countries; on the other hand, recent experience has shown the extent to which our own economic freedom is constrained by their activities, which it may often be difficult to reconcile with our own economic priorities. The fact that we are involved on both sides of the encounter may enable us to play a distinctive part in working out a more generally acceptable *modus operandi* for the future. In this kind of context the increase in aid, which would amount to about 0.4 per cent of our national income, would be a relatively modest consideration.

Modest, indeed, but Britain's attitude to the Common Fund proposal, which provoked the disregarded resolution at the Swanwick Assembly, is an indication of the mountains that will have to be moved before British economic priorities are determined generously in the context of world need. Herein lies a problem for the British churches. Their approach to world economic justice has so far been characterized by well-informed documents and arguments of a kind that would be—and have been—treated with respect in government departments. The aim has been to change government policy by means of rational persuasion and to avoid the presentation of proposals that would automatically be rejected as unrealistic. In other words, the approach has been 'political' and, from one point of view, it is encouraging to find the churches taking seriously the hard realities of political power and adopting the appropriate advocacy tactics.

But, by and large, these tactics have failed. And this, not because the arguments were faulty or the government ministers and officials insensitive to hunger and justice, but because the proposals of the churches were, in spite of their modesty, regarded as unacceptable to the electorate. This assessment was—and is—almost certainly correct. Which means that the churches have a responsibility for helping to educate and motivate the millions of British people who cast their votes at General Elections. Carefully marshalled facts and arguments, of which the contents of this chapter might be considered a fair example, undoubtedly have their place in the educating and motivating process. Yet the Christian Church has the vision of a world order in which justice and freedom and compassion are expressed in terms far beyond those suitable for a 'political' document. And the question to be faced—and doubtless disagreed about—is whether the time has come for the British churches to throw their weight behind those, mainly young people, who are pleading for a quite new world order and are inspired to sacrificial action by the prospect of its materialization.

This may seem politically inexpedient and unhelpful—

an indulgence to satisfy the radical conscience. Yet, as the poor nations themselves have discovered, it is often necessary to demand a lot in order to gain a little. And without the projection and challenge of a much broader vision, it is hard to imagine the British electorate voting for a New International Economic Order.

3. POVERTY AND PLENTY

Although matters related to 'Law, Freedom, Justice and Equality' were considered to be a major part of the 'Britain Today and Tomorrow' project, and certainly had a claim to high priority of treatment, the results of this part of the project were in many ways the least satisfactory. The large pile of papers consisted mainly of items submitted by individuals and groups working in isolation; hence the serious gaps, the frequent overlapping, and the lack of anything approaching a coherent analysis of the problems and their possible solutions. A frank introduction to the papers prepared their readers for disappointment: 'The topics under investigation are of the greatest importance to our British society and to the witness and mission of the whole Church. It cannot be said that they have been investigated with the quality of work which they demand.' Colin Buchanan, the theologian who had the difficult task of presenting the fruits of this study to the Swanwick Assembly, pointed out that most of the papers were on inequality, leaving three of the four subjects unexamined, and that the discussion was still at an immature stage. No one disagreed with him.

Most noticeably lacking, apart from any serious consideration of the relationship between law and freedom,[1] was a comprehensive attempt to grapple with the changes in Britain's economic and industrial strategy which are necessary to provide the wealth needed for the ironing out of the most serious inequalities and injustices. It is a sad, but apparently inescapable, fact that the majority of British people are only prepared for the less privileged members of society to have a larger portion of the economic

[1] On which Sir Norman Anderson's *Liberty, Law and Justice* is now available (1978).

cake at a time when the cake itself is getting larger. In a democracy it seems that social reform depends upon economic abundance; hence the need for the problems of inequality and injustice to be considered in the context of Britain's future prospects. This task has yet to be tackled.

Energy Policy: The Nuclear Debate

During the course of the project, though not directly related to it, the British Council of Churches did however make a substantial contribution to the public debate about British energy policy and the proposal that the government should authorize the building of a fast breeder reactor. Encouraged by the Secretary of State for Energy, Tony Benn, who had asked for the matter to be discussed as widely as possible before a government decision was made, the BCC arranged a series of Hearings in December 1976. During the course of ten hours, a distinguished panel of experts, meeting under the chairmanship of Dr. Hugh Montefiore (then Bishop of Kingston-upon-Thames, now Bishop of Birmingham), received fifty-nine written submissions and cross-examined some thirty witnesses on various aspects of the problem.[2]

The point at issue is how Britain can ensure a sufficient supply of energy in the year AD 2000. Experts vary in their estimates of Britain's likely needs and the energy resources that may be available within the world as a whole by the end of the present century. But current projections suggest that Britain will by then need to import energy. Uranium, the principal fuel of the existing reactors which supply electricity to the national grid, is becoming increasingly scarce. The present coal- or oil-fired power stations will continue to make a contribution to electricity generation for some time to come, but as usable sources of fossil fuels

[2] A full account of the Hearings is available in *Nuclear Crisis: A Question of Breeding*, edited by Hugh Montefiore and David Gosling, Prism Press, 1977.

become depleted it will become essential to conserve the remaining supplies for alternative uses. Hence the vulnerability of Britain's energy supply and the nation's future economic prospects.

In this situation the Commercial Fast Reactor, generally known as CFR-1, has many attractions—not least the fact that in its use of plutonium it actually produces (or 'breeds') more than it consumes when generating energy. But the CFR-1 has a number of serious snags. For one thing, it is colossally expensive to build: when first projected a figure of £600 million was mentioned, but by April 1977 this had increased to between one and two billion pounds. There are also unresolved problems regarding the disposal of the highly toxic waste created by this form of nuclear process. The concentration of so much energy in a few places, and the dependence of the nation upon an uninterrupted supply of energy for its survival, suggests the possibility of radical political change with a new emphasis on centralization of decision making and more authoritarian control of society. Furthermore the plutonium produced by the nuclear reprocessing plants associated with fast breeder reactors can be used for military as well as for peaceful purposes. Thus developments in this area are almost certain to lead to the international proliferation of nuclear weapons, since there is no practical possibility of the new methods of producing energy being restricted to the so-called Nuclear Producers' Club of the rich Western world.

The BCC Hearings at which these matters were discussed, with considerable expertise and some passion, led to no specific recommendations concerning future British policy, and there was a certain amount of criticism afterwards at the lack of attention to the moral aspects of the problem. But a full debate was held at the BCC Assembly in April 1977 and, after recalling the biblical imperative to exercise a responsible stewardship towards the resources of the world and the natural environment, the Assembly noted with regret the absence of any comprehensive long-term British energy policy and called on the government to develop such a policy. This should be designed to improve the forecasting of future energy needs, to promote energy conservation, to reduce the present wasteful competition between existing energy sources, to develop a range of alternative and complementary energy sources, to produce a more co-ordinated pricing of energy and to guide all major decisions on capital investment in energy.

The Assembly, having noted the unresolved problems and risks involved in the construction of the CFR-1, then called on the government not to authorize construction until the problems had been further explored and, in particular, a satisfactory solution found to the problem of waste disposal. The possibilities of international collaboration in production and marketing ought also to be investigated. Meanwhile, said the Assembly, the churches should be considering ways in which their congregations and members may develop for themselves, and encourage in the community, a more responsible private and public stewardship of energy.

So the advice of the BCC to the government is 'Wait'. But there is a risk involved in waiting, for even if there were an immediate decision to construct a CFR-1 it would not supply electricity to the grid much before 1995 and by this time Britain's own energy supplies may well be seriously depleted. In such a situation, the context of discussions about the creation and distribution of wealth would be radically different from that in which the churches considered these matters at the end of 1977.

The Cycle of Inequality

A valuable handbook for use by local churches, *Understanding Inequality*, was compiled by Neville Chamberlain (Executive Secretary to the Social Responsibility Committee of Lincoln Diocese), Eric Forshaw (Bishop's Chaplain to Industry and Commerce in Birmingham) and Malcolm Goldsmith (Bishop of Southwell's Adviser on Industrial Society). They used as the basis of their work a small paperback written by Frank Field, of the Child

Poverty Action Group, and published in 1974 under the title *Unequal Britain: a Report on the Cycle of Inequality*. This brought together the findings of all the major research reports published since 1945 and assessed whether or not Britain has become more equal.

For the purpose of official statistics, the government divides the population into 'socio-economic groups' (based on a variety of factors, not simply take-home pay). Frank Field based his study on a comparison of the position of people in classes 4 and 5 (semi-skilled and unskilled) with those in classes 1 and 2 (professional and intermediate). He traced his two groups from birth to death through eight different aspects of life and concluded that, while the poor are often better off now than they used to be (which is to be expected because the nation as a whole is much richer), so also are the rich: 'It is as if the poor have been placed on an escalator which gradually lifts their position. But the rich, too, are on board their own escalator which is moving just as fast, if not faster.'[3]

Without discussing the validity of Frank Field's analysis, Chamberlain, Forshaw and Goldsmith summarized his main findings, adding a little later material, and offered them as what they called a 'tool of analysis'. They said that their own knowledge of various reports and pieces of research supported his conclusions.

1. *Birth.* There is much evidence to show that children born to poorer parents have a much greater chance of dying at birth or soon after than those born to richer parents. Whilst the position has improved for both groups throughout the century, the relative differences have remained about the same. This is the beginning of the 'cycle of inequality'. Two newly-born babies, perhaps born in the same hospital at the same time, are already seemingly destined to grow apart because of the background of their parents.

2. *Education.* The home background of the parents affects a child's educational opportunities. The chances of an un-

[3] Frank Field, *Unequal Britain* (Arrow Books), p. 62.

skilled manual worker's child being a poor reader are six times greater than those of a professional worker's child. The chances of a social class 5 child being a non-reader are 15 times greater than those of a social class 1 child. Later, a lower proportion of children from poorer families goes on to higher and further education than from richer families even when their IQs are similar. And, as earnings are linked to length of education, this means that children from poor homes probably finish up on low incomes. A 1973 government publication showed that 44 per cent of men with degrees earned £3,000-plus, while 1.8 per cent of men with GCEs earned that much. (Today, when salary levels have doubled, percentages have remained the same.) Far from school correcting the cycle of inequality, the inequalities at birth continue to widen during school years.

3. *Income.* Surveys have shown that, on average, manual workers work about eight hours a week more than non-manual workers, yet they earn less money. The richest 30 per cent of the population receive a share of the nation's income three-and-a-half times greater than that received by the poorest 30 per cent. The surprising thing is that the income gap has not narrowed since the end of World War II. Nearly 100,000 families live on an income below the official poverty line, and these families are responsible for the well-being of 300,000 children.

4. *Work.* A man who has to work long hours, or is required to work shifts, cannot possibly have the same freedom in organizing his social life as a man who obtains high rewards for working regular hours and has long holidays. Unfortunately, Britain's industrial life still falls into two opposing factions, and different treatment tends to be given to the different groups—in terms of clocking-on, disciplinary procedures, fringe benefits, pensions, holidays and conditions of work. Not only are the lower paid (within these groups) disadvantaged at work: they are also more likely to lose their jobs than others. A 1974 survey, when the unemployment rate was 2.6 per cent, showed that pro-

fessional workers and supervisory grades had unemployment rates of 0.6 and 1.3, while personal service workers and unskilled workers had rates of 4.9 and 6.8.

5. *Health.* The government's General Household survey, looking at illnesses by type and social class, commented: 'All condition groups except diseases of the eye were more common amongst the semi-skilled and unskilled than amongst other groups.' Although working-class families use their local GP rather more often than other classes (though less for their children), they use the Health Service in general less than other groups, despite a higher incidence of illness. Part of the punishment for being poor is to have, on average, poorer health and lower life expectancy.

6. *Housing.* By and large it is the poorest who occupy the worst housing, and yet these families are faced with still greater inequalities, for out of their relatively low incomes many poor families have to pay disproportionately high rents. Unless the poor are able to gain a council house, they will have to depend upon the inferior private sector. Homelessness is the extreme point of housing inequality for the poor—the main cause being poverty, and the decrease in the number of houses in the rented sector.

7. *Wealth.* According to the Royal Commission on the Distribution of Income and Wealth, in 1974 the top 1 per cent of the population owned 25 per cent of the nation's wealth (i.e. marketable assets). This figure was reduced to 24.3 per cent in 1975. The top 5 per cent owned 47.4 per cent, and the top 20 per cent owned 78.1 per cent, leaving the bottom 80 per cent with 21.9 per cent. In other words, roughly one-fifth of the population in Britain own four-fifths of the nation's wealth.

8. *Death.* Inequality even reaches to the grave: social classes 1 and 2 have a longer life expectancy than classes 4 and 5.

Many British people, without access to facts such as these,

are likely to be startled, and perhaps disturbed, by them when presented in this stark form. So they should be. But the BCC's Division of Community Affairs submitted to the project a paper warning against the limitations of statistical techniques in understanding poverty—the limitations being those of tending to obscure the true character of poverty and of not indicating what remedial action is called for in particular cases.

One clear example of this is to be found in the concept of urban deprivation—the belief that poverty and disadvantage are rooted in particular neighbourhoods, where destitute, poor, mentally ill or criminal people seek refuge in each other's company. The belief that the problems of these people are then perpetuated into the future by families or whole communities has led to a desire to break up the areas where a 'subculture of poverty' exists. This understanding of deprivation—as an area problem calling for an area solution—has deep roots in church and other social work intervention in large cities. But, says the Division of Community Affairs paper, 'the promotion of policies of area discrimination misses out many of the poor. We are therefore forced to seek changes in national *policy* with regard to wages, income maintenance, housing, industry, etc. Area policies can only in part rectify spatial inequality in cities and may, by labelling, reinforce inequality and dependence, and scare off potential development.'

Another aspect of poverty which goes well beyond the statistics is discussed in a second Working Paper submitted by the Division of Community Affairs entitled *Poverty and Class*. This says: 'Poverty is a social pattern of rejection . . . It is not just a condition of people, but an interaction between people: it does not just happen to us, we do it to each other. In other words, "poverty" means "impoverishment": for it is the action and the suffering that are significant, the interaction that matters. Of course, part of the effect of the interaction is the condition of shortage, and that is often what is meant by "poverty". But it is only as we look at the action or interaction of impoverishment that we see poverty as a human reality. This is also to say that poverty is not just a material reality; it is a spiritual-material thing, a body-and-soul affair. It is . . . people rejecting one another. There are four elements in this rejection. First, people reduce other people, do them down, make them less than they are, dishonour them. Second, people remove other people, do them away, distance them, segregate. Third, people deprive other people—of resources for living. Fourth, people retard other people, inhibit their potential, stop them growing.'

The authors of this Working Paper then suggest that 'poverty in this sense is a main mark of British society. Our society is divided into groups which are graded on a scale of greater and lesser power. It is this grouping of people which gives poverty of impoverishment its particular form in our society: for it is principally across the lines between these graded groups that people reject one another . . . In this pattern of graded power, the power is not just social, it is socio-economic. It is social power, i.e. power over people, but it is also associated with economic power, i.e. power over resources. In this socio-economic power it may be difficult to say which is cause and which is effect—the power over people or the power over resources; but it is clear that they are linked and that the power over resources, the economic element, is very important.'

Incomes and Ethics

At this point in the discussion a group of theologians and economists in Cambridge, working for the BCC Directorate of Economic Studies, contributed a paper on 'Some Ethical Factors in Income Distribution'. Within the BCC's own constituency such a paper might appear to be somewhat superfluous, since the mere recital of the facts contained in Frank Field's analysis of *The Cycle of Inequality* is sufficient to arouse an awareness among Christians that something is seriously wrong with British society and that radical changes are called for. Yet this cannot be taken for granted among British people as a whole—possibly not even among church members as a whole—and, in any event, the intellectual as well as the emotional basis of Christian concern needs to be evaluated and articulated.

The Cambridge group begin by confessing that they have paid insufficient attention to the world setting of Britain's problems and assert that 'nothing at all is more important than to take a global view'. They also admit that they were unable to carry out a systematic study of Christian teaching in this area. But some kind of biblical authority was assumed, and the discussion appealed to other authorities too, especially the Graeco-Roman discussion of the nature of justice.

Thus the paper opens with the claim that 'prima facie, justice seems to imply equality except where a case can be made out in favour of inequality'. The authors consider three possible arguments for inequality—need, merit and 'the need to offer incentives or constraints to get work done which would not otherwise get done'. On the principle of need, they conclude that, since the biological needs of human beings are roughly equal according to age, and since psychological or social needs are either universal or idiosyncratic, there is here no argument for inequality of income: 'for either the need is universally equal and calls for equal treatment including equal income, or it is idiosyncratic and beyond the reach of assessment of equality/inequality, or it is of such a kind that income has no bearing on its satisfaction'. On merit, they say that one of the criticisms which can be directed against capitalist society is the largely arbitrary relationship between merit and reward. It is far from easy to compare one job with another. 'We are not convinced that some jobs inherently merit higher pay, when all allowances have been made for effort, longer training, poor conditions, unsocial hours and so on.' On incentives, they quote the majority view of the Royal Commission on the Distribution of Income and Wealth that there is no conclusive evidence of the influence of salary level and differentials on incentives, and that six studies of the effects of taxation on incentives are inconclusive.

Turning to the biblical evidence, the group says that, while the Christian tradition seems to imply some kind of equality through its doctrines of Creation and Redemption, it by no means follows that economic equality is to be regarded as implied. Of the Bible itself, 'Even if social equality is not directly within its ambit, there is enough in its teachings pointing in the direction to create a prima facie case for greater equality.' The biblical authors did not ask whether all people should enjoy economic and social equality for the same reason that they did not discuss the rights and wrongs of space travel: neither was above the horizon of possibility. Yet within the Bible there is the continuing criticism of the rich, very obvious in books such as Amos and the Epistle of James, the increasing tendency to look for greater virtue and spirituality in the common people, the dismissal of the monarchy and with it any idea that God is tied to a worldly hierarchy, the growing hope of liberation, a new exodus in which worldly injustices will be eliminated, the Magnificat which has been called 'the hymn of the universal social revolution', and the radical revaluation of values in the Sermon on the Mount, with its revolutionary social consequences.

The group next advance three arguments against inequality, examining it apart from poverty altogether. First, they claim that even if it is right for some to be rich, it may in fact be the wrong people who are rich. A popular entertainer or sportsman, or even the author of semi-pornographic books, may receive more in a few months than the average worker in a lifetime, while some of the 'dynamic entrepreneurs' who are most admired in one decade fall into disgrace in the next. Hence one argument in favour of a greater degree of equality is that it saves us to a proportionate extent from deciding who ought to be rich. Their second argument is 'the major Christian conviction that riches are dangerous', and they think that Charles Kingsley, though exaggerating, may have had a point when he said that the whole Bible was written to keep the rich in order, whereas the Church had taught that it was written to keep the poor in order. Then, thirdly, equality may also be necessary for the sake of true community. Great inequalities are a barrier to this, and it must be true that many rich people simply have no idea how the poor live; the converse is also true.

Questions about justice and equality cannot, however, be confined to issues related to the distribution of incomes since—as the group recognized—income and wealth are so interrelated, and their brief to look at incomes only proved to be a severe limitation: 'the whole issue of the relation between income and wealth needs to be discussed. Inequality of wealth generates inequality of income, since wealth can be used to produce income and also to confer non-financial goods which would otherwise have to be paid for. Inequality of income generates inequality of wealth, for obvious reasons. The question can clearly be raised: Which form of equality is more important?'

Next, as a practical provisional proposal, the group suggests that 'the income left after tax at the disposal of the richest should not be more than five times that at the disposal of the poorest'. They do not commit themselves to any particular means of achieving this greater degree of income equality, but they are clearly thinking of taxation and income policy, and in another paper contributed to the project the Directorate of Economic Studies makes three specific proposals for a long-term movement in the direction of income equality:

1. It is recognized that long-term measures to affect 'first-stage' income would involve the redistribution of the factors of production, i.e. of land and capital and those skills that can be developed by education, and that more medium-term measures could include wealth taxation and accessions taxation. But it is the shorter term measures which the Directorate has in mind, namely, incomes policy and the stipulation of maximum and minimum income levels.
2. Measures to adjust 'first-stage' income, thereby producing a 'second-stage' income, are already well known and are of two kinds: (a) income taxation, and (b) income main-

tenance. They are of course linked inasmuch as the cash benefits, of which income maintenance consists, are dependent on taxation as a source of public revenue. On income taxation it is argued that the case is strong for change in a more progressive direction, perhaps through raising of the threshold and through a more effective form of graduated scale. On income maintenance (pension, child, unemployment, sickness and supplementary benefits and family income supplement) expansion is favoured, and a move to a less discretionary system, and one that would combine more directly the tax-taking and benefit-giving measures. It is claimed that the present more discretionary system is administratively costly, personally humiliating and subject to misjudgement.

3. It is possible to take measures to remove the allocation of certain goods and services out of the realm of private income and private purchase into the realm of public provision. This is highly controversial, but the two main arguments for such public provision are (a) that certain goods are intrinsically public because they are part of the shared environment, and (b) that there is no guarantee that basic universal needs, like food, shelter, health and education, will be met by a system of private choice, either because some people have very small incomes and therefore have little choice or because they are income-less dependents (young, old or disabled) and for that reason have little choice.

These proposals lead immediately to the basic question of what kind of society is considered desirable in Britain. And in the context of a democracy 'desirable' must obviously embrace not only the views of academic theologians and economists, but also those of the electorate as a whole. The Cambridge group were clearly aware of this when they wrote: 'We found that two rival ideals of society seemed to lie in the background of our discussions. On the one hand there is the ideal of a more egalitarian society preserving so far as possible a free market economy and fostering small-scale property ownership by all—the elusive "property-owning democracy". On the other hand is the ideal of a more communal or communitarian life, in which the ownership of wealth and the undertaking of economic activity is largely the responsibility of the state, local administrative units and voluntary groupings, rather than of isolated individuals.' The group commented:

The former ideal seems to its critics backward-looking and impracticable as well as questionable even as an ideal. The latter is questioned by others because the increased scope for social enterprise and control seems to pose great threats for personal freedom. It might be that many Christians would accept, or even welcome, a planned Socialist economy so long as they were convinced that it was compatible with traditional Western freedoms; but they suspect that experience to date runs counter to such conviction. The practicability of greater equality within a free market economy and the seriousness of the threat to personal freedom in a Socialist economy both need to be evaluated. But beyond such evaluation there is much thinking to be done about which ideal accords better with a Christian understanding of man. Of course both are (in sociological jargon) ideal types, and in practice the immediate future must lie with some kind of mixed economy. We should like to see more attention given to the place of 'intermediate structures' in such a mixed economy—the units of administration and society which lie between purely local and intimate groups on the one hand and nations on the other . . . We are also aware that freedom needs to be spelled out in much more detail and that it is not a value which can be treated in isolation. Man also needs the security of knowing his position in the structure of society—of being saved from Durkheim's 'anomie' or normlessness.

Controversial Voices from the South West

If the churches are to be involved in the discussion of these fundamental issues, they will have to decide between contributing broad 'prophetic' statements, based on the general insights of the biblical and Christian traditions—justice righteousness, peace, loving one's neighbour, freedom and so forth—and a somewhat more detailed examination of the actual and potential socio-economic situation with a view to discerning at what points the general insights available to them may be applied to specific policies. The second course would certainly appear to be the more appropriate, both in terms of practical usefulness and of engaging in creative theological enterprise. The difficulty in this approach, however, is that the British churches are singularly lacking in members who have the necessary expertise to reflect theologically within a secular context, and one requiring a good deal of specialized knowledge.

Herein lies the importance of a contribution to the project made by the South West Group of the BCC's Directorate of Economic Studies. This consists of a substantial hard-headed paper, summarizing the aims of the United Kingdom during the next decade, noting current trends, and forecasting likely developments. It provides a valuable basis for *informed* Christian discussion and comment.

The group conceived the economic aims of the United Kingdom 1976–85 to be:

(i) To increase the amount of wealth in the world and thus provide enough resources for each person to live without undue anxiety for his material welfare. (The group rapidly dismissed the possibility of a perfectly balanced 'no growth state' for two primary reasons—it is not a possible economic policy; we need to grow in order to contribute to the economic prosperity of the developing world.)

(ii) To do this consistently with the known and projected availability of resources, without prejudice to the welfare of future generations.

(iii) To find a means of distributing income which ensures a moving together of the roles of command and of consumption.

(iv) To do this with careful regard to the acceptance willingly by the British people of a responsibility for the world's humanity, not just a private nationality.

(v) To develop a context of economic activity which makes

an equitable return for effort and skill; a context which makes the pursuit of sectional interest a more obviously destructive activity.

In the present situation of the U.K. economy, the group listed as the most significant factors: the balance of payments deficit; the inflexibility of an economy, the majority of whose employees are paid by an agency which in principle cannot go bankrupt; inflation; the chronic lack of investment; a recent history of investment which has not significantly raised productivity; a declining proportion of world trade; outmoded systems of labour relations; an extremely high public sector expenditure, combined with poor central forecasting procedures, lack of executive control and consequent inability to take appropriate decisions at the right time; very high levels of taxation; unemployment; the continued growth of money supply; and the uncertainty of economic analysis.

In a 1978 addendum to their paper, the group said: 'We view with some pessimism the attitudes which appear to be encouraged by changes in the economy since we discussed these matters in the summer of 1976. Britain's balance of payments has improved and the rate of inflation has declined; both developments are to be welcomed. But North Sea oil seems merely to induce a *folie de grandeur*, quite out of keeping with the country's true economic situation, the underlying structure of which is still in need of fundamental rebuilding. It can hardly be said too starkly: we are not on the brink of a bonanza.'

All these factors contribute, the group reckons, to a sense of injustice, of lack of opportunity, and thus to divisiveness, jealousy and indifference. There is evidence, too, of unwillingness to accept responsibility, to 'find a way through', rather than to create possibilities. This analysis of the present situation has, it may be noted, close affinities with the verdict of the report *The United Kingdom in 1980*, the result of an independent investigation carried out by the Hudson Institute Europe and published in 1974. The South West Group of the BCC Directorate next noted some international developments which impinge directly on the U.K.'s economy:

Since 1945 there has been international global peace, and increase in trade between politically and ideologically opposed countries; rapid prosperity growth in some European countries but an alarming indifference—maybe even a growth of indifference—to the plight of man in under-developed countries. It is also arguable that the term 'underdeveloped countries' requires more careful definition as time goes by.

The continuation of peace—a term meant to exclude the apparently necessary human habit of sabre rattling at small-scale localized wars—could be endangered by a number of events: savage world inflation; immense monetary problems; the growth of political, social or even ideological unrest, and dissatisfaction in certain 'backward' countries; drastic increase in the rate of decline of natural resources.

However, it does seem, despite what many economists argue, that world inflation is more under control than out of control, monetary problems are containable, plunder is acceptable. The group has assumed the continuance of an unsteady peace. However, the group does not believe that it will be a 'free' peace, either internally or externally. Peace is not a state of affairs which happens: it is a condition consequent upon human activity. The continued 'making of peace' is one of the priorities for any contemporary economic system. An expenditure on defence seems a necessary requirement if this condition is to be met.

Next, the group recognized that 'the way things are going' is also relevant to the discussion of the opportunities open to the U.K. in the 1980s, and the sort of possibility of change that can reasonably be proposed. They noted changes in public view on a number of social trends: educational standards; the value of the family unit; the status of women; regional autonomy; the status of authority; environmental concern; permitted sexual behaviour; technology and change. Each of these (and others could have been listed) has an economic dimension, the influence of which cannot accurately be predicted for the 1980s, even if it were possible to estimate it now.

The group was very aware that the range of choices open, and indeed the priority afforded to each social benefit, must essentially rest on political choice. There is a daunting list of social services which should grow—community welfare, education, housing, employee relations and social concern. In all such there are no imposed bounds to *qualitative* growth, and this simple fact must always be remembered when considering *quantitative* growth. Against that, there are some social trends which could be expected to gain strength:

(a) Greater responsibility for the total environment by corporations.

(b) Increased public influence, which may be expressed as action by central government on employer practices; alongside this we may also hope to see increasing responsibility on the part of employees to fulfil their contracts.

(c) Increased control by society (which means government and trade unions in this case) on general reward systems.

(d) The operation of practically any system—government, industry, medicine, the law, the church, the prisons—by consent.

(e) 'Small is beautiful'—the desire for the individual to have his feelings of individuality and contributions of skill and effort recognized and safeguarded.

The single most significant point which emerged at every stage of the discussion was that the United Kingdom could not continue its present style of operation much longer. In quite direct terms this meant that public sector spending would require to be reduced, certainly as a percentage of Gross National Product, and perhaps in absolute terms. This conclusion was not arrived at for doctrinaire reasons, but by the simple economic expedient of accepting that improvements in services—in the quality of life—have to be earned and paid for. Clearly at the moment this is not happening. It is vital that by the 1980s we have put this matter right.

The problem created by imbalance in the economy between public and private sectors is compounded by the fact that the electors are unwilling or unable to allow the government to legislate effectively in the economic sphere. Government by consent will grow, and make increasingly ineffective government economic legislation. The strong feeling of injustice, or at least dissatisfaction, with the present economic system, makes particular sections of the community more willing to trust to the divisive power of their private interests, rather than the 'honest brokerage' of legitimate and authoritative government. Hence the opportunities for leadership in government, as opposed to expediency, are likely to decline.

The acceptance of responsibility for individual welfare by the public purse has not been followed by a development of personal responsibility for the welfare of the public purse. Ways must be found whereby the individual can see where his money goes and what it buys. Only if this occurs will restriction on personal liberty be justified in terms of acceptance of personal responsibility.

The habits, customs and attitudes of 'the British way of life' will probably (the group believes) continue into the 1980s. A hundred years ago Britain had reached the peak of her muscle-power, particularly so far as world trade was concerned. From then until the First World War money, largely as overseas earnings, was reinvested and home investment was largely neglected. Heavy unemployment after the First World War polarized political differences, and the period between the two world wars determined the attitudes, beliefs and value systems, and some of the larger institutions, which influence us at the moment. The predominant feature since the Second World War has been the United Kingdom's graceful decline down the international league table. 'Great Britain' is now no more than a small island community. It is unlikely that the present system based on political democracy within the country will permit the seeding and growth of a resurgent spirit.

There has been a substantial change in the U.K.'s resources. There is now an above-average proportion of older people and no growth in the numbers of people in the working-age brackets. If the birth-rate continues to decline the population will thus stop growing and will then decrease. The research/investment ratio is well out of balance and this has permitted foreign countries, particularly the United States, to invest relatively more in the U.K. than in Continental Europe during the post-war years. There is only one apparent national resource to replace iron and coal: North Sea oil. The world lead in the creation and peaceful harnessing of fission-power has been allowed—perhaps even encouraged—to seep away.

Presently unemployment is felt to be high but this highly-charged emotional feeling may well be over-stated. Hours worked per employed person per year have fallen and appear likely to continue to fall. The capital investment per worker has increased, particularly in the 'merchant venture' sectors of industry. But labour relations are in a parlous state. Various likely estimates exist to show percentage per annum change in productivity, but one such model gives the 1973 to 1985 change as a decline in total hours worked, and only a 3.3 increase in total output achieved.

Management cannot be divorced from investment. The present low investment ratio figures stem from haunting problems in balance of payments. Low levels of demand, fewer economies of scale, and low growth in profits all result. A political ideology which has affected profit margins since the early 1950s points either towards considerably greater public ownership or the growing export of management skills, inventiveness and creativity. Little acceleration of management contribution can be expected under such conditions, as a vicious circle has been created.

All technology involves time-lag and there is often a net surplus of new thinking, which forces choice. The problem is that the direction of this choice is changed with the plunder of material resources. Re-cycling and substitution emerge as the most profitable and thus the most important

3

areas of technology. Too frequently, however, in the United Kingdom it requires some crisis or major disaster to prompt a new development, with the result that brilliant and commercially applicable new thinking is developed overseas, thus robbing the U.K. of a proper yield on the resources employed to create this new thinking.

Since the end of the Second World War, the U.K. has tended to underestimate the resources needed for new internal projects, with the result that fiasco has followed fiasco, with profits and reputation suffering. 'Prestige projects' is a new phenomenon, underwritten with an almost blind urge to maintain prestige regardless of economic viability.

Money really means the money supply and the balance of payments—where the United Kingdom has had a nightmare situation since 1945. Imports of manufactured goods have leapt away because of our own manufacturers' loss of competitiveness. Immediately after the war exports rose sharply, but from the early 1950s our share of world trade has declined and is, for example, now half that of 1959. The bright side of the picture is that the U.K.'s exports of services greatly exceed her imports and are indeed growing. Whether or not there is the capacity within the U.K. to change from these old basic industries (absorbing much labour of low skill) to the newer type of 'service of brain' export is highly debatable. Against this there is the battle of inflation, and the implications for the economy appear to be that internal spending and output must be restricted until the contribution from oil (already mortgaged) allows some minimal improvement in the early 1980s.

So far national planning has been a failure. Efforts to stimulate the traditional problem areas and to stop the movement of people from North to South have met with very limited success. Two attempts to introduce National Planning have been made, and the National Economic Development Council is a toothless reminder of these attempts, but Britain does not possess the reliable mechanics of the planning systems such as those in France and Belgium.

Some aspects of democracy will change—for example, the rule of the administration by influence from outside bodies rather than by the response of elected parliamentary organizations. Some form of government 'hand on the tiller' in wage and associated payment systems will persist. It is reasonable to expect that class divisions will be eroded (but not much) and that class militancy will decrease. Since the group holds that a high rate of economic progress is necessary before fundamental social changes can take place, it concludes that the very modest growth which is possible for Britain cannot even support modest social progress towards an egalitarian society in the true sense.

The group, having recognized that it had painted a dismal picture and that some at least might suppose the recommendation of objectives to be a waste of time, none the less moved on to make certain proposals.

It will be necessary to educate the community so that it understands that the national economy is limited and that improvements in personal situations may have to come from voluntary action rather than from state intervention. The relief of loneliness, for example, is now within the means of any person, without incurring any additional expense. Clearly the rate of quantitative growth will be minimal, but this should not preclude our society from recognizing that *qualitative* growth is obtainable at a rate which is not directly in sympathy with quantitative growth.

We have to accept responsibility to the community as individuals so that we may as a community begin to pay for what we already have. The essential improvement in qualitative growth will come from personal initiative and affectionate delight in service. The organization of social service may lead to the death of kindness; whereas a little more human affection would release resources for those capital goods which affection is unable to secure, such as housing and hospitals.

If this analysis of the present situation, current trends, and likely developments in the 1980s is reasonably accurate, the U.K. will (the group believes) need to address itself to the following challenges:

(a) Government must tackle and beat the problems of inflation and balance of payments deficits. Before these problems are dealt with no other solutions to other problems are feasible.

(b) In order to attempt to eradicate inflation, labour legislation to discipline behaviour is an essential ingredient —the present patchwork of responsibility is too unsure.

(c) The curbing of expenditure, rather than the raising of additional punitive taxation, appears to be the only action that will bring about a decrease in the public sector deficit.

(d) The transfer back to the individual of some of the public services in the social field is essential. We need the curbing of the spawn of bureaucracy in local authorities; and the running of public-owned industries on commercial lines, which may mean making available equity for public subscription and thus commercial accountability.

(e) We need, too, an increased sense of partnership between government and private industry.

(f) The formulation of long-term economic objectives is vital, despite the tendency of politicians to seek short-term political expedients as a substitute. If this is to succeed, considerable improvements will be necessary in forecasting techniques, and in the ability of those with the knowledge to educate the layman. An informed society is a necessary requirement for sound long-term decision-making to be possible in economic affairs.

(g) The supply of realistic and mobile labour is essential, in both blue- and white-collar activities.

(h) The introduction of more appropriate marketing methods is needed to establish demands, particularly overseas.

(i) The introduction of inflation accounting is overdue.

(j) Private transportation must be seen to be an essential symbol of personal freedom and unless some substitution can be made for it in that sense, then it must be allowed to continue.

(k) No community can continue responsibility towards its individual members unless the individual members develop a new sense of responsibility towards the community. Our gloomy conclusion is, therefore, that there can be no valuable increase in distributable wealth, or real increase in our growth rate, apart from a development of this sense of responsibility. Further, and more optimistically, if the development of this sense of responsibility were to occur, we should not need much by way of economic 'good fortune' to have within our grasp a considerable increase in real wealth, which it would then be the task of the community to use responsibly.

It is too easy, the group adds, to say that the Church has to take a lead in reform. The Church is weak and therefore could not do the task on its own. Furthermore, its own polarization of theological attitudes into leaving it all to 'them', and doing it all 'oneself', means that institutionally the Church merely reflects the problem that society faces. What the Church should be interested in is *persons* and they are the result of responsible participation by the individual in community. Much depends therefore on both the willingness of the individual to share, and the willingness of the community to encourage sharing and not destroy it.

Since both aspects are involved, the Christian community is concerned both with the structures of community and the motivating of individuals. Therefore it has a duty to involve itself meaningfully in the changing pattern of the total socio-economic political environment. And as one vital part in this process, the Church must begin to reflect on its own use of resources, the ways in which institutionally it encourages or discourages personal responsibility for ideas, behaviour, relationships. Whether the Church is a 'participant' community is, for example, a matter which gives pause for thought. Whether the Church has been interested in quantity or quality might also be given some attention, as also the tendency to squander or render useless scarce and expensive resources. In the way that society awaits an upsurge in available wealth before giving adequate attention to responsible behaviour, so too the Church waits for a revival—as if there was no present vitality to be mobilized and re-directed, given a little leadership and insight. So the Church's preaching of responsibility naturally begins at home through the acceptance of responsibility.

Industry has notoriously a bad press, whether it be management or trade unions, or the finance and banking houses, public or private. Quick profits have been made at the expense of the community's well-being; high wages have been acquired for the few at the expense of opportunities for the community at large—or jobs for others. However, it may not be too optimistic to see signs of new responsibility in industry at large. Whether or not the policy is right (and many could be found to support either view), the will of the majority to make the Wages Agreement work in the interests of all is impressive.

Further, it is increasingly clear that management sees itself having concerns and interests outside its own immediate sphere. As the Church, another misunderstood institution, has tended to talk rather than listen, so also industry in the United Kingdom has to emerge from its period of hurt, to engage in public discussion on public matters regarding the quality of our society.

The group felt that it is not without real significance that the first collective and organized move in such a direction has come about in a country where the contribution of the private sector remains appreciated and valued. The chairman of the Aspen Institute in the U.S.A., himself a businessman of distinction, has written:

The head of every major corporation is being made acutely aware that he and his fellow-executives are caught in a hurricane of change which is smashing at the stability and progress of this country [the U.S.A.]. For their own survival and the survival of our society, the challenges and responsibilities which centre on leading members of the business community must be met not simply by the improvement of management techniques, but by opening up new lines of communication between leaders of the business community and other major segments of our national life, and by examination of our institutions, concepts and values.

In Britain we must look for such involvement to develop and grow, for 'industry' is not a separate part of the structure of society but at its heart. Again, we must also hope for the emergence of a new type of trade union leader who sees his role as an interpretative one, as well as a protective one. Plainly, in the terms in which we are talking—of responsibility and understanding—industrial leaders are not merely concerned with profits, nor can trade union leaders be concerned merely with the cash-benefit returns to their members.

It was in the area of the activity of the state that the group felt most disquiet. For if a good argument could be made that the originators of economic surplus wealth—and this, in a Western society, remains the private sector of industry—should take a lead in encouraging responsible use of resources in the interests of the community at large, it certainly is incumbent upon central government not to act in such a way as to frustrate responsible choice. Indeed, it should encourage the required mobilization of spirit and energy. The squandering of resources, of money, time and talents, and the lack of will to deal with the problems, do not give us much confidence that central government will develop this responsibility. The fact that so many are dependent upon central government for their livelihood means that representatives in Parliament act more like delegates, sensitive to constituency or sectional interests, rather than to the real interests of the whole community. In this situation can one hope that fundamental economic and social questions will be tackled?

Although the economic future of the United Kingdom seems bleak if the present situation continues, things may change—or be changed. For essentially, the group observes, economic systems are *human* structures and, though these are difficult to change, they can change. Perhaps there is a traditional role here for the Church among other structures. Man is not entirely the product of his past history; neither is he completely at the mercy of the forces that operate on him in the present. On the contrary, the future **is** an open possibility waiting to be chosen. Our emphasis is on the notion of responsibility because we believe we can choose. A hope which makes it possible to take the reality of choice seriously provides the basis for freedom and confidence.

There the group ends its report. It seems fair to assume that its analysis of the present economic situation in Britain and of current trends in society at large will not command universal assent. Forecasting the future in a rapidly changing world is a hazardous occupation for any group of people, and Christians can lay no claim to infallibility in this area of prophetic judgement. There are no doubt alternatives to those outlined in this particular report. And it is certain that the presuppositions of the group and its prescriptions for the future will arouse serious criticism from Christians who are qualified to tackle the issues with the appropriate level of expertise. So also will the views of the Chairman of the BCC's Directorate of Economic Studies, who published an important book shortly after the Swanwick Assembly in which he championed the unfashionable Christian causes of economic growth and the profit motive, and the virtues of a consumer goods society.[4]

Yet the fact remains that the paper submitted by the South West Group was the most substantial contribution made to this part of the 'Britain Today and Tomorrow' project. Its contents were not seriously challenged at the Swanwick Assembly, for the simple reason that they were not seriously debated. Thus the paper lies in the tray of 'unfinished business', claiming no authority beyond that of the group who obviously took a great deal of trouble over its preparation. But it demands to be answered, and in terms as realistic as those employed by its West-country authors.

[4] Owen Nankivell, *All Good Gifts*, Epworth Press, 1978.

4. LIFE AND THE DOLE

Within the wider debate about the causes of Britain's present economic malaise and the long-term economic objectives and policies needed to cure it, there is an immediate problem which is causing a great deal of personal hardship and raising issues of a far-reaching character. This found expression in an important report prepared for the 'Britain Today and Tomorrow' project by a Working Party on Employment and Unemployment.[1]

The *Department of Employment Gazette* publishes monthly figures of the number of people unemployed, which receive wide publicity through the press and broadcasting, and are the subject of much social and political comment. But the basic causes of the present high level of unemployment, the distribution of unemployment in the regions and age groups, and the effects of unemployment on individuals and communities are not generally recognized by ordinary citizens, including church members, and the report is concerned, among other things, that the facts should be more widely known.

The present level of unemployment in Britain—about $1\frac{1}{2}$ million people, representing around 6 per cent of the total labour force—cannot of course be compared with the position in the 1930s. In 1932, for example, unemployment reached 2.8 million, which was 22.1 per cent of the available labour force and 6.1 per cent of the total population of the country. None the less, the present level is higher than anything experienced since the Second World War, and much higher than anything anticipated by those brought up in the post-war era. During the 1950s and 1960s, unemployment stood at 2 per cent, representing just under 400,000 people—many of whom were changing jobs or

[1] Now published as *Work or What?* (Church Information Office).

thought to be unemployable. Between 1970 and 1972, the period of the last recession, unemployment rose to a level of 3–4 per cent, representing 600,000–800,000 people. But in 1975 the figure of one million had been reached, and in the summer of 1977 this had risen to 1,600,000.

The picture in Britain today is not very different from that in Western Europe as a whole. In mid-1977 the percentages of unemployed were: West Germany 4.6, the Netherlands 5.3, France 6.4, Denmark 7.2, Belgium 0.1, Ireland 12.3. The position in North America is much the same: United States 6.9, Canada 8.0. Disturbing though these figures undoubtedly are, they can hardly bear comparison with those of the developing world where, according to statistics published in the *New Internationalist* in September 1976, some 300 million—35 per cent of the total labour force—were either unemployed or underemployed.

In Britain, as in most other Western countries, young people have been the worst affected. In 1967, 25.9 per cent of the unemployed were under the age of 25, in 1971 the percentage had risen to 31.1, in 1975 to 41.9, and in 1976 to 43.9. Throughout 1977 there were 450,000 unemployed in the under-25 age group, quite apart from the fluctuating number of school-leavers, and in July 1977 almost exactly half of the 252,000 unemployed in the 20–24 age group had been without work for at least three months. Among young coloured workers unemployment rose by 450 per cent between February 1974 and February 1977, by which time the total number of unemployed coloured people under 25 had reached 19,000. The increase in unemployment in the population as a whole was 130 per cent during the same period.

There are also significant regional variations. In the Home Counties, figures of just over 2 per cent are fairly normal, whereas 10 or even 11 per cent of the labour force are registered as unemployed in Liverpool, Wrexham and Wearside. The period June 1971 to June 1976 was moreover a time of significant change in the pattern of employment in Britain. The number of people employed in mining declined by 13 per cent, in agriculture by 9.7 per cent, and in manufacturing by 9.5 per cent. But there were increases of 17.6 per cent in financial, professional and miscellaneous services, and 12.4 per cent in public administration and defence. Manual workers are now probably less than half the total labour force.

The causes of the present high unemployment in Britain are several. The recession exacerbated by the oil crisis of 1974 has not only caused the closure of small, and sometimes quite large, firms, and the slimming of the labour force in others: it has also prevented the degree of expansion needed to absorb the increasing number of young people and married women entering the labour market. There was a considerable bulge in the birth-rate in the late 1950s and early 1960s which has worked through to the school-leaving ages and, in part, accounts for the high proportion of young people among the unemployed. Economic uncertainty and new legislation designed to protect workers against unfair dismissal have combined to make employers think twice before increasing their work forces—often preferring to offer overtime work to existing staff, rather than to take on additional people. The 'hidden' cost of employment often acts as a disincentive to the recruitment of staff, since the costs of recruitment, training, extra supervision, holidays, days lost through sickness, pensions, national insurance, and so on are thought to add as much as 40 per cent to wage costs.

Again, cuts in public expenditure have had their designed effects, creating high unemployment in the construction industry, and also bringing unemployment and a sense of insecurity to men and women with professional qualifications who were quite unprepared for their employment to be terminated before retirement. But most significant of all in the long term have been the structural changes taking place in the industrial sector, where machines are increasingly replacing human hands and brains in the manufacturing process. One of Britain's most successful major companies, Imperial Chemical Industries, is planning to spend £800 million on investment in new plant over the next few years; at the same time it will be re ducing its work force by 4 per cent per year—a loss of nearly 30,000 jobs in ten years. The effects of these necessary developments on a particular region have been clearly described in a report from North East England:

The era of domination by primary industry—coal mining, shipyards, railways and heavy engineering—is slowly coming to an end. But new industry has come. Government grants have provided new factories. Trading estates have been developed. The North East Development Council has been created to co-ordinate action on a regional scale. Foreign employers have built new extensions to their overseas businesses, though they shut them down again just as quickly when the wind blows cold at home. An urban nuclear power station has been built.

There has been major investment in the area. Imperial Chemical Industries have put £400 million into Cleveland in three years. The British Steel Corporation has invested £2,000 million over a decade. Government grants and aid have revitalized road networks and built new towns. The area called Teesside itself is a community of relatively modern origin. Middlesbrough did not exist in 1830. The river Tees was largely undeveloped until ten years ago. Now the scale of industry is vast and dramatic. The oil and chemical plants dominate the skyline and march with their advanced technology into the next century. 100,000-ton tankers and bulk carriers berth in one of Britain's largest ports.

This technological change is everywhere. It is normal, constant, and yet disturbing and hurtful. Some find it exciting and life-giving, but for others it has become a new and widespread cause of redundancy and unemployment. It affects managers and scientists as well as the less skilled. New investment brings more sophisticated technology and with it fewer and fewer jobs, cutting the labour force right across the board. In one case, £1 million invested produced a mere 1.5 jobs. Higher and higher qualifications are being demanded by this new technology and the lot of the semi-skilled and the unskilled gets worse. In Cleveland it is abundantly clear that unemployment is written into the very fabric of industrial development. Structural unemployment like this cannot be coped with by mere palliative measures which stave off its immediate effects.

Government, Churches and the Unemployed

The government is of course well aware of the problems and has adopted a number of policies designed to reduce unemployment. Its broad industrial strategy, aimed to reduce inflation and to make the economy more competitive, is undoubtedly leading to fewer jobs and higher unemployment. But in the long run, without efficiency and competitiveness, unemployment could be even higher. The difficulty here is that many factors are beyond government control. Improved export performance depends on a general international economic recovery. It is anticipated that in Britain alone there will be nearly two million more people needing work in 1991 than there were in 1971, and it is difficult to see how any industrial strategy will achieve sufficient growth in employment opportunities to meet this scale of need.

Regional policies, designed to attract new industries to areas of high unemployment, have had some success, but the disparities between various regions are still considerable and the types of industry attracted to these areas are often capital-intensive rather than labour-intensive, as the report from the North East indicates. The Working Party responsible for *Work or What?* believe that regional policies which take into account the special requirements of particular areas need to be further developed, though another school of thought (represented in the Hudson Report) believes that Britain's economic recovery depends on investment being concentrated in certain key productive areas, like the Midlands, and not, as they would see it, dissipated over wide areas where the wealth-producing returns are likely to be comparatively small.

The government has also promoted a number of schemes to blunt the edge of unemployment. The Temporary Employment Subsidy has encouraged some employers to retain people who might otherwise have been laid off. The Job Creation Programme and Community Industry have provided additional work, particularly (but not entirely) for young people. The Job Introduction Scheme has helped to ensure a better deal for disabled people, and the Job Centre Programme has tried to minimize the length of time taken to fill vacancies. Most of these schemes have been introduced relatively recently and rapidly, and they have met with mixed responses. The costs to the government have been considerable, though it is necessary to set against these costs the amount that would otherwise have been paid out in unemployment benefits. It is always important to examine the *net* position, and in this context there is some evidence that fewer public expenditure cuts might have provided greater benefits than the millions of pounds spent on helping the victims of those cuts. However, the general verdict of the Working Party is that all the government schemes have helped to alleviate the problem: 'The achievements of the Department of Employment and the Manpower Services Commission should not be under-rated. There is potential, too, in many of the projects which could be developed further.' The work of training and re-training carried out by the Training Services Agency, with its twenty-four Industrial Training Boards, is also significant.

The churches, too, have not been idle and the report includes an account of the various ways in which Christian people have responded to the problem of unemployment in their own localities. These responses are classified under the headings Analysis, Work Creation, Training, Education and Industry, Counselling and Creative Protest, and the authors say: 'Our purpose is not to claim that Christians have done more than other people. It is rather to show the great variety of projects in which Christian people have had a share and which could be repeated in other places.'

One such project in North East England, which has provided a basis of experience for similar developments elsewhere, is described in the report. It is the Stockton Portrack Workshop.

As soon as the Job Creation Programme was announced in October 1975, all the church leaders in Cleveland were called together by the senior chaplain of the Teesside Industrial Mission to meet the Regional Head of the new scheme. There had already been experience of Community Industry which began in the area in 1972, but starting projects under this new Programme without experience and skills was a formidable hurdle. To begin with, no schemes at all emerged from the churches! Eventually the Industrial Mission sponsored a churches' decoration and repair project, and a dozen congregations joined in. The next step was a plan to start a toy-making workshop, for which scrap timber was available. But there were no premises to do the work in. Then an old canteen on a site cleared for development by British Steel Corporation (Industry) Ltd. became available. Special schools for handicapped young people were contacted. Numerous negotiations and discussions were also conducted with the Headmasters' Association, with the Local Authority, and with the Social Services Department, which had its own plans for a disabled workshop. Finally, an ex-training manager turned freelance management consultant was found to head the scheme and the Portrack Workshop was in business.

The Regional Head of the Job Creation Programme gave help with the necessary paperwork and project definition, and in August 1976 the Workshop was officially recognized. Seventeen insurance policies were found to be necessary! The County Planning Department helped to fix this insurance cover, put the Workshop wages on to its computer and offered other administrative help. Now, in addition to making toys, the Workshop also refurbishes school desks and some 75 a month are produced to the complete satisfaction of school staff. Recycled solid beech desks are often preferred to more modern substitutes.

Disabled people, for whom this Workshop has been designed, suffer particularly in times of high unemployment. Where such charitable workshops do exist, people expect to buy things from them for next to nothing. They are not often seen to be employing people with special skills and an equal right to work alongside everyone else. The

Portrack Workshop has been determined to produce high quality goods and to market them on a competitive basis. It is now a thriving small business employing 44 people.

Commenting on this and other Christian responses to unemployment problems, Professor George Wedell, who has special responsibility for employment and unemployment issues with the European Community in Brussels, said: 'There is a good deal more Christian (and other) initiative on the micro-level in the United Kingdom than in almost any other country. This is remarkable and should be recognized by government and harnessed more fully.' He went on to warn, however, that 'the problem transcends the capability of voluntary effort'.

The Working Party next discussed the question: What has been particularly Christian about these responses? And they answered:

In some cases the projects we have described have been initiated by Christian people. In others Christians have shared in the work of essentially secular agencies. But within all these types of response the Christian spirit and motivation can be detected:

—The basic concern for the neighbour in need has led to involvement in projects to alleviate that need and to prevent its occurrence in the first place.

—Analysis springs out of a desire to know the truth about the human situation.

—Work creation and the innovation of new forms of creative activity is based on the belief that man shares with God in shaping the world and having dominion over it. The divine image in man is reflected in such activity.

—Training and education involve the enhancement of human potential and the development of skills and talents implanted in man for him to use both for the glory of God and for the service of other people.

—Counselling gives expression to the Christian concern for the person and confirms the validity of each one of us in the sight and love of God.

—Creative protest reflects the deep-seated prophetic strain in the Christian faith, crying out for justice and righteousness in human social relationships.

Before moving on to make their own proposals for dealing with the unemployment crisis, the group outlined the values which they believed to be an expression of their vision of what ought to be:

First, we value *truth* and the realism in policy-making which comes from facing it squarely. In the employment situation in Britain today we have detected deep-seated structural changes taking place. We need to face this truth and plan accordingly. Advancing technology is rendering old skills and old industries increasingly obsolete. It is affecting the traditional manufacturing areas more heavily than the rest of the country. Increased investment in industry will not of itself solve the social deprivation that goes with high unemployment. The problem will not go away when trade picks up. We believe that fundamentally new thinking is needed if we are to respond adequately. We applaud the variety of schemes devised at great cost to alleviate the short-term effects of unemployment, but we must recognize that on their own they are not enough.

Secondly, we value a *concern for the disadvantaged and the poor*. We have seen that unemployment persistently affects those least able to cope in our society. Yet our Christian faith demands that we care particularly for these vulnerable groups. We cannot claim to be a society motivated by Christian values if we fail to pay special attention to those who suffer most among us. We have noted that various selective measures are provided for them, but the extent of the problem is such that we need to discover new ways of proclaiming and delivering release to those held captive by it.

Thirdly, we value *human fulfilment*. We see that this takes place chiefly in community, and we value work as a creative opportunity contributing to this end. It is important because it enables people to do something for others, to serve and to participate, and these are basic requirements for human growth and development. The sense of belonging both to smaller groups at work and to the wider community is fundamental to the good society. It is the fact that unemployment prohibits this that makes it so unjust. At the same time, we recognize that some work is dehumanizing and that there is a need for certain aspects of the work experience to be radically changed. But our theology speaks to us about the dignity of work, about Christ the worker, and about the possiblity for us to share with God as co-creators. We value the opportunity for people to express themselves, to grow, to share and to serve, which work provides. We believe that this should be available to all, irrespective of colour or creed or country. We place a high value, therefore, on a policy of full employment.

Fourthly, we value *human equality*. We have discovered that unemployment is a deeply divisive element in modern society. It divides country from country, region from region, group from group, and person from person. It forces additional and disturbing inequalities upon us. We believe that all men are equal in the sight and in the love of God, and that our failure to share equitably the resources of the world and the available work is a denial of this basic truth. Fundamental new thinking is needed here, too, if we are to discover how to bring this sharing into the structure of our society.

Fifthly, we value *world brotherhood*. We have been uncomfortable in our realization that Britain is inextricably bound up in an international context. We could not banish poverty from this country on our own. We need other nations for our food, our raw materials, our trade and for the enrichment of our culture. Our common humanity, in this age of mass communication, forces us to face the truth that we cannot be free until the whole world is free with us. Our Christian faith confirms this value in the doctrine of the universal fatherhood of God. We are all brothers and sisters in the worldwide family of man. We have to seek solutions to our problems together.

Proposals for Action

In the context of these values, the group makes five specific proposals.

1. *The facts* of our changing economic situation should be made more widely known and should be honestly faced. Without widespread analysis and knowledge of the truth, and open discussion of it, there can be little chance that the full gravity of the situation will be appreciated or that adequate measures to cope with it will be taken. We envisage that widespread debate might take place in the churches, in synods, councils and conferences at international, national, regional and local levels. The pressure that could be exerted as a result, on government agencies, Members of Parliament, employers' associations, trades

councils, places of education and on a variety of other organizations, could be considerable.

2. *Further substantial selective measures* are needed to help those groups which suffer most as a result of unemployment. We look for greater special provision for young people under 25, for those whose expectations are of manual work in manufacturing industry, for black people and members of other minority ethnic groups, for the disabled and for those who have been out of work for long periods already. We see no justification for the continued inequality in opportunity for young girls, for the persistently uneven spread of the burden of unemployment across the regions of the country, nor for the seriously declining state of the inner cities. We are glad that the Manpower Services Commission has achieved as much as it has, but we look for more. We support the development of special schemes to create new work, building on the experience of the Job Creation Programme. We wish to see such schemes concentrating on socially beneficial projects, publicly valued, well managed, and contributing noticeably to the education and training of those who are taken on by them. We wish to see further special provisions of this nature.

3. *A new 'life ethic'* calls for research to give significance to our common productive process. Current disillusionment with the state of industry, the alleged low esteem in which it is held, the lack of motivation of many school-leavers faced with a career in industry, the recent reluctance of students to pursue engineering subjects at universities and colleges, and the widespread inability of politicians to understand and to control the working of the economy, are all symptoms of the absence of any clear agreement about the ends which this economic activity serves. The Protestant ethic gave a strong justification to work and produced results in terms of prosperity which appeared to confirm it. Today a new social purpose is needed. It should be rooted in the fulfilment of the potential of human beings and should build on an understanding of our common interdependence. It should enable us to demonstrate the value we place on human beings and the respect we have for the

created order as a whole. It should help us to see the proper relationship between work and leisure, enabling us to define the difference between them and illuminating the contribution of one to the other. It should deepen our understanding of the link between education and employment, so that the studies young people are engaged in at school, the training they receive at work, and the retraining they may experience later in life may all be seen in relationship to each other. Finally, it should clarify the ends of economic activity, and help us to make sure that the means employed are consistent with them. We see a valuable role in this endeavour for our theologians, and we encourage the churches to set aside further skilled resources to explore these questions. Without such a 'life ethic', which can give meaning and coherence to our economic activity, we shall make little progress towards a better society.

4. *Alternatives must be found to the dominant industrial products, methods of working and organizational styles of today*. We have noted a long-term shift from manufacturing to service industries. We do not regret this. Service industries are valuable in themselves and are often labour-intensive. They have a high human content and are geared directly to the meeting of human need. While we wish to assert the dignity and value of manual work, we also see a chance for the growth of human skill and satisfaction in other forms of employment. We welcome the increased opportunity for work for women as a whole. We recognize the liberation that is provided for them through sharing in the socializing benefits of the working community, and the opportunity to provide more for their families. We see this trend as an increase in sharing in our society which contributes to greater human equality. But we look for more radical alternatives, too. New products that serve human need without wasting scarce resources, polluting the environment, or costing more to produce than they represent in value added to society, need to be further developed. New methods of working which give priority to those who operate them need to be devised. Alternatives to continuing

115

repetitive, meaningless, unskilled, physically unpleasant work, should be energetically pursued. New forms and styles of organization need to be developed, too. We welcome the trend towards smaller organizational units, more widely shared decision-making, workers' co-operatives and participative styles of management. We wish to see more fundamental thinking about these ways of giving expression to our interrelatedness, and more experiment along these lines.

5. *These objectives should always be considered in their international context.* We believe that studies done by other groups into the relationship between world justice and our own economic plans in Britain are of fundamental importance. We support the demands for a New International Economic Order which are struggling to find expression at international economic discussions, such as those of the U.N. Conference on Trade and Development, and of the European Economic Community, at meetings of the Ministers of the Commonwealth countries and at the World Employment Conference held in Geneva in 1976. Difficult though it may be, the group believes that this issue must stay on the agenda of a society that is serious in its concern for world brotherhood and the future of employment for all men.

A Radical Change

The group's proposals are nothing if not ambitious in their aims and far-reaching in their implications. Many will applaud them but have difficulty in seeing how they can be implemented within the foreseeable future. Thus there is an obvious danger that they will be consigned to the ever-enlarging library of excellent but impractical ideas. And, lest this should be the fate of their work, the group concludes with an exhortation to further action. 'The conclusion to our report is not the end; it is a beginning . . . We invite you to take action, where you can, on the proposals we have made. What you do today will help to

nould what others experience tomorrow.' They also affirm
heir own belief in the possibility of change and improve-
nent in the human condition:

Ve believe that we are in a situation of hope. Our study has
hown that people can change the circumstances in which they
ind themselves, even though this may seem hard to accept. We
ave described new towns planned and built, investment in
echnology on a vast scale, national schemes administered by
overnments, and major trends in society. Against this back-
round, the power of the individual or the small group may seem
ninimal, and impotence rather than hopefulness the chief response.
Sut many of the local projects we have reviewed depended on the
nitial vision of ordinary individuals. The Christian Gospel does
iot promise easy success and we do not wish to underestimate the
problems of overcoming unemployment. But the possibility of
enewal, new life and victory held out to us through the resur-
ection of Jesus does give us encouragement in the struggle for a
better future.

The report was warmly received by the Swanwick
Assembly and, since its publication in booklet form, has
been recognized elsewhere as a significant contribution by
the churches to the discussion of a major problem. One
notable omission from it, however, is any serious consideration of the possibilities and difficulties involved in the
wider sharing of the available work. At the present time
three-fifths of all male manual workers average ten hours
of overtime a week. Most male workers are expected to
work until retirement at the age of 65. Relatively few
people are allowed more than three weeks' paid holiday a
year. Is there no way by which working hours can be
generally reduced through the elimination of overtime
working, a shorter working week, longer holidays, sabbat-
icals, and earlier retirement? The problems involved in
these ideas are considerable but, if the broad outlook is
one of ever-decreasing demand for labour, even greater
problems seem certain to emerge if the work and the wages
are concentrated in fewer and fewer hands. Changes here
will require much skilled organization, and some sacrifice

from those who are benefiting from the present arrangements, but justice in modern society does call for skill and sacrifice and it will be strange indeed if this particular challenge can be dodged indefinitely.

On the other hand, it already seems strange to non-economists that $1\frac{1}{2}$ million people should be unemployed when so much work remains to be done to make Britain a better place in which to live. Any suggestion that working hours should be reduced, when urban renewal programmes are being slowed down or abandoned and when it seems almost impossible to obtain the services of a plumber or a window-cleaner, seems faintly absurd. And, although there are sophisticated explanations of this paradox, its simplicity invites the question: Does the widespread unemployment now being experienced in the Western world signify the breakdown of the capitalist economic system?

The Working Party report stated: 'We see the importance of intervening in the organization and structuring of the social order. We see the importance also of developing alternatives that will profoundly affect the workings of the dominant industrial and economic aspects of that order.' The Swanwick Assembly, through one of its Hearings, said that it supported 'the development of comprehensive national policies to deal more adequately with long-term employment problems'. It also expressed its belief in the need 'for the development of an acceptable system for the distribution of income and wealth'.

These are bold and necessary words. And they have political implications of the most serious kind which need to be worked out and plainly stated. 'What kind of a society do we want?' asked the Archbishops of Canterbury and York in their 1975 Call to the Nation. The reply from the British Council of Churches could surprise them.

5. NEIGHBOURLY LOVE AND CHARITY

Although individual Christians have opted out of society in order to live as hermits, there is broad agreement among Christians that men and women are meant to live in some kind of relationship with others—in communities of various kinds. Such an agreement depends on no particular religious insight, since it is plain for all to see that human beings are interdependent and need to be involved with others if their physical, mental and emotional needs are to be met.

Within the religious sphere itself, community has been a factor of crucial importance. The calling of Abraham to be the founding father of a great nation provides the basis of the religion of the Old Testament, and of the Jewish community today. Jesus chose twelve men to be the pillars of a new community in which the dynamic love he taught might be experienced and which could become the model of all true human community. The marks of such a community may be summarized in the ideas surrounding the concepts of accepting, sharing, caring and growing, and for the Christian the parable of the Good Samaritan has illustrated what membership of the human community involves in practical action.

Hence the Church's long-standing concern for community health and its own involvement in community affairs. In Britain the Church was one of the central features of community life throughout the Middle Ages, providing a sphere in which individuals learned to live together and also a supernatural cement to give cohesion and stability to society as a whole. This did not survive the Industrial Revolution, but until almost the end of the nineteenth century the parish church was a focus and expression of community life in the remoter parts of rural England.

Since then the Church itself has shared in the general upheaval brought about by the movement of large numbers of people from small villages to large towns and cities. Its own life has become fragmented, its role in society less certain and its Good Samaritan work expressed in personal rather than social categories. The dramatic changes in society during the late eighteenth and the nineteenth centuries outstripped the capacity of the Church for change, though the best work of the Victorian slum parson, the Nonconformist mission and the Salvation Army introduced some expressions of humanity and community in many dark and desolate places.

Now, in the final quarter of the twentieth century, the British churches are sharing in a general attempt to create, recover and improve community life in a variety of settings. But they seem to be hampered by the fact that no one quite knows what constitutes true community life—especially since the sociologists moved into this field. One of their number, after identifying ninety-four existing definitions of community, came to the conclusion that 'beyond the recognition that people are involved in community there is little agreement on the use of the term'.[1]

One thing is, however, quite clear: it is useless to think of community in terms of the model provided by a rural Utopia of the past. Most people, apart from the very old and the very young, now spend their lives in a variety of relationships in a number of different locations, based on the demands of work and the choice of friends, activities and interests. In the larger cities it is common for people enjoying a rich variety of work, recreation and friendship to have no meaningful contact with their immediate neighbours. On the other hand, there are some who are less mobile or have less choice and are more dependent on contact with those who reside in the same locality. Thus any discussion of community and any work to further community must take account of the complexity and pluriform character of modern social life.

None the less it is now possible to identify two quite

[1] G. A. Hillery, 'Definitions of Community: Areas of Agreement' in *Rural Sociology*, Vol. 20, pp. 111-23.

different contributions to the improvement of community life and, while these sometimes overlap, they normally spring from different conceptions of what constitutes a healthy community.

Community Care

This is related to social casework and personal community service, which have honourable histories and are by no means redundant at the present time. The provisions of the Welfare State do not cover every personal need, nor is it conceivable that they ever will. In any event, individual care or assistance—exercised locally and spontaneously in response to immediate need—has an important contribution to make to personal welfare and community health. Traditionally, the British churches have encouraged their members to engage in this kind of activity as an expression of their Christian discipleship. In recent years, some local churches have organized Good Neighbour or 'Fish' schemes in order to channel personal service to all the individuals known to be in need in particular areas. There is scope for more work of this kind, which is in effect an extension of family or neighbourly care.

It is necessary, however, to be aware of certain dangers involved in caring work of this kind. Paternalism, which may demean the recipient of aid, is an obvious trap, though not so obvious that many good-intentioned people avoid falling into it. Another danger is that excellent first aid work may obscure the need to deal with the fundamental cause(s) of a particular community problem. And in both of these instances there is the near certainty that individuals or groups will lack the opportunity to assess their own needs and contribute to the solution of their own problems.

Community Work

It was partly in order to avoid, or at least minimize, these dangers, but chiefly to widen the whole concept of community care and development, that a number of significant changes in the basis of social work began to emerge in the late 1960s. These changes have encouraged the growth of what is now known as 'Community Work'—defined in a British Council of Churches report as 'an area of activity which explores the means whereby citizens can be encouraged to act collectively in order to identify their own community needs and to make their contributions to the meeting of these needs'.[2]

Such a broad definition provides an umbrella for a wide variety of activities, but common factors in Community Work are the involvement of members of a particular community in meeting their own needs and the changing of some aspect of society to facilitate self-help or to prevent a problem recurring. Sometimes this involves collaboration between a local government authority and one or more voluntary organizations in order to adjust and improve the existing system. An example of such collaboration was contributed to the 'Britain Today and Tomorrow' project from Leeds:

Caring about the Elderly

The South inner area of Leeds was developed rapidly in the nineteenth century to provide cheap 'back to back' housing for workers near the textile, heavy engineering and other factories of the locality. The housing was tightly packed and, as the families had grown up together, there was little scope for children to settle near their parents. This meant that in due course there was a large concentration of people over pensionable age. As these people died or became too frail to live independently, the houses they vacated provided some of the cheapest accommodation in the city. Newcomers therefore tended to be poor, with large families—and some were coloured.

In 1971 a new social welfare team was introduced to the

[2] *Community Work and the Churches*, 1976.

area and the new workers were immediately faced with a flood of requests for assistance from the neighbourhood. In an attempt to meet these requests voluntary visitors for the elderly were recruited from the local church, and, as it happened, these volunteers lived in the neighbourhood. Many were themselves of pensionable age. The local churches appointed a minister who had been trained in community work to serve in the area as part of a team ministry.

It soon became obvious that the problem of the care of the elderly was overwhelming—the number of people of pension-age ranged from 40 per cent to 80 per cent of the total population of the districts of the area—and in the face of mounting difficulties it was apparent that the local people were developing a dependency on the new social service office and its workers. The way in which the voluntary workers from the church had been organized reinforced this trend and by-passed a great deal of the informal caring work already going on. The social workers pressed the minister to provide a lunch club on the church premises, but this was resisted as an inadequate response to the level of the problem. What is more, it would have continued to build up passive dependence among the elderly.

After spending some time living in the area and meeting people informally, the minister began to discuss the problem with the church members, social service workers, decision makers and other interested people. In turn they conducted further investigations into the way in which local people saw the problem. Small groups discussed possible solutions. The purpose was not to persuade people that the church, the minister or the local authority had a solution that should be accepted, but to help people to see their situation and the nature of the problem more clearly, and to share information and develop ideas for a solution.

Eventually the community groups and church members began to work on the idea of a centre which would act as a focus for work with the elderly in the area and provide day-centre facilities. It was decided that the church building would make a suitable base, a quick decision in favour of the scheme for the conversion of the building was made by the church, and an application was made to the government for financial aid to carry out the work and provide running costs. A group was formed to ensure that there was steady pressure on the relevant people to secure a positive decision, and the process was helped by the sympathy of the local Member of Parliament who was Secretary of State in the appropriate government department. This action-group managed the centre when it was first opened, but a democratic structure was soon evolved with annual elections.

The activities in the centre have reflected the self-help approach. Rarely do groups sit and listen; often they are mastering new skills which a busy working life crowded out—swimming, painting, dancing or learning about welfare rights. In the same building there is a playgroup run by local mothers and developed on the same principles. This provides a natural meeting across the generations and an opportunity for those new to the area to meet older residents. Some pensioners help with the playgroup, some mothers with the centre. Of course, some personal caring work among elderly people has to be organized: there are those who are ill or may have just returned from hospital. But this personal work is seen as an integral part of the 'giving and taking' relationships set up in the area and is a long way removed from the traditional 'us doing something for them' approach. And, though there has been and continues to be a dependence on outside bodies for financial assistance in the running of the centre, the fact that it is managed and staffed by local people, rather than by local authority appointed officials, seems to have increased its impact and its contribution to the life of the community as a whole.

If this 'success story' is a challenge to the leadership of the British churches (how many churches are prepared to become involved in community work of this kind and to encourage ministers to be trained for it?) the general approach is one which bishops and moderators can support without overmuch anxiety. But what are they to make of another report which found its way into the 'Britain Today and Tomorrow' project:

Welland Residents' Association, Peterborough

This Association was formed in June 1973 on a new council housing estate comprising 350 dwellings—houses and flats. Owing to pressure on the housing waiting list, tenants were moved into completed dwellings before such basic amenities as footpaths, street signs, public telephones, playing areas and shops were provided. But there was a nucleus of people who were not prepared to accept living in this situation with their families and, in the words of the present chairman of the Association, 'The spontaneous combustion of oppression threw up a group'. In this context, 'oppression' is defined as 'domination by the public sector ruling class: local government officers and Councillors'.

The current aims and objectives (and problems) of the Association have been described by the chairman in a paper originally prepared for the Brazilian Bishops' Project International Study Days for a Society Overcoming Domination'. It is a classic example of a structural conflict model of Community Work and, though not dependent on any specifically Christian insights, does require a response from Christian bodies claiming to be concerned with the development of healthy community life:

We have concerned ourselves with two main aspects of function—
1. To get amenities for our estate.
2. To involve as many people as possible in participating in their own affairs, for we have felt much of the trouble has been apathy amongst tenants. We feel bad government exists because ordinary people are disinterested and allow mismanagement.
We have done rather well in the amenities struggle, but we do not congratulate ourselves for we have not done well in getting tenants to fight for their own rights. We have studied our failure in this respect and we can now enumerate reasons for people not participating in the management of their own lives:
i) The committee of ten has been taken up with amenities business and has neglected personal contact work. It is hard to get more than ten volunteers to an annual general meeting.

(ii) Our resources in terms of people and money have been too limited. We need a local community paper for regular free distribution—a communications line.

(iii) Tenants do not understand rights issues or local government. They are generally the product of an education system which has made them into semi-literate factory fodder, especially neglected in terms of education about the individual and society.

(iv) Tenants accept oppression as their lot. We see this as the overlap from the old cloth-cap days of a clear-cut class system in which one 'knew one's place'.

(v) Tenants are afraid of government. They cannot assert themselves positively, particularly when language is impoverished; and they have an ingrained fear of eviction.

(vi) Tenants often have severe personal, economic and social problems. Oppression extends from national government practices to denigration of each other through personality conflict problems. How can they be interested in community health and welfare, and participate in it, when they are so frustrated, ignorant and unhappy in themselves? In many cases their potential has been grossly under-used, to their disadvantage. They are too creative for a mundane job, or frustrated in promotional chances by lack of confidence, mean management or prejudice.

(vii) Many tenants are deluded. They do not think they are oppressed by anyone or anything. They believe what the advertisements tell them and what the government says. In fact, they are quite contented, happy people. Perhaps then they d not represent the oppressed, feeling nothing about that condition or the world. Complacent, not apathetic.

(viii) Tenants falling into any of the above categories militate against themselves—a form of internalized self-oppression.

From these findings, it is clear *how* local government can exercise unacceptable power themes. *Why* they do it is a second question. A senior official may not set out to dominate anyone, but the structure of government and the pressures placed upon him lay down the pattern for the emergence of a dominant personality practising oppression. The two clearest examples of this practice are—

(a) Pursuit of rent arrears methods which include approved harassment techniques.

(b) The form taken by the Tenancy Agreement regulations which are in the main petty oppressive articles (nearly 40 items in Peterborough), and include no indication of the landlord's responsibilities to the tenant, though some of these were laid down in the Housing Act 1961.

Any of these regulations can be used to bring pressure to bear on an unpopular tenant. We can see the sense in this if he is making life intolerable for his neighbours; but we are more interested in *why* the tenant needs to misbehave, or *why* he cannot pay his rent. Yet the official is able to exercise domination and it is this fact which bothers us. We know it is partly tenants' inertia, but it is also due to inertia on the part of people who are elected to the Council.

Councillors do not exert the power vested in them by the people very competently. This may be due to working too hard at too many commitments, but it is also due to lack of sufficient interest in and education about processes of local government. Like the tenants (self-inflicted), they exercise oppression through inertia. We have observed Council meetings where Councillors have been baffled by figures and where they have not challenged officials for explanations. We have heard questions being given baffling answers, yet the Councillor did not press the matter further, perhaps for fear of seeming stupid.

It might seem that we are being hard on officials and accusing them of slipshod management at a time when their job is made especially difficult by economic restrictions. But we argue not so. In 1976 Peterborough City Council increased rents to raise an additional £549,000. Of this, £449,000 was to replace Rate Support, while £100,000 was intended for the Repairs Account, to raise from £48 to £56 the cash available for repairs on each of 10,000+ properties. Yet repairs are not being done, except in cases of dire emergency or when Councillors are continuously chasing officials. Therefore, the tenants are paying much more— the rate was increased too—but getting much less, and overall cuts in public sector expenditure have deprived them further. Oppression by deprivation occurs as much as oppression by domination.

The Welland Residents' Association is not depressed by this overall condition. Our issues are local, though related to wider issues, and we understand that we live in a society geared to profit not needs. Our aim is to work on priority issues—whittling away at the problems, pressing on relentlessly.

At present, the city rubbish dump—for the waste materials of 180,000 people and factories—is planned to be placed next to our estate. We must fight this. Last year we failed to rally our people on the rents issue because we did not have enough personal contact with neighbours. Our aim now is to get the message across more clearly to everyone: the ultimate target being to inform them enough to realise they are free to participate in the management of their own lives.

Collectively, the British people are free to act, since the instruments of the State—armed soldiers and police—are inadequate to match collective resistance. Yet the people are afraid; they cannot see the light about collectivity—even at local level. They say, 'Well they (the Council) will do this or that whatever I say.' But this is an unnecessary admission of defeat and we, the Residents' Association, say we will not endure defeats; If there is to be domination, then we shall be doing the dominating—we, the people, expressing ourselves through a collective unit. Oppression can only be overcome by informed resistance to oppression.

The aims and methods of this Residents' Association are clearly based on certain convictions about the nature of community and the distribution of power within a local community—and presumably in society generally. It is a long way from the Church's traditional involvement in community life, and indeed some distance from the Leeds elderly persons' project where 'partnership' rather than 'liberation' appears to have been the primary motivation. Yet if the British churches are to be seriously concerned about the character of community today and tomorrow they can hardly avoid some of the awkward questions raised by the Welland Residents' Association. This in turn requires consideration of the theological perspective within which church leaders and others might examine particular situations and pieces of community work. Here the report of the BCC's Working Party on *Community Work and the Churches* offers certain suggestions, though it is at pains to emphasize that creative theology must emerge from a community worker's experience, rather than from an abstract theoretical basis. Even so, there are some biblical and traditional insights that cannot be ignored:

(i) The prophetic tradition emphasizes that social justice, integrity and *shalom* (peace) are as important, and often more important, than correct worship.

3

(ii) The tradition of man as co-creator of the world gives man a co-responsibility for its development.

(iii) Jesus, 'the Son of Man', as the criterion of what it means to be human.

(iv) The recognition that God is at work liberating men, and that the Church must gather at the points of this activity.

(v) The mission of the Church to express solidarity with the outcast, deprived and powerless.

(vi) The priesthood of all believers which demands participation and leadership by all the fellowship, not just those who are ordained.

(vii) The concept of *koinonia* (fellowship) implies participation in the social, political and economic orders.

(viii) The Kingdom of God as a present reality.

(ix) The Good News as the bringing of abundant life.

(x) The worshipping, gathered and eucharistic community as a model for the wider community.

(xi) The ministry of Jesus:

    (a) Asking the right questions.

    (b) Encouraging people to answer from their own experience and resources.

    (c) Intervening in situations.

    (d) Opposing all that dehumanizes.

There is, it would appear, nothing in this list of biblical and traditional insights that would preclude an individual Christian or a local church from becoming involved in the work of a body such as the Welland Residents' Association. Indeed there is a great deal in the list that might reasonably be expected to drive Christians in precisely this direction, and the main report on 'Creating Community' presented to the BCC Swanwick Assembly in November 1977 said quite plainly that 'the creation of community demands changes, not just in personal relationships but also in the institutions, power and economic arrangements of society'.

The New Black Presence

Nowhere has the need for such radical changes in British society been made more clear than in the report of a

British Council of Churches' Working Party on Britain as a Multi-Racial Society. This report, published in the early part of 1976 under the title *The New Black Presence in Britain: A Christian Scrutiny*, was not planned as part of the 'Britain Today and Tomorrow' project, yet finds a natural place among the thinking provoked by the project and still stands as one of the most penetrating analyses of the racial situation in Britain to be produced by any responsible body —ecclesiastical or secular.

The group responsible for the report met under the chairmanship of Gus John, himself a native of Grenada, who came to Britain in 1965 and now serves as Director of Youth and Race in the Inner City Project of the National Association of Youth Clubs. Other members were of Caribbean and Asian origin, and among those of British origin a number had had many years of working in Africa or the more deprived inner-city areas of the United Kingdom. Their broad conclusion was that Britain's race problems in general, and the plight of the coloured immigrants in particular, are a symptom of a deep and long-standing malaise in British society as a whole. Stated in their own words: 'The basic issue is not a problem caused by black people: the basic issue concerns the nature of British society as a whole, and features of that society which have been there long before the recent phase of black immigration. The black communities are the groups which have been most recently exposed to the demands of the British way of life, and they are exposing features of that way of life which may be painful to recognize. In certain very revealing ways, they are holding a mirror to British society, in which members of that society can see themselves. The urgent question, therefore, is not "What shall we do about the black problem?" but "What is British society like?" and "What sort of Britain do we want?" '

The mirror provided by the black presence certainly does not reflect an attractive picture of British society at the present time, and the Working Party invited its chairman to delineate the main outlines as these appeared to him. This he did with a bluntness of speech not normally encountered in church documents, as the following extracts from a document submitted to the Working Party clearly indicate:

Britain saw black immigrants as little more than second-class production factors; as labour stock whose yield could be maximized, given the social circumstances they would encounter . . . higher rents, higher HP, in fact the privilege of being black entitled you to work longer hours and pay more for everything.

Because of the society's attitude to and way of seeing black people, it was felt that it was quite acceptable to consign them to urban areas already disintegrating with decay, and rumbling with the conflict generated by dispossessed groups aspiring towards a more humane way of life. Black people were lumped, lock, stock and barrel with the white working class. The society then turned round and blamed the blacks for the urban decay and for the results of social inaction and unplanned urban growth on the part of successive governments.

Refusing to come to terms with its own history and to accept that it was essentially a racist society, Britain laid its increasing social problems—most of which were a function of the racialist nature of the society—at the door of 'the alien wedge' . . .

If one were to examine institutional structures in this country and how they relate to black people, one would find disturbing evidence of malpractice, of racism, of black people being included out, and of procedures and policies which render black young people and adults quite vulnerable. This is reflected in institutions along the whole spectrum from education, housing, social services, etc., careers, opportunities, to black people within the police force and in the British armed forces . . .

From where I stand, working with twelve youth and community work projects, all concerned with black people in twelve inner-city areas, I find the system's method of coping with the situation of young black people quite horrifying. The police rightly claim that they have a job of work to do, and presumably that job takes on new dimensions with every batch of black school-leavers who join the ranks of the unemployed. We have long arrived at a situation in which it is necessary for schools to teach young people, formally and seriously, not only how to survive on the dole but also how to survive in the 'nick'; in other words, education for unemployment and education for incarceration . . .

Against this kind o background how does one relate to the concept of integration? Given the experiences of black people in

Britain to date, given the manner in which institutional racism plays havoc with people's lives, granted society's inability to look at how it is mirrored in the experience of its black population, let alone accept what it sees and what that experience tells us, is it surprising that black people treat Community Relations and the idea of harmonious community living with pronounced cynicism? To wish to integrate with that which alienates and destroys you, rendering you less than a person, is madness. To accept the challenge to join it and change it from within, when it refuses to accept that you are there in your fullness and refuses to acknowledge the results of the interaction between you and it, is double madness . . . In the light of the totality of our experience and not just the British experience, community relations as the race relations industry defines it is not just a luxury but a downright humbug. We, as black people, need to realize the dangers facing us as a racial minority in this country and take action to confront our condition. This we cannot do if we continue to expend our energy within irrelevant programmes which only serve to confuse the real issues facing us, and at the same time enable the oppressive system to continue the pretence that there is a genuine concern about our situation as a racially oppressed minority . . .

For us, as black people, the choice is clear. Even if the Church, encapsulated as it is within the oppressive culture so that it cannot stand with the poor and oppressed, refuses to proclaim the Gospel of deliverance that Christ preached (Luke 4:18), and accept the mission that the Gospel enjoins, a mission which poses the Church as a contradiction to the status quo, we as black people could do no other than identify with the struggles for liberation of the oppressed peoples of the world.

The Working Party accepted Gus John's analysis, while recognizing that black people are not always unanimous in their evaluation of British society, and that Caribbean attitudes are sometimes different from those of Asians. But the personal experience of the Working Party members and the investigations carried out as part of their study for the report led them to identify certain elements within the disorder of the black communities in Britain:

1. Large numbers of potentially creative young people defined, labelled and stigmatized by being condemned

to spend years in schools for educationally sub-normal children, and emerging finally to incur the disrespect and rejection of society as opposed to being allowed to earn a wage.

2. Even larger numbers emerging each year as semi-illiterate school-leavers doomed to exist on the fringe of society.

3. Young people without roots and without hope, often unemployed and homeless, gradually drifting into a life of crime.

4. Conflict between these young people and the police force and other control agencies, with a high proportion being removed from society into custodial institutions.

5. Parents incurring humiliation and blame for not caring for their children or for dealing with them too harshly, losing all hope and self-confidence and creating further problems for the social services.

6. The co-opting of potential leaders into organizations that are intended to control discontent and to do ambulance welfare work, so that they are not available to engage more radically with the structures of society which are based on exploitation and which create the casualties in the first place.

7. The white working class clamouring in some sections for repatriation and denial of citizenship to black people, and in other sections expecting black people to join them in alliance without taking upon themselves any concern for the black people's own claims: black people working harmoniously alongside white people on the factory floor, but being excluded from joining them after work in working men's clubs.

Reflecting on their findings and analysis, the Working Party reached the conclusion that the experience of many black people in Britain today is not basically different from that of many white people, though their rejection and sense of isolation is undoubtedly exacerbated by racism. But the main problem is the pyramid shape of British society itself. This condemns large numbers of people to a permanent position of disadvantage—worst schools, worst housing, worst medical facilities, worst social and recreational amenities. These form the base of the pyramid, and above them are to be found more privileged groups whose affluence, life style, opportunities and influence increase as their numbers become smaller. And although the privileged minorities depend so greatly on the rest for their privileges, the large number who constitute the broad base of society are always made to feel 'outsiders'—and it is at the base of the social pyramid that the overwhelming majority of black immigrants have found themselves. Hence the judgement of the Working Party:

To be working class meant, and still to some extent means, to belong to a nation that is not the real nation. In England particularly, rich and poor, scholar and peasant do not share a common culture to the extent that they do in parts of the other nations of the British Isles. It is perhaps this kind of barrier-system within English society, rather than straight poverty, that immigrants have found most frustrating. They did not come to this country just to be the bottom of the heap: they feel that this was not the purpose for which they were invited, nor for which their parents were invited: and in the countries from which they came there is not the same kind of subtlety and deviousness in the system which puts people at the bottom of the heap.

At this point the Working Party discerned what it believed to be a significant difference of attitude between the black immigrants at the bottom of the social heap and their white working-class colleagues: for, whereas the British working classes have been assimilated to the system and do not, on the whole, see themselves engaged in a struggle against oppression, the black people are not prepared to be assimilated to a system which they regard as oppressive. Therefore they have little sense of solidarity with the disadvantaged of British ancestry and little confidence in the Labour Party as an instrument of justice and liberation. And so the Working Party reached the crunch issue: 'Perhaps the sharpest question which has come to us in our investigation is this: Is it possible for a British type of society to exist except as a heap with a group of people at the bottom? Is it possible to be so interested in success, without a group of failures who can make success credible?'

No answer to this key question was forthcoming in the report. It is reasonable to suppose that the members of the Working Party were unanimous in hoping that the pyramid structure of British society might one day be replaced by something more just and humane—and this sooner, rather than later. But, since they lacked the skills necessary for turning hope into a policy of revolutionary change, they made no specific proposals on the point. Instead, they concentrated on two issues which could perhaps be regarded as preparing the way for a new British social order in which minority groups and other distinctive communities can play their part in the life of the nation and receive a fair reward for the contribution they make.

The first of the Working Party's hopes was that there might be a movement towards a pluriform concept of society. The idea that immigrants from other racial and cultural backgrounds will eventually be assimilated into British society, either by accepting a permanent position at the bottom of the heap or by conforming to middle-class social norms, must be rejected—as indeed it has already been rejected by members of the immigrant communities themselves. Instead, the various racial and cultural groups should be encouraged to maintain and develop their distinctive identities, and contribute their particular insights and gifts to the life of the nation as a whole. Of course, such a suggestion is threatening to those who benefit from what they regard as the present 'unity' of those who inhabit the United Kingdom. It can easily be dismissed as 'divisive' and fear can be aroused by talk of 'unassimilated minority groups living in ghettos'. Yet the development of the right kind of pluriformity now appears to offer better prospects for success than schemes for assimilation which seem certain to fail.

At this point the Working Party suggested that the pluriform approach, far from being an unfortunate necessity and a second best, would lead to 'a richer and more inclusive British life', and they called attention to a number

of areas of personal and community life where vigorou
black communities might have something to teach the
indigenous white population. The cultures from which
Britain's new black citizens have come retain many in
sights into the character of human interdependence and the
relationship between man and nature, all of which i
highly relevant to Western ecological problems and the
increase in heart disease, alcoholism and other stres
disorders. The way in which Asian families care for thei
sick and elderly people could have something to say to the
whole of British society about its methods and standards o
personal care. So, also, could the African handling of deatl
and their support of the bereaved. And as the indigenou
British become increasingly assimilated into their industria
and technological culture, with its dehumanizing demands
the assistance of those for whom this is a new, and ofter
shocking, experience might well lead to a more adequate
evaluation of what is taking place in Western society.

These are some of the Working Party's hopes for the
future of race and community relations: 'This country ha
an opportunity for its national character to grow and b
renewed on a scale such as it has not known for many
centuries.' But such a growth and renewal requires a
radical change of outlook on the part of the British. I
means, first and foremost, a willingness to recognize—
especially in England—that the so-called liberal tradition
with its many achievements and its great benefits to thos
who have been able to play the game according to the rules
has masked another face of society, which is illiberal and
degrading to the poor, the marginal and to the under
privileged alien. It will also require a readiness to allov
the new black communities to determine the terms and
characteristics and boundaries of their own identity
'People are not free if there is a more powerful group c
people who insist on defining them and keeping then
contained within that definition.' And in the quest for a
more just society the freedom of the black communities t
claim certain economic, social and political rights will hav
to be acknowledged. There is no possibility of building

new pluriform, yet integrated, society if one or more sections of it are—or feel—dependent upon the generosity and goodwill of the rest.

Enough has been quoted from official reports and documents to indicate that at the leadership level the British churches have adopted a radical stance in respect of community work, and especially in their assessment of the underlying causes of Britain's race problem. It is normally the case that those who serve on the full-time staff of bodies like the British Council of Churches, or join specialist working parties, are not representative of their constituencies as a whole and often take positions that do not win universal support. Yet, in the case of *The New Black Presence in Britain*, it has to be noted that this remarkable report was introduced to an official Assembly of the British Council of Churches on 6 April 1976 by the Bishop of Liverpool (the Rt. Revd. David Sheppard) in a commendatory speech in which he said, 'I go along with the view that black people have not brought problems to Britain but have revealed the problems our society had.' Moreover, the Assembly itself, which is made up of a highly-respected cross-section of the leadership of the churches, having debated the report, passed *unanimously* a resolution expressing its gratitude to the Working Party for 'a stimulating paper which demands careful reflection by Christians' and urging 'member churches to encourage their departments, committees, local congregations and members to use this opportunity to listen to an expression of the black experience in our society'. This resolution went on to 'accept the challenge which it presents to us and to our understanding of, and obedience to, the Christian faith, and asks the Division of Community Affairs to bring recommendations to the Assembly for dealing with implications arising from the document'.

Fine words and high aspirations on the part of the BCC Assembly, but before the churches' critique of the existing structure of British society is taken further, and its recommendations for the development of community work underlined, it may occur to some outside observers that a number of questions on these topics might usefully be addressed to the churches themselves.

The first relates, again, to the extent to which the official documents are in any sense expressing the views of the churches as a whole. For it does not seem to the diligent listener to episcopal sermons or to the reader of local church magazines that one of the primary purposes of the Church is to subvert the existing social and economic order. And the Working Party responsible for *The New Black Presence in Britain* was clearly aware of this when it wrote:

In the past the churches have been sources of inspiration and of power for social reform. But the churches have also contributed to the conditions from which people need to be liberated. They have become trapped into being a device for congratulating the powerful on being powerful. Long before the latest large-scale black immigration, the churches connived at a system in which some people have been relegated to the margins of society and deprived of a voice. More recently, they have become pre-occupied with questions of their own survival, and this means that they have a strong inclination to hope for the survival of society's present order and structure.

The truth is that the radical critique of British society is being voiced by a small minority of Christians who are within the prophetic stream of the Church's life. And what they are saying is being listened to sympathetically by a much wider body of church leaders and members who are genuinely concerned about the plight of black people and the poor. At the Swanwick Assembly, the Archbishop of Canterbury led the signing by all the members of a powerful statement condemning racism in general and the activities of the National Front in particular. Yet the radical viewpoint is in grave danger of being stifled by sympathy, for it has yet to be seriously debated within the British churches. Approving nods are substituted for real grappling with issues which, if resolved and carried into action, could have only the most dramatic, and painful, consequences for the churches and their members. Again, Gus John makes the point with some force:

A preoccupation with community relations and racial harmony is unjustified and misplaced unless it is seen as a natural outcome of the struggle for equality, liberation, human dignity and racial justice. The Church must choose to identify with and wage that struggle not in order that blacks might be given a better deal, but on its own terms and out of an active self-interest. If the Church is happy about the society which black people experience in the manner described, then it has nothing to say to black people—or to whites for that matter—and it deserves to be condemned with the oppressive system. If it is not, then it is imperative that it engages the values of society and works towards a re-ordering of society in accordance with the vision of social justice and the deliverance of the oppressed, which, as Church, it must have in Christ.

The Churches and Community Work

The issues involved in a statement of that kind are far too important either to be ignored or taken for granted. They call for the most rigorous examination, and if the churches cannot accept the analysis of the present social situation made by Christians like Gus John they have a duty to say so. But, equally, if they do accept such an analysis, they have a duty to take action on many fronts in order to assist in the effecting of change.

Since the debate on the basic issue has not yet taken place, much less been resolved in favour of radical action, it is hardly a matter for surprise that the churches' own involvement in significant community work is somewhat limited. Which is not to say that churches are not undertaking important work in some places. The Leeds project for the care of the elderly, described earlier, is an expression of insight and imagination. Elsewhere, some local parishes and congregations have made their buildings available for community work, and in some instances a community worker has been appointed in preference to an assistant minister. There are Neighbourhood Centres, established and supported by local churches, and providing specialized advice (legal, housing, welfare rights) in addition to per-

sonal counselling. And in a few areas groups of churche
have initiated community work on a wider, perhap
borough, basis. In addition, there are individual Christian
—clergy and lay—who are employed as community
workers or regard themselves as community workers. The
involvement of the churches in community work cannot be
assessed simply by whether particular efforts are based on
church premises or operate under church auspices.

Yet, having acknowledged all this, the fact remains tha
the Church's contribution to community work is small
and represents only a tiny part of the resources it could
make available for work of this kind. In 1968, the report of
the Calouste Gulbenkian Foundation, *Community Work and
Social Change*, drew attention to these resources and thei
possible exploitation: '(The churches) command a network
of many men and a number of women working full-time
and of premises unrivalled by any other voluntary body . .
They have in the past carried out a number of social wel
fare and educational activities which have since become th
responsibility of the community as a whole . . . In common
with other voluntary bodies, many of whose activities hav
been taken over by statutory authorities, there has been a
tendency for the churches to try to cling to these particula
activities rather than to explore those new areas, such a
community work, where there is as yet little statutor
provision . . . Although the formal breaking down of
traditional barriers and the engagement in community wor
takes time, there are many clergy to whom this work woul
be welcome if they were trained for the job and given
clearer mandate for it. This may well apply, too, to man
women church workers, and indeed to many lay members
Here then, in the churches, their congregations, thei
premises and their sometimes still powerful voice in socia
affairs, is a significant potential source of communit
work.'[3]

That was said in 1968, and eight years later the BCC
Working Group on the subject reported, sadly: 'Th

[3] Quoted in *Community Work and the Churches*, p. 8.

churches have done little to really develop this potential'. Their report complained that church leaders were doing little to encourage in a systematic way community work in the churches; in fact, where a community work approach had been initiated this was sometimes destroyed by the churches' failure to make the right kind of subsequent appointments. It was also noted that, of the British churches, only the Methodist Church has established a special committee (the Community Development Group in the Division of Ministries) to promote community work insights and to encourage and sponsor community work training.

The importance of the churches' greater concern for community work was stressed again at the Swanwick Assembly. The churches' 'enviable possession of local manpower, immediate resources and nationwide communications' was noted, and 'the need of the churches to examine their current deployment of people and plant' was urged. Various community work issues were remitted to the BCC's own Division of Community Affairs 'for examination and appropriate action', and the churches were urged to provide the funds needed for the continuation of the central work already in hand.

Among the issues remitted to the Division of Community Affairs was a crucial one concerning 'the validity of the churches' current involvement in "community" work, with their frequent emphasis on individual needs at the expense of corporate needs'. But here was a matter that cried out for a full-scale debate among the church leaders gathered at Swanwick, since it contains the clue to the churches' lack of involvement in community work of the more recent, radical and comprehensive kind. Of course, the British churches are essentially conservative bodies and, as the Gulbenkian Report was aware, it takes time for traditional barriers to be broken down. But there is a more fundamental issue—with profound theological questions at stake—concerning the Church's relationship with human society.

It is not necessary to argue here that such a relationship

exists and that the Church has a responsibility for preaching and living the Gospel within its framework. The question is whether the Church conceives its responsibility in individual or corporate terms—in care and concern for individual men and women in need, or in the influencing and changing for good of society as a whole. The answer, no doubt, is that the Church must do both and that the categories are not mutually exclusive. Yet, for a variety of reasons—theological, historical, cultural—the British churches have in recent centuries laid the greatest emphasis on work among individuals. And this emphasis remains the most powerful driving force in the Church's social work at the present time. Lively local congregations are well organized to meet personal need, and often do so with real dedication and love, but the idea of becoming a force for changing certain elements in the social structure of their neighbourhood is quite alien to them. Relations with the Local Authority may be excellent, and there may well be close co-operation with professional social workers, but the whole picture of community life is never subjected to a Christian critique, nor is an attempt made to grasp the realities of power.

This failure to deal with communities as a whole extends far beyond the immediate issue of local community building, and includes all those other communities—industrial, commercial, educational and recreational—to which individuals belong. And the called-for adjustment of thought and action has become a matter of the greatest urgency. Nowhere more so than in the realm of local community work, where most of the churches' resources are still to be found; though once action is initiated on a corporate basis the inter-relatedness of all the communities that constitute modern society becomes increasingly apparent.

Yet the weaknesses—theological and practical—in the British churches' approach to community work do not mean that the churches are obliged to accept as infallible every new sociological theory of the subject; neither should they feel bound to approve and become involved in every form of community action. There is a need for evaluation in this, as in every other, sphere of life, and it is at this point that the churches can make a very valuable contribution, though it cannot be emphasized too strongly that the degree to which attention is paid to their views will always be directly related to the extent to which they have first-hand experience of the issues under consideration.

In the report *Community Work and the Churches*, the BCC Working Party attempted tentatively to work out realistic and authentic ways of relating human issues which are thrown up by involvement in community work and appropriate aspects of the Christian understanding of being human. They noted several points which might contribute to a Christian critique of community work, the first of which concerns the potential implied in the conviction that men and women are made in the image of God and are sharers in the love of God. Inasmuch as community work enables men and women to prepare themselves for mature relationships it is a divine business with possibilities and resources to match. Therefore nothing is ultimately impossible.

The potential is however in each and every man and woman, so Christians have a particular concern for the working out of a practical balance and tension between the individual's needs and the community's needs, knowing that they are inter-related but not yet equivalent. Christians have therefore to insist on pressing an analysis of situations and resisting over-simplification. In considering particular circumstances 'Christians will draw from the Bible in general and from Jesus in particular an understanding of God's concern for the poor and the oppressed, and of God's role as the disturber of all that keeps men and women from their full and free share in a richness of community and life'. This may involve community workers in opposing oppressing structures, institutions, processes and values which prevent people from attaining maturity. But, since this opposition is expressed in the context of the universal and unconditional love of God, there must be concern for the oppressors as well as for the oppressed.

Christians, while always stressing the divine potential in

men and women, will also be conscious of human sinfulness and aware that attempts to perfect human nature are bound to be provisional and incomplete. This suggests the need for realism (not to be confused with cynicism) in community work, and the recognition that any one form of work or association must have its limitations. 'Community' itself can be exploited as a form of tyranny or manipulation, and particular groups can be as selfish as those they are fighting against. The Working Group believes that 'a proper understanding of sin and of eschatology should enable the constant overcoming of failure and frustration, and the constant renewing of hopes not yet fulfilled or once again denied'.

Since the close of the Swanwick Assembly, the issue of race relations has become even more prominent in the national debate about Britain's future. There is, it is believed, political capital to be made out of the racial prejudices of many British people, and statements by Conservative Party leaders in the early part of 1978 have increased the fears of the black communities and hindered the work of all those who are committed to the building of a multi-racial society. The position of the BCC in this matter is clear, but it can hardly be re-affirmed too often, since the racist elements in Britain show all the signs of gathering strength. If, at the end of the day, it could be shown that the churches had offered the slightest encouragement to racism, or compromised with it in any way, or failed to expose it as un-Christian and a grave evil, their credibility as agents of true community would be completely destroyed. The warning of Gus John, on page 139, demands to be heeded.

6. THE COST OF FREEDOM AND PEACE

Change is now normal; and one special feature of modern society is the inter-relatedness of the different facets of change. The highly complex mechanism needed to control a shrinking world is extremely sensitive to change. Movement in one sphere tends to activate the rest, often in unforeseen ways. The rapid advances in technology which have been a feature of the last twenty-five years have changed the lives of everyone in the Western world, and also had repercussions elsewhere—creating the need for changed political and economic structures to accommodate new possibilities and demands. There are now very few areas of life where it is possible to propose a 'simple' change: the consequences of the proposal need to be traced and evaluated in many different directions. Neglect or carelessness in this part of the planning may be held responsible for many of the problems in modern society.

In the deliberate search for social change, it is normally possible to detect two distinct approaches. There are, for example, those among the underprivileged and disadvantaged who wish to have a fairer share of their nation's wealth and, to this end, are prepared to work for change within the existing social and political framework. This involves them in all kinds of political activity and they are prepared to work, often with heroic patience, for long-term goals. The pattern of social change in Britain has followed these gradualist lines and, although the Labour Party is sometimes believed to have socialist intentions, its policies have generally been designed to win or retain the support of those occupying the 'extreme centre' of the political spectrum, as well as offer something to the less privileged elements in society whose interests it traditionally represents. The fact that none of the post-war Labour governments has seriously tackled the question of House of Lords reform is clear evidence of the non-revolutionary character of the British Labour movement.

But there is another approach to social change which is less patient, and is expressive of a commitment to the building of a particular form of society which is believed to have intrinsic worth, for example Western democracy or a socialist or fascist state. In this case there can be a deliberate desire to break down the existing social structures—sometimes by means of physical violence. Those seeking radical change of this kind tend to flourish either in a static society in which inequality is rife and there is mounting discontent, or in a rapidly changing society where there are tensions between groups, anxiety and rising expectations. When the foundations of society are being shaken, then there is a tendency towards polarization and confrontation leading to violence. At the moment it is too early to judge how far the increased support for the National Front in certain areas of London and Birmingham, where deprivation and rapid social change (including racial factors) have gone hand in hand, is firm evidence for the shaking and undermining of the foundations of British society. But, superficially at least, the signs are not encouraging for those hoping for non-violent change.

An interesting example—with a happy ending—of the delicate situation that now exists in certain urban areas of Britain was brought to the attention of the BCC Working Party on 'Violence, Non-violence and Social Change'.

During the evening of 4 June 1976 an Asian student, Gurdip Singh Chaggar, was killed in a brawl outside a café in Southall, in West London. His assailants were a number of English youths but the incident appears to have been entirely fortuitous and the accident occurred when tempers were raised about girl-friends. There were, however, many of the ingredients for civil disturbance present. Southall's indigenous population had been weakened by out-migration and the area lost its civic status in 1974; in the absence of a community council, authority appeared remote. The immigrants were divided between Asians, mostly Sikhs, and some West Indians. Among the Asians there was a generation gap—the older people retaining a loyalty to their roots, the younger wishing to become full participants in British society, but feeling oppressed economically. There was clear evidence of the arrival on the scene of extreme leftist groups willing to capitalize on the situation. In time the extreme right, doubtless, would also have appeared. The police appeared to some observers to be over-reacting to the possibility of further incidents. The situation could have turned very ugly.

Yet matters did not get out of hand. Fortunately, Southall had sufficient stability not to fall apart. After an early spontaneous demonstration demanding revenge, the energies of protest were channelled into anti-racism and community solidarity. Significantly, the local political and religious leadership were active and involved. The church leadership took the lead in organizing and running the main protest march, subsequently using the emotional energy to promote a community association and other positive aims. In the end, what could have been an explosion became a means of community growth. The existence of a healthy community and the skilful intervention of local leadership before extremists could exploit the situation undoubtedly made all the difference. Unfortunately, these protective and creative elements are not found everywhere.

The problems arising from living in a rapidly changing society, which is a relatively new experience for the human race, led the BCC Working Party on 'Violence, Non-violence and Social Change' to pose three important questions:

1. *Is present British society in such a state of flux that it is not able to sustain much more, especially induced, change?* There are signs in all kinds of conservative reaction to the social developments of the 1950s and '60s that people need time to get their bearings or to recover their equilibrium. However, any such issue cannot be predicted; it is a matter of judgement, and there are those who believe that the British social fabric has a knack of adapting itself and can sustain the present pressures.

2. *Is present British society so structured that only a radical break and reconstruction can overcome the injustices in it?* No one denies there is room for improvement in society. What is questioned is the possibility of improvement within the present system, and this is bound up with ideological differences about the legitimacy of graduation, the nature of power, and so on.

3. *Is it more desirable to go for social aims at the expense of the social fabric or is it better to retain law and order as the best framework for social development?* This is directly related to the question of violence as a tool of social change (and to a lesser extent of any use of confrontation). To use violence is to decide for chaos as preferable, if it can be a means to what is believed to be a good end, and the judgement is to some extent dependent on how much value is placed on what already exists.

The Working Party, having noted the dangers of violence and social collapse, and observed that the normal Christian understanding is to accept violence only as a last resort when it is absolutely clear that no other way is open, went on to suggest that 'on balance, while being committed to social change for the realization of social justice, particular aims must be seen against the need to accept responsibility for the whole of society. There is wisdom in restraint and gradualism, and therefore in limiting the tools of change. Moreover, change in a stable social context is less likely to end up in dictatorship of left or right. It may be that we should seek not only a just and responsible society but also the flexible and representative society. It is important to work for greater and valid democracy as this is part of social justice.

Here, then, is a clear commitment to 'restraint' and 'gradualism', and—by implication—the rejection of violent change in British society. This is what might easily be predicted of a group of representative churchmen, or indeed of any typical group of British citizens, and the commitment is made in the context of a society in which violence appears to be increasing and is believed by some to have become endemic.

Yet the present problems in British society are not so easily disposed of, and the gradualist approach cannot always avoid conflict, with the risk of violence. Anne Power has described[1] a community work project in Holloway, in North London, where the Quakers set up Friends' Neighbourhood House in an area where unemployment, bad housing, urban renewal, poor services and migration all make for frustration and resentment. 'There was a warden but no other staff. It was an open door, a base, and because it was open people came in, and one thing led to another, so there is now a network of groups and activities throughout the neighbourhood.' These include area playgroups, an adventure playground, tenants' groups, immigrants' groups, housing action committees, teenage meetings, conservation area politics. There is frequent recourse to direct action and demonstration, which requires great care in a volatile situation where violence, as an uncontrolled force, is just round the corner.

Manifestations of Violence

In this story there are various areas of conflict. One of these is between the local groups and the Greater London Council, the authority for housing and planning. It involves confrontation, ranging from statutory procedures to direct action, over grievances: 'It is the beginning of answerability to the people directly affected by policies drawn up without consultation.' Another area of conflict is between the older inhabitants and the growing number of middle-class house purchasers who wish to live nearer central London. This has brought in the property developers, a rise in house prices and a clash of style. Initially, there were also clashes between the police and teenage groups, but as a result of meetings between the police and the young people a certain rapport was established, the police became more discreet, and now there is much less fear on both sides. Much frustration in the area has now

[1] Anne Power, *I Woke Up One Morning*, BCC, 1974.

been channelled into creative action, but the possibility of violence erupting is always there.

The role of the police in this and other difficult situations is frequently misunderstood—a point made with some force in a contribution to the Swanwick Assembly by the Committee on Police in the Community. After pointing out that contemporary emphases on the value of pluralism and diversity are difficult to reconcile with received views of the function of law as the instrument of a society determined to enforce a single model of behaviour, the Committee observed that, although the police are not responsible for the making of the laws they are required to enforce, nevertheless they tend to be identified with them and attract any unpopularity which attaches to a particular law itself. 'There is therefore a sense in which the police become scapegoats for unresolved disagreements within society as a whole concerning particular aspects of social behaviour. They carry our sin.'

The need for a closer relationship between the policeman and local people is, therefore, a matter of considerable importance. 'The advantages of the foot beat-system over the Panda car are evident.' The Committee added: 'One implication of this which requires further examination is that the exercise of discretionary powers by the police may need to reflect local attitudes to what is acceptable, provided that members of a local community have adequate opportunities for expressing their attitudes towards unsocial behaviour.'

It is important, however, to distinguish between various forms of violence and their underlying causes. There is, for instance, a difference between the violence displayed by hooligans at a football match and that employed by those intent on breaking up a political march. The violence of the bank robber is different again. And because these forms of violence have different motivations and causes, the methods of control have to be different too. In a critical, but not unsympathetic, appraisal of the Working Party's paper, Adam Curle, Professor of Peace Studies at Bradford University, listed five distinct manifestations of violence:

1. Ideological violence, as practised by the PLO, IRA, Red Army faction, liberation forces such as Frelimo, or of any who are violent (even though their motives may be mixed) for the sake of a cause. Part of the confusion surrounding this aspect of violence is that its practitioners are viewed as heroes or terrorists depending on which side one favours—Joan of Arc, T. E. Lawrence, the French Maquis were patriots or war criminals respectively to their friends and their enemies. An additional confusion is that success brings legitimacy, for example, Jomo Kenyatta and, again, Frelimo.

2. Structural violence, which is the sort of violence embedded in unjust or grossly unequal social systems. Here the violence is not directly physical (although it invariably has physical corollaries, such as high infant mortality; even in Britain infant mortality differs significantly between socio-economic groups 1 and 2, and 4 and 5), but involves economic, social and political deprivation and discrimination. For extreme examples, see South Africa and still, in many respects, the southern states of the U.S.A.

3. State or institutional violence by which those hostile to or disliked by the authorities are restrained or punished. It often heightens as a result of ideological violence (see the awesome dilemma of the West German authorities being reluctantly pushed towards distasteful repression). But it may also be the occasion of ideological violence, as in the case of the Tupamaros in Uruguay.

4. Violent crime, which is self-explanatory.

5. Pathological violence, which is normally a destructive response to present, or more usually past, pain, fear and confusion in which individuals inflict on others the hurt they have themselves experienced (or feel they have experienced).

Violence in Ireland

As Adam Curle recognizes, several or all of these types of violence may be perpetrated in a given situation, of which

a classic example is to be seen in Northern Ireland—th
most acute and dramatic instance of violence and conflic
in the United Kingdom at the present time. In its con
sideration of this particular issue the Working Party wa
considerably helped by an important report *Violence i*
Ireland produced in 1976 by an Irish Council of Churche
and Roman Catholic Joint Group on Social Questions
This report identified several factors in the history o
violence in Ireland, in which religion and politics hav
always been closely intertwined.

The basic cause of the present problem is the cumulativ
failure, extending over nearly three centuries, to find a way
in which the people of two nations, cultures and religion
can be integrated within a relatively small geographica
area. The existence of the 'double minority' (Roma
Catholics with their own national aspirations forming a
minority in the North, and Protestants with their own
national allegiance and fears constituting a minority in
Ireland as a whole) has produced a situation which has
so far, defied a political solution.

This is not the place to consider the history of th
conflict or the way in which Britain has attempted to
handle 'the Irish problem', but the sequence of event
during the last two decades is of some significance. Following
the failure of its fairly small-scale campaign of violence
during the years 1956–62, the Irish Republican Arm
abandoned physical violence in favour of a politica
approach. This was of an extreme left-wing character and
aimed at uniting the Catholic and Protestant workers o
both North and South who would, it was hoped, find a
common cause in their positions of underprivileged, ever
though the reasons for their respective positions might b
different. In theory at least, there was every reason fo
supposing that Ireland could support a large socialis
movement, and that the existence of such a movemen
would divert the long-standing religious/cultural/nation
alist conflict into a simpler bosses/workers conflict whic
would, when successfully concluded, not only improve th
lot of the workers but also provide the basis for a unifie

Ireland. This was by no means an unworthy objective, though it did not take sufficient account of the historical factors in the conflict and the difficulty of replacing these with new political aims.

In 1968, however, the civil rights movement sprang up in Northern Ireland as an expression of a contemporary world-wide concern for social justice. There was ample scope for its activities, since the Catholic population was underprivileged and discriminated against, and—in common with civil rights movements elsewhere—the Irish protesters used the techniques of confrontation and demonstration. The IRA was not involved in this new movement, but the emergence of a group of people who had chosen the way of violent confrontation in preference to the gradualist approach presented a challenge to it. The result was a split and the formation of the 'Provisional IRA' who were, and are, committed to violence in the hope that this will make the province ungovernable, lead to the withdrawal of the British 'oppressors', and pave the way for a united Ireland ruled from Dublin. Government measures combined with police and military activity designed to contain the violence exacerbated the situation, with the result that between 1968 and the beginning of 1976 more than 1,000 people were killed, nearly 26,000 people (one person out of every sixty for the whole population of Northern Ireland) made claims for personal injury, and 105,000 claims for damage to property (amounting to over £200 million) were made. The psychological, moral and social effects of the violence cannot of course be quantified, but the authors of the report are in no doubt about the overall effect of what has taken place since 1968:

The evil fruits of violence would in themselves be enough to show its intrinsic evil in the Irish situation. It may take generations before the terrible moral and spiritual price for these years of violence is paid. The sanctity of human life, which is a central Gospel principle as well as a basic human value, has been seriously eroded. The consequences for the future of Christian society in Ireland, indeed for the future of ordinary civilized living, are grave indeed. No conceivable political result could justify it.

Irish experience could well stand as a conclusive demonstration of both the evil and the ineffectiveness of violence as a means of desirable social change.[2]

These are strong words, spoken with great authority out of a situation in which violence, non-violence and social change are daily realities and not simply matters for abstract reflection. The conclusion of the authors is that non-violence is a pragmatic necessity, for the legitimate aims of protest are not possible through violence or in a violent society; that without prejudice to the long-term needs for justice and peace there is 'a moral obligation to support the currently constituted authorities'; and that the churches must progressively free themselves from their past identification with particular political stances. They move on to propose a seven-point programme for the churches in Ireland 'as their specific contribution to the elimination of violence and the achievement of reconciliation':

1. *The churches and their members must act justly themselves.*
   This includes justice within and between the churches, and in the churches' relations with the wider community. They must not seek unjustifiable privileges for themselves, or remain silent about injustices in order to secure political support, or to retain the support of certain interests or groups within congregations. Sensitivity to how things appear to those outside the churches is also required.
2. *The churches and their members must uncover injustice fearlessly.*
   This concerns the activities of political institutions and other interests or groups in the community. A suggestion is made that an Irish Centre of Christian Social Investigation be established, on an all-Ireland basis, to monitor and investigate the basic grievances of discrimination and injustice related to the occurrence of violence, to alert the churches to the danger of permitting their worship to be exploited for political and

---

[2] *Violence in Ireland,* Christian Journals Ltd., Belfast p. 49.

military reasons, and to scrutinize the counter-insurgency role of the armed forces.

3. *The churches must be prepared to come to the aid of victims of injustice.*

This involves collaboration with other voluntary bodies who are concerned with individuals who have been caught up in the evils of society, and also with the strengthening of community life through the provision of better housing, adequate incomes and more recreational facilities. Special emphasis is laid on support for family life, for young people, and for those under duress.

4. *The churches should encourage and prepare their members to take all legitimate action to overcome injustice.*

The emphasis here is on education programmes concerned with the political and social implications of Christianity for Irish society. But it is also envisaged that the churches will not hesitate to give a direct lead to public opinion on issues of justice. Support by the churches for a Bill of Rights to protect various minorities is suggested.

5. *The churches cannot escape the obligation to give guidance to their members about methods of direct action alternative to violence, and not open to the same condemnation.*

This is a new field for the churches and their members, but non-violent techniques need to be pioneered and advantage taken of the experience in these techniques gained elsewhere.

6. *The most distinctive task confronting the churches is to promote and support reconciliation.*

Much work needs to be done in proclaiming the Gospel message of forgiveness, patience, peace and reconciliation. And specific attention must be given to the issues of Mixed Marriages and Separated Education.

7. *The churches must encourage community development and reconciliation.*

This is a wide field and includes helping to release the latent forces in the community of goodwill, enterprise, concern and talent which may have been unexploited or unrecognized. Political leaders should also be encouraged to seek a just agreement with their opponents rather than victory over them.

The programme ends by 'reiterating the futility of calling for reconciliation and peace in the community in the absence of full reconciliation between the churches themselves . . . If the churches are true to their Lord they will individually and jointly lift up their hearts in prayer for guidance and help, and do together all that conscience does not compel them to do separately. Both in their corporate acts and in the conduct of their members, the churches must now demonstrate that a reconciled relationship between them has become a constant factor in Irish society.'[3]

This report has not escaped criticism in Ireland (no report on so controversial and explosive a subject could be expected to), but its analysis of the situation has been widely accepted as valid and perceptive, and the Roman Catholic hierarchy have, with only minor comment, endorsed the major thrust of its recommendation. In the rest of the United Kingdom, the report is seen by the churches as a very significant document, and no one standing outside the Irish situation would wish, or dare, to quarrel with its courageous verdict and proposals. If it is true that the Irish churches were somewhat slow to awaken to the danger in their midst, and their own involvement in the causes of violence, they have moved considerably during the 1970s.

The question arises, however, as to how far the lesson of the as yet unfinished Irish experience can be transferred to other parts of the world. The authors of the report, writing within their own painful experience, are in no doubt that violence cannot be justified in Ireland at the present time, and they also conclude that this experience demonstrates the evil and ineffectiveness of violence as a means of desirable social change elsewhere. But is this conclusion a valid one?

[3] *Violence in Ireland*, p. 89.

Violence in Southern Africa

Many Christians in Southern Africa and Latin America, while sympathizing with those caught up in the Irish violence, might well feel that their own situations are very different and call for quite different treatment. This certainly appears to have been the view of a BCC Working Party report on *Violence in Southern Africa*, published in 1970. Surveying the position of the black inhabitants of South Africa, South West Africa (Namibia), Angola, Mozambique and Rhodesia (Zimbabwe), the Working Party came to the conclusion that 'the history of Southern Africa in comparatively modern times has throughout been a tale of conflict. It is violent history and, in the areas considered, the present political systems are maintained solely by political force, without social cohesion, or general consent. If liberation movements are now violent, this is no new manifestation but the continuation of a long and bitter struggle for liberty and independence.' Since the white governments of Southern Africa are determined to preserve the present situation as long as they can, continues the report, 'this makes them, in the eyes of many Africans, an occupying enemy power, as the Nazis were in France. To such an occupying power, many Africans see resistance as the hard, the courageous, and the moral course and collaboration as the easy line of expediency dictated by fear.'

Thus the report moves on to endorse the concept of the 'just revolution'. It recognizes the claim that the racist régimes cannot be broken in any other way. In any case it is not for British Christians to forbid recourse to arms when they have their own defence forces. While non-violence would be preferable, it can be said to have failed. In discussing the possibility of non-violence, the report points out the sacrifice and discipline that it demands. It sees it as an option none but heroes can take, especially when the response is known to be brutal, and 'since we know that sacrificial non-violence is only likely to be acceptable to individuals, we cannot accept it as a practical means of achieving an end ... Unless we can provide a better strategy for change then we cannot both declare our solidarity with freedom fighters and refuse to help them.'

What is the alternative? The report recognizes that there can be no blanket endorsement of any strategy because, however well-intentioned, those involved in the struggle can become dehumanized, use excessive force or be corrupted by power. In a fallen world there has always to be room for the prophetic word of judgement: 'It seems likely', the report says, 'that only a church within the revolution can help to humanize it. A church that is trapped into deifying revolution and making gods of its heroes has merely updated the pagan worship of war. To be within a revolution and from there to speak prophetically to it, may be both illogical and terrifying. It is at this point that it may simply be necessary to be foolish for Christ's sake.'

Seven years after the publication of this report, it is possible to examine its analysis and conclusions in a somewhat different light. Broadly speaking, the analysis stands. But it is necessary to set against the belief in 1970 that the use of force by African revolutionaries had 'no immediate prospect of success' the facts that Angola and Mozambique were liberated from Portuguese rule, and the Smith régime in Rhodesia was driven to make the 1978 agreement with nationalist leaders. In none of these instances would the violent actions of freedom fighters have been sufficient on their own to bring about change. Other, external, pressures were needed as well, but the internal violence and border threats have been—and continue to be—highly influential.

Nor was it foreseen in 1970 how soon world interests would be sucked dangerously into the conflict. Of course, world interests have been involved in Southern Africa for many years—largely providing moral, economic and, sometimes, military support for white racist governments—but the substantial part played by the Cubans and Russians in the liberation of Angola and Mozambique was a new factor, and provoked a much more serious concern for

Southern Africa on the part of America. The liberation of Angola led to a civil war, and the two former Portuguese territories now have Marxist governments whose concept of freedom is not the same as that of the Christian missionaries who drew the attention of the world to the vicious and inhuman ways in which the then Portuguese government was trying to retain control of its African possessions. Another consequence, quite unforeseen, was the violent, though almost bloodless, revolution in Portugal itself—the repercussions of which were felt in neighbouring Spain and may have helped to create the conditions in which, on the death of Franco, a democratic society replaced a repressive fascist régime. Within Rhodesia competing African groups, some of them with Christian leaders, including a bishop, are engaged in a struggle for power as the days of white supremacy draw to a close. The South African government, faced with change and instability uncomfortably close to its own borders and the mounting hostility of world opinion, appears to be retreating into an even more clearly defined *laager* which it is determined to defend against all comers.

All of which has happened within a mere seven years and is intimately connected with the use of violence in the cause of social, political and economic change. It is much too early to form a judgement on what has happened in a story of change which is still far from completion. British people who are concerned about the effects of violence in Southern Africa, and the degree of instability that follows the overthrow of established political orders, may find it helpful to reflect on how much violence and instability preceded the development of their own democratic institutions. Equally, those who support the freedom fighters will do well to note how rapidly violence escalates and how unpredictable are its consequences. And as the cauldron of Southern Africa begins to boil more threateningly, the futility of facile judgements made from a safe distance becomes more and more evident—though the British people have not yet fully discharged their responsibilities in that part of the world, and the British churches have a special concern for black and white Christians held in the tension between the struggle for justice and the yearning for reconciliation.

Violence in Defence

Somewhat nearer home are the problems associated with Britain's own defence policy. Obviously, it is not the intention of Britain, or of NATO, to take an initiative by launching an attack on some other nation or group of nations. But the maintenance of armed forces and nuclear weapons implies that in certain circumstances they might be used; hence, the ethical problems associated with violence and non-violence cannot be dodged by those who are concerned with Britain's defence policy.

The most substantial piece of work undertaken by the British churches in this field appeared in 1973 in a BCC report entitled *The Search for Security*. This report draws attention to the growing realization of the absurdity of modern all-out war as an instrument of justice and ultimate peace. At least pacifists and non-pacifists can be agreed on that. And the report goes on to point out that the classical 'just war' doctrine when properly understood is not primarily a sanctioning of war but an attempt to limit it. War is always evil and if entered into as a last resort must be restrained as far as possible; war is never permissible for aggrandizement or oppression.

The report, very properly, devotes most of its attention to alternatives to war, the best ways of ensuring stability and reducing the occasion for war. The concept of *détente* between conflicting power blocs is important in this context, and so are efforts to control the growth and spread of armaments. Herein lies the significance of the current strategic arms limitation talks, SALT. Above all, security is not simply defence but requires trust and justice, and a framework of international law within which conflicts of interest can be resolved by peaceful means.

At this point, the report—surprisingly, it may seem—has

some hesitation over world government as an ideal. It suggests that such a world institution could easily become a repressive instrument in the hands of élite groups. Rather there need to be checks and balances, and independent and trusted international organizations. Thus, while the powers and role of the United Nations as a peace-keeping body need to be strengthened, there is also a need for means for regional and world consultation—a kind of world democracy.

All of which is, inevitably, a long-term objective. In the meantime, where do Britain's responsibilities lie in relation to her own defence arrangements and her involvement in NATO? What kind of contribution should Britain make to international security? These and other related questions were discussed by members of the British section of the Council on Christian Approaches to Defence and Disarmament, and an edited version of their discussion was contributed to the 'Britain Today and Tomorrow' project. Since the group included pacifists and non-pacifists, no agreed answers were forthcoming, but the lines of the moral dilemma facing Christians were quite sharply drawn.

It was argued by some that the defence of the United Kingdom is based on the North Atlantic Alliance in the belief that it is only through the collective effort of like-minded nations that the West can ensure its freedom and, in deterring aggression, contribute to world peace. Whatever its intentions, the Soviet Union's capability for exerting political pressure on the West by military means is growing. Britain's contribution to NATO may be small, but her geography and facilities are important to the Alliance, and her involvement is significant in a European context and as a sign of willingness to share with the United States in the moral and ethical burdens of nuclear ownership.

Behind this argument lies the conviction that, while it is important for Britain to play a full part in international efforts towards disarmament, unilateral disarmament is not a morally responsible option: 'The difficult path to a more certain peace must be taken in steps rather than leaps.

From a position of military balance, with a convincing capability for conflict management on both sides, the next step should be a balanced reduction in arms. Negotiation from military weakness only encourages appeasement.'

Against this pragmatic position, the group considered the pacifist case derived from the belief that 'those who seek to follow Christ may not deliberately inflict hurt or harm on another, physically or mentally or in any other way, even for a just or righteous cause'. Moreover, in the long term, force and violence almost always cause more problems than they solve. One possible policy decision derived from this belief would be Britain's withdrawal from NATO and in due course from the Alliance, followed by a considerable reduction in Britain's own defence forces. This would place Britain in a similar position to Sweden and Switzerland which rely on the protection of NATO, and shelter under the massive American nuclear deterrent, but it is the pacifist hope that the British withdrawal would sooner or later lead to significant moves towards disarmament on a much wider front.

Christian Perspectives

There is a clear division among Christians, not only in Britain but throughout the world, as to whether violence may, in the last resort, be met with violence. In general, it appears that although the response of non-violence is being made by an increasing number of individuals, and is deeply respected by others as an authentic personal vocation, there is no substantial support for non-violence as an appropriate response for corporate groups, such as nations, which have wider responsibilities than those normally embraced by individuals. For Christians there are profound, and unresolved, theological issues involved in this division and there is little prospect of a consensus being reached within the foreseeable future. But as an aid to further discussion, the Working Party responsible for the 'Violence, Non-violence and Social Change' section of the project produced a statement of 'Christian Perspectives' which may be summarized as follows:

1. *Conflict is part of created human experience.* The freedom of human existence can only be based on mutuality and love. Relationships are built out of the variety of human experience, needs, hopes and fears. Each of us is different. Sharing means therefore discovery through differences, diversity and conflict. Part of human maturity is the ability to accept and deal with this openly and with joy.

2. *Conflict is occasion for sin.* There is a pervasive failure, passively and actively, to bear the burden of being human. Instead barriers are built and social relationships sour. The sinfulness of the human condition must be taken seriously, but it is a fallen state, not the ultimate truth, for man is created for community and communion. Hence the call to overcome the damaging conflicts of past and present and to struggle for the future. And hence the need to take a positive attitude to the state, which is too often conceived in negative, static terms, as a means of controlling sin. But the state has also a creative, dynamic function, enabling human freedom and righteousness. Thus, while the state can be opposed and attacked, the Christian will normally wish to work through the structures of society (Romans 13). The Bible does call for revolution (Exodus) but it also calls for righteousness among the people (the prophets) and patience in the face of evil (Revelation 7).

3. *We live by covenant.* The bond between God and his people is that of calling and response, of saving and acceptance. The key concepts are responsibility and *shalom* (peace). We respond to and accept responsibility. If God has accepted us, then we must accept each other; if God has redeemed us, then we must accept any and all, however far we are apart. We have to have a theology that is big enough to comprehend all mankind, to believe that there is no beyond, no 'outside the pale'. To condemn another is to deny hope. More positively, the covenant between God and man brings *shalom*—the peace of God, woven out of justice, of care for the down-trodden and the stranger, where power is responsibility and service. So there is always

a call to strive against injustice, cruelty and oppression, and to build up a compassionate and serving society. These two concepts are not always easy to hold together. Yet the Christian must endeavour not to shut the doors of reconciliation and renewal.

4. *We are under judgement.* The Kingdom of God is always beyond us and the present is therefore always under judgement. This means that the Christian cannot be finally identified with any ideology or system or analysis. He is free to use the tools to hand and the insights from human science, but they must be used in the service of the Kingdom. He is utterly given to achieving certain penultimate goals, but knowing that the final outcome is beyond his reach. The only demand is for obedience—varying from one person to another—and the doctrine of forgiveness points to the acceptance by God of unworthy human effort and the promise of renewing grace and providential care.

5. *We are saved through the Cross.* The Gospel is about the overcoming of enmity (Ephesians 2), being a victim of violence and overcoming through absorbing hate and anger (I Peter 2: 21ff) the triumph of conflict, a defeating of the power of evil (Revelation 12) and challenging the powers that be (Cleansing of the Temple). Even when trying to live in obedience, Christians are involved in human solidarity in sin. It is not that one way is good and another sinful, but that whichever way we turn we can only rely on the mercy of God. To feel obliged to become involved in violence does not make it good but underlines our involvement in a fallen world. Dietrich Bonhoeffer once said: 'If any man tries to escape guilt in responsibility he detaches himself from the ultimate reality of human existence, and what is more he cuts himself off from the redeeming mystery of Christ's bearing guilt without sin and he has no share in the divine justification which lies upon this event. He sets his own personal innocence above his responsibility for man and he is blind to the more irredeemable guilt which he incurs precisely in this.'[4]

[4] Dietrich Bonhoeffer, *Ethics*, English translation, SCM Press, 1955, p. 210.

6. *What of the Church?* It is necessary to recognize the 'greatness and misery' of the Church. It bears the name of Christ, it is the people of God, the household of faith and therefore, rightly, the Church is looked to as the locus of the Word of God. Yet at the same time it is representative of broken humanity, tied down to the history and prejudices of time and place. The Church cannot help but be caught up in the distinction of class and nation, sharing the hopes and fears of the society in which it is found. It cannot help being made up of ordinary people who are influenced by the many different forces at work in their lives. But this is not to be seen as other than how the Gospel must be found—embedded in the reality of the world, giving hope and comfort, judgement and freedom within the web of living.

Within the Church there will always be a *variety of ways* in which God's word will be heard. The Christian mind, grappling with the Word of God and the contemporary world, struggles to articulate obedience. There will be many voices—some from those engaged in noble sacrifice, others more humble and obscure. In our day we can even expect prophecy by committee or report. In the matter of violence and change we have to listen to those engaged in the struggle across the world, while testing the spirits.

The Church—locally, nationally, internationally—should be a workshop of grace. Within the Church are to be found the conflicts of the world, a wide spectrum of humanity. Unfortunately, there are certain weaknesses—for example, the middle-class and conservative bias of much British Christianity. Nevertheless there is a chance to show how, in the household of faith, it is possible creatively to hold tensions and resolve conflicts, to show that violence need not destroy. For God speaks through the pioneers—the heroes who inspire and point the way forward, by whom the rest of us are judged, who each in his or her own way has sacrificed all in obedience to what was seen as God's call.

The Church lives for the Cross, though most Christians want only its healing and glory. Christian faith demands a loyalty that is above party or clan. We should expect to find the scars of rejection while trying to struggle with the burden of human existence. Above all, the Church is the body of Christ. The Church's greatest asset is its members—men and women deeply and sensitively formed in the school of Christ, living a pilgrimage for him, with their fellowship of mutual healing and strength, through which can be expressed the reality of the hope of the Gospel. The Church offers renewal, a glimpse of heaven, a call to service and witness. The Christian is committed to the world for Christ's sake. But in the end the only gift we have for the world is to be true to the Gospel in so far as we are able. For the rest, we can only rely on the mercy of God.

After these theological affirmations, the Working Party moved on to draw some general conclusions from its study and to make a series of recommendations.

Violence is a complex concept, as much a social condition as a mode of action. Acts of violence—intuitive or deliberate—are usually only an expression of a whole pattern of violence or threatened violence. Therefore it is important always to recognize what is implied in the use of violence. Violence as a tool, if it is found acceptable or thought necessary, must be a last resort because it represents the last line of defence or attack. For many, even this is not acceptable and adherence to pacifism or non-violent means is binding. But in either case the intention is both the containing and overcoming of violence.

The primary need is to reduce violence. This means attacking the roots of violence through effective pursuit of personal and communal justice. It also means enhancing the search for peace and the effective means for keeping and promoting peace-keeping at all levels, including a high priority for non-violent action.

There needs to be a much greater public awareness of the nature of violence, its effects and causes, of how to combat it, support for the forces of peace and just order. This includes the need to understand the political and ideological implications for and against the use of violence, and of the threat of collapse of social structures.

Of the twenty-one specific recommendations, nine are addressed to the nation and twelve to the Church:

The Nation

(i) We urge recognition of the strains and stresses in British society which are modifying and moulding the liberal democratic structures that have evolved over the past centuries. We look for a just and responsible society, and the evolution of adequate means of participatory involvement at all levels of government and other decision making. A humane society is a belonging society.

(ii) Positive discrimination of resources should increasingly be given to areas of tension in our society, especially the inner-city and immigrant areas, to promote a sufficient level of community health and creative stability.

(iii) Statutory authorities should be encouraged to devolve powers of decision as widely as possible and to devote resources to encouraging community participation in policy-making and implementation. Bureaucracy needs to become more responsive to demand, and services to be more readily accessible and flexible.

(iv) British politics has tended to be dominated by short-term aims and electoral pressures. Much more attention in public debate ought to be given to the wider long-term issues involved in adjusting to rapid and radical social change.

(v) Peace-keeping is an essential part of social cohesion. This implies the building up of a tradition and resources for non-violent action, especially in response to violence. Consideration should be given to the proposals contained in a report of the United Reformed Church, *Non-Violent Action* (1973), which include the training of the army in non-violent techniques; the training of volunteer reservists for non-violent peace-keeping operations; the setting up of non-violent training schools by the churches; an increase in the numbers of the police and in the spread of the population to be found among them.

(vi) Careful consideration should be given to the introduction of a Bill of Rights, though the case for this is not agreed. Alternatively, adequate legal provision should be made to defend minority rights.

(vii) The functions of Commissioners of Complaints should be widened to allow more freedom in redressing grievances, and moves to make the processes of law more accessible and speedy should be encouraged.

(viii) Education has a serious responsibility in moulding opinion and creating communal awareness. History courses should not stress war and violence as positive virtues, and should put our national history into world perspective, including attention to the history of civilizations other than our own. Religious education, without prejudice to any beliefs, should reflect Britain's multi-faith society.

(ix) Further research is needed into the effect of the media on society. Care should be taken to maintain a responsible attitude to the portrayal of violence.

The Church

(i) The Kingdom of God, which is both God's gift and for which we have to strive, is both justice and peace. The Christian is therefore committed to the prophetic demand for a just society, and also to the redemptive activity of reconciliation and renewal. While each situation demands a particular response and there are different paths of obedience, both these must be kept together whatever the strain. God is the God of order, not chaos; of judgement and mercy.

(ii) It is imperative that 'all in each place' should be ready to learn from those in other situations, with a desire to listen for the Word of God in our own time—though it is recognized that in the end each has to make his own decision.

(iii) At the theoretical level there must be continuous Christian exploration of the nature of the 'just and responsible and participating society'; the nature of human community; and the nature of violence, the just war and the just rebellion. There is a need for a deeper Christian critique of political and social ideologies as well as a readiness to use the tools of political and social analysis.

(iv) We would recommend investigating the desirability of the setting up of a British 'Christian Centre of Social Investigation' (along the lines suggested in the report *Violence in Ireland*) as a means of furthering Christian thinking and relating to wider society. This could be done by correlating and enlarging work now done in the British Council of Churches, the churches and other bodies.

(v) The churches should continue to stimulate responsible public debate about the issues facing our society. The immediate need is for this to happen as widely as possible at the local level and to popularize work already being done at national and international levels.

(vi) Priority should be given in the deployment of resources to areas of social deprivation. The churches can, even in a weakened state, be an important community resource and should be enabled to carry this responsibility.

(vii) Within a community, or within a region, the churches ought, ecumenically, to plan their strategy and to discover how to relate creatively to the needs of their community. For this local or regional Councils of Churches could provide a focus (cf. 'The Missionary Structure of the Congregation' project). This could allow for a better use of resources and a link between specialized ministries.

(viii) The ordained ministry provides an important community service with the advantages of freedom and flexibility. Clergy should be encouraged to accept and use their role as community leaders. They should be more adequately trained for this in both initial and in-service education.

(ix) The local congregation should be encouraged to be actively engaged in community building, using resources for example, buildings and members' talents); offering programmes in relation to local needs, and fostering creative developments (for example, community newspapers).

(x) One of the ways in which the churches, at every level, can contribute to community understanding is as a meeting point, committed yet independent, where groups can meet across the barriers that divide them. Dramatically, this may mean the daring and risk of living in Northern Ireland, but it is equally true and valuable in areas where tensions and conflicts are less formidable.

(xi) There is a need to help people to face the issues and threat of violence, and to build up a reserve of understanding and wisdom. This is not easy apart from an immediate need; nevertheless, there are means for building up such an awareness, and discussion can clarify issues. Local issues challenge us to decide what our Christian responsibility is. There may be opportunity to provide training in confrontation and non-violent action.

(xii) The centre of Christian faith is fellowship in the Spirit, through Christ with God the Father. The development of a deep and relevant spirituality is of paramount importance. Much attention must be given to the quality of worship, study and devotion that will enable Christian people to be able to witness under the pressure of contemporary living.

So the British churches, in common with the major Christian communities throughout the world, are not much nearer to a common mind on whether, and in what situations, the use of violence may be justified. This should occasion no surprise since the differences of conviction on this point go back at least as far as the fourth century, when the Church became significantly involved in the life of society at large. What can be said, however, on the strength of the evidence presented to the Swanwick Assembly, is that the churches in Britain are becoming much more sensitive to the causes of violence and far more knowledgeable in the ways that violence can be handled if it breaks out on a fairly small scale.

Another unresolved problem is that significant changes in the structures of society rarely take place without some degree of violence being involved. There is no reason why the past should dictate to the present or the future, but the patterns of known human behaviour indicate with some clarity that the emancipation of enslaved individuals, groups or nations is not normally achieved with the willing o-operation of the oppressors. Individuals groups and nations do not seem to be inspired with a spirit of generosity that drives them to share their privileges and wealth with others without external prompting and pressure.

In this report the British churches are proposing a number of radical changes in the structure of British society, and in the ordering of world affairs. These proposals involve massive transfers of power and wealth from the privileged to the under privileged. Naturally, it is hoped that this can be achieved without the need for anyone to resort to physical violence. But a nagging and painful question remains: Is it not unrealistic to the point of naïvety to suppose that it can and will?

7. THE DECISION MAKERS

There is nothing new about a situation in which most people exercise only little power and influence outside their own family circle. This has often been the case though there are exceptions: the pattern of life in primitive tribal societies suggests that there individuals could play a significant part in the making of community decisions. What is new in the twentieth century is that more people are *aware* of their lack of power. Equally significant the wider distribution of power—particularly in the political sphere—which has characterized the nineteenth and twentieth centuries, has made it much more difficult to discover where power is actually located. Under a despotic king or even a benevolent feudal lord, the power structure of society was relatively simple, as unfortunately it so remains in most parts of the world today, but the development of democracy has broken the simplicity of the earlier system without—so far—producing a pattern of government which indicates clearly where power is to be found and how it can be corporately exercised. Hence the current belief that power always resides with some 'other' individual or group —giving it an elusive will-o'-the-wisp existence which is not subject to effective control.

In Britain, for example, the Prime Minister is believed to have very great power at his disposal. Provided his majority in Parliament is secure he can in theory alter the laws, impose taxes and direct all the forces of the state. Yet his role in government is quite different from that of a President. The doctrine of Cabinet responsibility means that the Prime Minister cannot survive long without winning at least the acquiescence of his senior Ministers He must also keep his party together, and in enforcing unpopular measures must bargain for the support of all the major interest groups involved—something which M

Edward Heath discovered to his cost following his confrontation with the coal miners in 1974.

The same is true in a lesser degree of Ministers of the Crown. These enjoy considerable theoretical power in that they are responsible for the implementation of government policy through their huge departments. Yet if they are to fulfil this role they must acquire real mastery of the issues and exercise effective control of their senior Civil Servants. The modern practice whereby Ministers tend to move from one department to another after a stay of maybe eighteen months or two years makes such mastery impossible, and readers of the *Crossman Diaries* are left in no doubt as to the tensions that can arise between the wishes of a Minister and those of a Permanent Secretary.

In theory, of course, the Civil Servant has no power and occupies the humble position of 'your obedient servant'. His or her role is to advise and to carry out instructions. But if a senior Civil Servant advises against a certain policy and produces strong evidence to show that a certain line of action is impracticable, the Minister who makes the proposal is in a difficult position, especially if the Civil Servant has more information at his disposal than has the Minister. Which is not to say that a top Civil Servant would consciously suppress or misrepresent relevant evidence, but stereotyped patterns of thinking could have the same effect; and the consensus methods employed within a department, added to the self-perpetuating style of the Civil Service through recruitment and promotion procedures, undoubtedly increase this danger, So, in practice, the Civil Service has great, if negative, power; and the same is true, on a smaller scale, of permanent local government officials.

Another check upon, or stimulus to, Ministerial action is provided by the political parties, of which Prime Ministers and Ministers are members. These parties are responsible for winning the votes that place a government in office, and each has its own ideas concerning the policies that ought to be pursued. In practice, governments do what they believe to be right or practical without constant reference to their parties, but it is unlikely that any government could, or would, embark upon a major innovative change without first securing the approval of its party machine. It is also the case that ideas are sometimes first put forward within a political party, and later carried forward into legislation. The parties also choose candidates for parliamentary and local government elections, and the exercising of this particular power is not without its anomalies and tensions.

Military power in Britain is still firmly under government control, and likely to remain so while the system of constitutional monarchy remains, since the Services' deep tradition of loyalty to the Crown, rather than to the government, arguably keeps them at a distance from intervening in politics. Nevertheless, the way the armed forces respond to their assignments, for example, possible action in Rhodesia and actual involvement in Northern Ireland, has a profound influence on political possibilities. Similarly, the police, while existing to maintain law and order, have found themselves increasingly pushed into a quasi-military role and this, combined with a number of other factors, has weakened their traditional identification with the community. Hence the belief of many coloured immigrants, trade union pickets and public demonstrators that the police often take the law into their own hands and exercise a power for which they have no authority and which, in some circumstances, constitutes a serious threat to personal freedom.

Those responsible for wielding economic power in Britain are, like everyone else, subject to law and their activities are subject ultimately to parliamentary constraint. But in a capitalist society, where vast amounts of wealth are at their disposal, they exercise very considerable power, not only over those engaged in industrial and commercial activities, but also over national economic policies. In a mixed economy of the type that successive British governments have tried to operate since 1945, major problems are likely to arise when the interests of the holders of economic power conflict with social policy—for example, when investment is directed towards the building of office blocks in preference to the renewal of industrial plant, or when foreign exchange dealings lead to the weakening of the national currency. The socialist instinct to 'capture the commanding heights of the economy' is correct inasmuch as there can be no overall social control while economic power remains in private hands. The position is further complicated by the fact that certain transnational corporations, whose activities are so widespread and influential, are virtually immune from control of any kind.

Curiously, the British public—or at least that part of it represented in the British churches—is less worried about the activities of those who hold economic power than it is by the activities of the Trade Union movement. Since the fall of the Conservative government, following its confrontation with the miners in 1974, and the collaboration between the successor Labour government and the leaders of the main trade unions over pay restraint, it has been commonly held that the trade unions have great power—even to the point of holding governments to ransom. But the position is more complex than this, for the power to force high pay rises is confined to a small number of key industries where the strike weapon is particularly effective. Elsewhere the trade unions are too small and too divided to exercise a great deal of power, and the Trades Union Congress itself has no direct control over individual unions; it is a representative and consensus-seeking body. Within the unions themselves, a particular power problem often arises from the fact that only a small proportion of the members are interested enough in union affairs to attend the meetings at which officials are elected and national policy decisions discussed. The result of this is that power accrues to few hands and is not always subject to adequate control. But without the activities of the trade unions there would certainly be a massive imbalance of power in British industry, and all in all it seems fair to say that the negative power of the unions, to obstruct and to force employers and governments to think again, is greater than their positive power.

The power of the media is hard to assess—partly because their influence is most likely to register at the unconscious

level, and partly because their most popular form, television
has arrived on the scene too recently for conclusive research
to have been undertaken. As far as the press is concerned
its power to influence public opinion and action directly is
often greatly exaggerated—not least by newspaper owners
and some journalists. In a totalitarian society, where all
forms of communication are subject to censorship, ordinary
people are of course easily misled. But in a free society
where there is no censorship and a fairly large number of
newspapers and broadcasting stations, manipulation is far
less easy, since news items and editorial opinions are subject
to cross-checking. In any event, a large number of newspaper readers and television viewers are more interested in
being entertained than in being educated or indoctrinated.
So the most that can be said of the press is that it can
probably push its readers a little more quickly along the
road they have already decided to travel. Even so, it is a
matter for some concern that virtually all the British newspapers are controlled by one particular (the most wealthy)
section of society, and are used to promote its interests. In
the case of television, the greatest concern has been expressed about the portrayal of violence and explicit sex, but
there is no conclusive evidence about its power to influence
personal behaviour in either of these fields of human
activity. There seems to be a greater likelihood of television
exercising an influence in more subtle, less direct ways—
by the setting of social standards and norms. Yet even here
individuals are exposed to many other influences which
reduce the power of the media.

Until comparatively recently, the churches themselves
exercised a fair amount of power in society. The Archbishop
of Canterbury and the rest of the Anglican bishops were
listened to with respect when they spoke on national affairs
and were considerable figures in the areas covered by their
dioceses. In the early years of the present century it was not
unknown for Liberal Prime Ministers to consult Free
Church leaders about legislation affecting areas of social
and personal conscience. But the churches no longer
command any coherent power base. The Archbishop of

Canterbury is virtually the only church leader left with some *ex officio* influence. A few other bishops and some leaders of other churches are listened to with respect, but this is because of their personal qualities rather than any office they may hold in the Church. At the local level, some clergy and ministers are influential in community affairs, and in certain black areas of South London the churches are felt to have at least moral power and to use it for justice. Economically, the churches have virtually no power and are for the most part struggling to find the money needed to sustain their modest efforts. The Church Commissioners administer a substantial amount of money on behalf of the Church of England, and have been criticized for not using their investments as a power lever for the application of economic pressure in South Africa, but the income of the Church Commissioners is not sufficient to meet even half the stipends of the Church of England's clergy.

Britain's Powerless People

It is clear from this brief survey that in Britain power is quite widely dispersed, and is in certain areas subject to various checks and balances. Some of the individuals and groups who may appear to have great power at their disposal, often turn out to possess very little. Other, little noticed, individuals and groups may be more powerful than anticipated. But the BCC Working Party report on 'Power and Powerlessness', while not ready to acknowledge the existence of a 'power élite' in Britain, did acknowledge this: 'In Britain the "top people" tend to be linked by education in the independent sector and, to a surprising extent, by intermarriage—a by-product in part but not entirely of our endemic class-stratification.' The group added: 'There are certainly some grounds for seeing Britain today as a federation of interacting institutions, many of which are headed by people whom personal wealth, family background and education make sympathetic to each other but arguably not enough to the feelings of the majority of citizens.'

Power is notoriously corrupting of those who wield it and oppressively dehumanizing for those who are the victims of its misuse. But power is not to be feared or rejected out of hand as inherently evil. In some form it is essential to human fulfilment, both individual and corporate, and indeed to survival itself. What has been called the 'aggressive instinct' serves vital purposes in humankind—exercising power over the environment to secure food and shelter, and within the group to create social organization. Civilization is based on the exercise of intellectual power in solving technical problems and in the arts. Moreover, to possess some power is indispensable to believing in one's own value, for power is the means to achievement. Very often quite simple levels of achievement are enough to bring satisfaction, but those who are denied any control over the most fundamental areas of their ordinary life, who do not have even a margin of decision about how and where they live, or what job they can take—or any job at all—are being robbed of their humanity. The result, in individuals and groups, may be either apathy or impotent rage, expressed in futile violence, or both in alternation.

Power is necessary to genuine freedom, therefore the power generated within a society must be distributed as widely as possible, not clung to by a minority, however capable or well-intentioned. Power must enable others, both individuals and communities, to grow in power and share in its exercise. Any over-concentration of power is not merely dangerous but unjust, and once established is notoriously hard to break up. In Britain today power is more widely shared than in some other parts of the world, but many people—including a high proportion of thoughtful Christians—believe that a further redistribution is needed, and that the abuse of power is still widespread and too easily tolerated. The Working Party identified five areas where such abuse is to be found.

1. *Manipulation.* This shows itself in such features as the appeal to low values, for example, in advertising or in political slogans such as 'doubling the standard of living in 25 years'. The media promote attitudes which perpetuate

the present bases of power: consumerism, status, violent domination. In search of power, extremist groups indoctrinate their members with political philosophies, the implications of which they are quite unequipped to appreciate. Equally, official rhetoric protects the status quo with talk of 'consultation' and 'open government' which has little substance in fact. Catch phrases such as 'unity not uniformity', or 'the ministry of the laity' serve a similar purpose in church life.

2. *Force.* Physical violence is part of the British scene in a way unthinkable even fifteen years ago. But physical violence achieves nothing. Whether used by the National Front or the Socialist Workers' Party, by the Provisional IRA, the UDA or the security forces, it can only preserve or change the holders of power, never the system. The system cannot be changed with its own weapons. 'The more there is of real revolution, the less there is of violence; the more of violence, the less of revolution' (de Ligt).

3. *Structural Violence.* This occurs when there are gross inequalities of wealth and power; the worship of materialistic and technological progress in ways that make dehumanization inevitable, for instance, in mass production techniques; the assumption that efficiency can flourish only in a system of murderous competition. There is mental violence dealt out every day to thousands by the 'insolence of office'. The BCC Working Party reports: 'We have examined cases where all one can say is that the authorities have treated the poor and deprived like dirt, leaving letters unanswered, denying them the most basic information (for example, about rehousing plans), refusing interviews, threatening tenants with eviction (quite illegally) if the first offer of a new home was turned down, misinforming them about available accommodation, going back on arrangements said to be firm. Such cases are not typical, and no doubt the incidents described looked quite different from behind the clerk's desk. But that is the point. Power, even petty power, can so easily destroy awareness of other people as human beings like oneself.' And the group adds:

Examples of the abuse of what little scope Britain still has for pursuit of self-interest by unilateral action are to be found in the way, during our tenure of the Presidency of the EEC Council of Ministers, British negotiators determined to back a handful of issues which were blatantly to our domestic advantage, for example, to bring the joint European Torus (atomic energy) project to Culham, to keep farm prices down whatever the cost to other interests in the Community, and to pursue a narrow self-interest in regard to our oil reserves. A chronic abuse of remaining British domination is our unwillingness to meet the developing countries half-way in negotiations in the North/South dialogue about the sharing of the world's resources. Our refusal to concede the fact that Iceland's dependence on the rapidly depleting fish-stocks of the North Sea has unavoidable implications for Britain's traditional diet and the livelihood of our fishermen is another example; as is the determination of the British Treasury and Ministry of Defence to pursue a vigorous arms sales policy, whether or not the Third World purchasers ought to be spending precious resources on such commodities.

4. *Accumulation.* Here the abuse of power is shown negatively in reluctance to distribute or relinquish power, as in the refusal of the police to contemplate independent investigation of complaints, or the habit in local and national government of stigmatizing those who question or resist as 'troublemakers'. Positively it is seen in such things as the aggregation of wealth or control of the media.

5. *Idolatry.* When power becomes the object of idolatry the results are disastrous. If there is nothing higher than the state, any tyranny can be justified in the state's supposed interest. This situation is sometimes disguised by speaking of 'the people'; but 'the people' and 'the state' are by no means identical, and many a revolution has resulted in ritual worship of the people, the oppressed, the revolution itself, and left the powerless as weak as before. We urgently need a theory of the legitimacy of government which will do justice to new insights into human rights and to the state as less than God.

If these are some of the main ways in which power is abused, it follows that each in its own way, and sometimes in combination, creates or adds to the powerlessness of particular groups of people. Of course some powerlessness is inevitable in human life. It is an illusion to suppose that the world can provide everyone with that to which he or she aspires, and the sense of powerlessness relates to subjective as well as objective factors: some feel deprived not absolutely but in comparison with others or with what they have experienced earlier in their own lives. Context is also important: we may be powerless at work but not at home, and vice versa. And deprived groups are not always minorities—women, for example. All of which provides no excuse for accepting the present distribution of power, but rather a strong motivation for seeking greater justice in the use of the available power in society, and sensitivity in its application.

The most blatant areas of powerlessness in Britain today are those of unemployment and poverty, and where these are combined with colour or youth they become particularly acute (see chapters 4 and 5). But for everyone there are areas of structural and personal powerlessness which inhibit the growth of a truly corporate society and, all too frequently, are the cause of personal frustration and unhappiness. The BCC Working Party identified several such areas, the first of which involves what it describes as 'the elusiveness of the centres of power'.

At a time when more people wish to have a say in matters that affect their lives, such as the closure of a local hospital, transport facilities, types of housing, play areas for their children and so on, it is becoming more difficult to pin down—much less influence—the point of decision-making. What seems at first sight to be the key link in the chain, for example, the Local Authority, turns out to be subject to a national government decision made several years earlier, when none of the people to be most deeply affected were aware of the implications of a particular plan of strategy. Thus, if allotments in London's dockland are taken away to create a lorry park, this may have been rendered virtually inevitable when certain much larger decisions on industrial policy were made years before. This leads the Working Party to the conclusion that 'in a planned society the vote is an irrelevance, so far as most issues are concerned'. Hence disillusionment with politics and the all-pervading vision of life in terms of 'us' and 'them'.

Another prime problem is 'official mystification'. An Anglican bishop resigned from his Regional Health Authority in despair because the technical jargon of the documents made the lay members completely ineffectual. For all practical purposes, decisions were wholly in the hands of a tiny élite of experts. The same is often true at other levels: information about such things as re-housing projects, when given at all, too often comes in vague terms or legalese. No effort is made to communicate with people at their level of education; nor, for that matter, is there any attempt in school or adult education to equip people for participation in the planning of their lives. It is generally assumed that they have nothing to contribute to the decision-making process, and that the issues involved are too difficult for them to understand anyway.

This is not to suggest some sinister, carefully engineered plot to retain power in the hands of the few. A great deal of power concentration is due to unchallenged, and therefore unexamined, assumptions. Thus in the decaying inner-city areas, the professional social services, whose development is rightly seen as an expression of a more compassionate society, all too often increase the sense of powerlessness because their efforts only succeed in creating a population of passive clients for whom everything has to be decided by the bureaucracy. In such districts, matters like housing and schools are inevitably a numbers game to which personal needs and preferences, if indeed there were time to discover them accurately, are purely incidental. (For illustrations of pioneering efforts to involve local people in decision making, see chapter 5.) But in urban communities at least the effort is made to provide facilities of some kind, even though these be inadequate or not really what the people would themselves choose. Different, but equally tragic, cases of powerlessness are the dying villages of Britain, where people are being driven from their homes because planning decisions, remote from the actual human situation, have led to the withdrawal of most of the supporting amenities—public transport, schools and post offices—with the inevitable result that shops, pubs (and often churches) follow suit.

In general it may be assumed that powerlessness and wide-ranging deprivation normally go hand-in-hand, and this is confirmed by the Working Party's conclusion that 'the children of the poor are more likely to die in infancy. The child of an unskilled manual worker is six times more likely to be a poor reader than the child of a professional person. So far from education correcting inequalities, the gaps in attainment actually widen during school years. All illnesses, except those of the eyes, are commoner amongst the unskilled and semi-skilled, and their life-expectancy is lower. At work they receive fewer fringe benefits, shorter holidays and poorer pension provision, and are more likely to lose their jobs. Unless they are in Local Authority housing, the poor pay a higher proportion of their income in rent than the better-off; and the decline of private sector housing has increased the incidence of homelessness. In concrete terms, these statistics mean such things as living in a polluted environment; inadequate basic diet; disturbed children because father is out of work and so mother has to go to work; the child-minding racket; under-educated and under-motivated youngsters finding their only outlet in truancy, vandalism and petty crime; over-worked doctors prescribing endless palliative pills; the handicap of belonging to a "bad area" which the rest of the world dismisses as inhabited exclusively by criminals, prostitutes, layabouts and troublemakers.'

Jesus and the Powerless

This analysis of the location of power in Britain and the effects of its abuse or maldistribution on the powerless might well find acceptance among social scientists and others who are aware of the broad pattern of life in Britain today. But in seeking answers to some of the main problems discerned, it may be wondered whether the churches, as exponents and expressions of the Christian faith, have any distinctive contribution to make. Here it is necessary to record that the Working Party's efforts to reach towards a 'Theology of Power' do not appear to have been excessively strenuous, but three points are made, the first of which is concerned with the ambiguity in the attitude of Jesus to power.

Although Jesus seems to have eschewed the use of power, it would be quite untrue to suggest that he never at any time made use of power. His personal and moral power was astonishing, shown in the variety and number of people who attached themselves to him, and in the barriers of social and religious convention that he smashed to make this possible. That he had intellectual power is revealed in clarity and depth of thought given perfect and memorable expression in words. That he had para-normal powers, principally of healing, is beyond reasonable question, and the New Testament itself speaks of these as 'works of power'. The gospels also indicate that he used his powers of thought and speech frequently in strongly aggressive and denunciatory ways, and saw God, for all that he was the Father of the poor, as also the ultimate avenger on the hypocrite and on those who oppressed their fellow human beings. It was because Jesus was a powerful figure that it was thought necessary to crucify him.

The willingness of Jesus to be crucified is, however, seen as clear evidence that physical violence was the one course that he rejected. 'If Jesus is in any sense the "beloved Son in whom I am well pleased"—and Easter must surely mean that at least—then God's will for human life is that violence and coercion are out. Emphatic, even aggressive, presentation of what is believed to be right may be in; such behaviour is necessary to the realization of the human individual, and the community must recognize and accept this, and not insist in the interests of the rulers or the status quo on a meek, total passivity. Turning the other cheek is usually necessary only if you have done something to make someone strike you on the one.' This brief assertion of non-violence as the only possible course for the Christian needs, however, to be compared with the more extended consideration of the issues in chapter 6.

The third point made by the Working Party is that, in order to find God's will, it is necessary to look not just at revelation or the teaching of Jesus but also at the world for which God is responsible. When we do so we find that the Golden Rule, 'Whatsoever ye would that men should do unto you, even so do ye unto them', requires among other things that the powerful should create conditions in which the powerless can be human, which means exerting in their turn legitimate forms and degrees of power. The group concludes: 'Our job as Christians is not to deny power or renounce it, but to work for a world in which everyone, poor and rich, minorities and majorities, can enjoy legitimate power.'

Power for the Powerless

Looking at the world in a quest for remedies for powerlessness, the Working Party identified certain experiments already taking place in deprived or relatively-deprived areas of Glasgow, Liverpool, Coventry, Southampton and Portsmouth which seemed significant and pointed a way forward. These are all taking place within the community action movement and the lessons which emerge appear to be remarkably consistent.

The first is the elementary one that there must be means for people to make their needs and viewpoints known. This is not as easy as it sounds. Apathy and diffidence are hard to break down. Good ideas are there, but the capacity to articulate and argue them to professional administrators and politicians is itself a power people often lack.

A second and absolutely fundamental point is that, both in identifying needs and then in meeting them, it is self-defeating for outsiders to analyse the problem and lay on solutions. The whole object is to give people themselves some power and control over their own lives. They may need help in 'conscientization'—that is, in becoming alive to the realities of their situation; but that does not imply the injection of theoretical needs, or of needs that might be felt by someone from a different background. The people immediately involved must formulate the needs and they must meet them in their own ways. The role of the outsider is simply to facilitate, and any helper must remember constantly that it is all too easy to crush in the powerless the incipient will to help themselves.

A major part of community action is concerned with information, both its discovery and its dissemination. It is virtually impossible for those without some professional knowledge of where to go and what to look for to find out such things as planning decisions, the legal position on particular matters, council debates and so on. Even relevant news from other neighbourhoods has to be searched for. When information is available, it has to be spread. Duplicated news and comment broadsheets or magazines, and sometimes an Information Centre, are key items in building up a community from scratch.

Also crucial at the early stage is the creation of confidence, which means, in effect, having some success. This can be difficult where progress depends on negotiation, and a community is in a weak bargaining position with nothing to offer. But any start, however small, can be enough. A simple matter like fixing up and running a play area can have startling significance. It will have meant carrying a point with the Local Authority; finding that even without much education people can organize and run a project; taking a new pride in one's own culture, like the Liverpool community which completely redesigned a play area because 'our children don't play like that'.

All may go well if problems are not severe and authority is co-operative. But what if they are severe and the powers that be are awkward? Consensus and co-operation then break down, and give way to conflict and confrontation. Major problems are beyond solution by a local community because they may involve such things as land values, interest rates, industrial policy, and government expenditure. If its case is ignored, then in order not to be crushed out of human significance, a local community must protest, lobby, hold public meetings, interrupt local councils, organize rent strikes, and so on. Christians who raise hands of horror at such methods may not realize that what they are watching may not be blackmail and intimidation but the only way some people have of reassuring themselves of their own human dignity.

There is always the temptation for those who are oppressed to challenge the powerful at their own game with their own weapons. The effect of this, even if successful, is to oust one power group by another; it does not change the system. 'There are other means. We have before us a large number of examples of non-violent community action and its successes in other countries, such as France, Sicily, the United States and Latin America.' Love for one's enemies is fundamental to real change.

The Working Party goes on to emphasize that 'it would be mere romanticism to pretend that such initial efforts of the powerless to gain power do not depend crucially on help from the powerful. Constantly what turns the tide in the early stages proves to be the support of the media (Glasgow), of the police (Glasgow), of government money (Coventry), of qualified people prepared to work for low salaries as "civil servants to the working class" (Coventry).'

The lessons learned from community action experiments are obviously helpful in the search for ways of enabling individuals and groups, hitherto powerless, to exercise some real degree of power in their own immediate neighbourhoods. But, as the Working Party noted earlier in its report, a great deal of power is now exercised at a considerable distance from local communities and all too frequently vitiates local initiative and responsibility. If, for example, a decision is made in the American headquarters of a transnational corporation to close down a factory which provides the main source of employment in a North of England town, it is difficult to see what those involved in the factory can do to influence this decision or to reduce significantly the hardship which the decision may cause to individuals and to the local community as a whole.

The question arises, then, as to how far local community action can provide a model for correcting imbalances of power on a much wider scale—even in situations falling well short of the problems created by transnational corporations. The Working Party was aware of this rather urgent issue but, beyond noting that a 'redesigning of the kind of economy we want to manage' is required, left the matter in the form of eight difficult questions:

—How is a stress on the need to create real community through small units to be reconciled with the need for larger units of power within Europe and the world to foster understanding?

—How can participatory democracy be reconciled with efficient central planning?

—What are the best levels for different sorts of decisions (the devolution issue)?

—How many decisions can any one person realistically be involved in anyway?

—How can understanding between government and electorate be maximized in a highly technical society?

—What is the ultimate core of agreed principle and purpose which gives government its ultimate authority?

—If all participate in decisions, ought not all to participate in the consequences (for example, by taking a cut in time of loss)?

—We can see successful changes of the power structures in limited situations; how can these lessons be applied on a larger scale?

These and other basic problems of approach cannot—obviously—be resolved by theory in advance, but only by practical experiment. As the group said, 'We none of us know, or can know, the concrete reality of the society towards which we journey. We shall find out by discussing and correcting our vision as we go along. There are also dangers on that journey of which we are well aware, not least in the manipulation of the powerless for their own ends by the powerful, who seek only more power for themselves. But for the first stage we suggest, in the light of all we have examined, the following steps for Britain today, on its way at least to the immediate tomorrow:

1. The churches (which are not without power) must express their active solidarity with the powerless, and the first point on the Christian agenda is to transform society, and this applies at the level of the local congregation in their local community.

2. Christians must be ready to give up power and privilege. For example, we should actively foster higher prices for raw commodities such as cocoa, coffee and tea.

3. Those who are in positions of relative power and privilege should use their power to enable and facilitate the powerless to help themselves (for example, the Coventry workshop).

4. There is a need for positive discrimination in favour of the powerless, for example, women, blacks.

5. There should be a movement in the direction of the greatest possible measure of participatory democracy, for example, village and neighbourhood meetings, industrial movements such as the Scott-Bader Commonwealth.

6. There is need in all our internal reforms to bear in mind the needs of the Third World, and to press for Britain to come up to the United Nations' requested figure of 0.7 per cent of the Gross National Product for aid, and that this figure should be genuine aid, not tied, or loans at interest.

7. We should encourage those measures of electoral reform and devolution which enable more people to determine their own lives.

8. Education for participatory democracy must begin during school-years.

9. The churches must set their own house in order, and see that within their own structures power is more widely shared.'

Although placed last among the steps deemed necessary, this final point about power in the churches can hardly be dismissed as unimportant. The 'Britain Today and Tomorrow' project is not concerned with church reform. Yet the internal affairs of the churches cannot be entirely ignored, since certain changes are required if the churches are to make an effective contribution to the life of society as a whole, and if they are to speak with authority about the big social issues of the world in which they are placed. 'Physician heal thyself' is a fair retort to church leaders who call upon politicians to solve problems which they themselves have hardly begun to face within their own ecclesiastical domains. And the churches do have a number of unresolved problems about the distribution and exercising of power: some of which are made the more difficult by the unwillingness of many Christians to acknowledge that churches are communities in which power actually exists.

In their forms of government the churches experience many of the dilemmas about power felt in other institutions. The Roman Catholic Church is an exception here, inasmuch as power is largely concentrated in the hands of the hierarchy, and sometimes exercised quite ruthlessly. The rest of the British churches have something approaching democratic forms, with elected assemblies, conferences and synods. But these are often criticized for their unrepresentative character (encouraged in some cases by the demands they make on busy laity), for the undue influence that accrues to partisan interests, and in some churches for the powers of veto that reside in small groups. As in all representative bodies, those who serve on committees and have the time and interest to master the paperwork tend to become the most powerful, and provide formidable backing for the 'establishment' line normally presented to the large assemblies—some of which meet only once a year. And what is true of the churches at the national level is equally true of their local expressions where the minister or priest and a few articulate lay people form their own bureaucracy and establishment and dominate the life of the congregation. On the other hand, most local churches do enjoy very considerable autonomy and have real freedom to order their life according to neighbourhood needs; the tragedy is that this autonomy and freedom is rarely exploited to the full.

In the matter of finance—normally a sound guide to the location of power in any community—the British churches are in a state of transition. Hitherto the great majority of local churches have been responsible for raising most of their funds and meeting most of their expenses. Church of England parishes have been buttressed by centrally-administered endowments, but these were attached to particular places and so enhanced, rather than diluted, local autonomy. Now, however, financial retrenchment is leading to much greater centralization of funds, thus placing more power in the hands of a few. One serious consequence of the shortage and centralization of funds is that innovative expenditure is often the first to be axed, and a good deal of this expenditure is related to the Church's engagement with secular society. The transitional character of the churches' present financial operations makes it impossible to forecast the ultimate patterns of income and expenditure, and much will depend on whether inflation can be brought under control, but it is important to recognize that financial changes involve changes of power.

Another area in which the presence of power is not always recognized lies within the sphere of theological research and reflection. Intellectual power now tends to be found outside the main structures of the Church and many leading theologians hold university rather than ecclesiastical posts. This leads to the suspicion of theologians as being out of touch with church needs and 'real life', and to resentment when the freedom of the academic environment produces unorthodox speculations—especially if these receive wide publicity. Bishops and other pastors then feel drawn to adopt a protective role in relation to the laity, and the charge that Christians 'value only love, not truth' has real foundation.

The reluctance of the relatively powerful to relinquish power is also seen in the life of the churches, most notably in the token power allocated to the majority of ecumenical bodies. The central questions of the deployment of manpower and physical resources are still firmly under denominational control, and the unwillingness to share buildings, even to the extent of building new ones cheek by jowl, would be comic were it not so wicked. In South London there is real bitterness and bewilderment among the Black churches at the refusal of the established churches to lend them facilities. A comparison of the budgets of the main British churches and that of the British Council of Churches provides an illuminating commentary on the relationship between denominational power and ecumenical commitment.

In general, it may be said that the Working Party responsible for this section of the project favours considerable development in what has come to be called participatory democracy. It has no ready-made answers as to how such development can be achieved, especially in the area of central government, and takes refuge in the belief that many insights can be discovered only by experiment. This is by no means an unreasonable line to adopt, and in any case the churches lack the expertise necessary for working out how power can be shared in particular situations. The unsatisfactory blend of authoritarianism and democracy in their own life is proof of this.

None the less there remain certain issues in this important area of concern which need to be faced, and could well be tackled in the next phase of the project. The generally unfavourable reception accorded to the Bullock Report on industrial democracy has by no means disposed of the crucial question of how individual men and women can be more closely involved in decision-making processes which often have far more direct consequences for their personal lives than the decisions made by their representatives in Parliament. If the Bullock solution is unacceptable, another must be found to take its place.

The same may be said of the proposals made from time to time for the reforming of the House of Lords. There is a widespread, but mistaken, belief that the House of Lords no longer plays a significant part in the making of important political decisions. If this were true, the case for reforming this element in the parliamentary process would be even stronger, since there is almost certainly a place for a second chamber. Such a chamber had better be effective. The present position is that a non-elected, and in no sense representative, body has an important influence on legislation, and the difference of attitude exhibited by the House of Lords when the Conservative Party is in power is a cause for legitimate concern by radical social reformers. The churches are well equipped for looking closely at this particular issue, since 26 Anglican bishops and many more distinguished laymen from all the churches have seats in the House of Lords, and their views on the relationship between hereditary power and participatory democracy could be quite illuminating.

On the wider front, two further questions need much closer attention. The first concerns the conflict between economic and political power. While it may be a grotesque exaggeration to say that British governments are prisoners of the City of London, there is enough truth in such a statement to justify unease. And, since the City of London is itself being obliged to relinquish more and more of its power to international corporations and institutions whose objectives may or may not coincide with British interests, the case for investigation becomes even stronger. The second question is an old one, but still highly relevant: Is democracy, by its nature, conservative and also inefficient in its operation? If consultation is really widespread and power is truly shared, can society as a whole move much faster than its slowest members? And if a rapidly-changing world requires quick decisions—not simply on industrial and commercial matters, but over a wide range of social concerns—can these wait until the will of the people has been ascertained? Upon the answers to these questions will depend the possibility of achieving many of the objectives recommended in other parts of this report.

8. THE GREAT AND THE SMALL

Among all the questions concerning the distribution of power in society, the debate about the devolution of power from Westminster to Assemblies in Scotland and Wales provided the most vivid example of pressure for change during the course of the 'Britain Today and Tomorrow' study. Here is no theoretical set of proposals, based on an idealist vision, which can safely be dismissed as impracticable or postponed until circumstances seem more favourable. Here is legislation.

The demand for devolution has come entirely from Scotland and Wales. Apart from a relatively small number of politicians and social thinkers who advocate a more regionalized form of government throughout the United Kingdom, the English have been—and continue to be—content with the present arrangements. Since they are generally believed to be the main beneficiaries of these arrangements, this is hardly surprising, though historical and cultural factors are probably more significant.

Although the Church of Scotland began to express, through its General Assembly, a desire for a greater measure of self-government for Scotland as long ago as 1946, and has pressed for the matter to be considered on various occasions since then, the most substantial contribution to the debate by the British churches as a whole came with a report on *Devolution and the British Churches*, presented to the spring 1977 Assembly of the BCC. This was the work of the Archbishop of Wales (Dr. Gwilym Williams), the then Convener of the Church and Nation Committee of the Church of Scotland (the Rev. W. B. Johnston), and the Secretary-General of the General Synod of the Church of England (Mr. W. D. Pattinson).

After providing a brief account of the history of devolution and a 'plain man's guide' to the proposals of the

Kilbrandon Commission and the doomed Scotland and Wales Bill of 1976/77, the authors prefaced their own views with a significant quotation from W. E. Gladstone. He remarked, in the Irish Home Rule Debate of 1886, that:

The passing of many good laws is not enough in cases where the strong permanent interests of the people, their distinctive marks of character, the situation and history of the country require not only that these laws should be good, but that they should proceed from a congenial and native source, and besides being good laws should be their own laws.

They went on to state their own position quite clearly: 'In our view the conditions that Gladstone described as applying to Ireland then apply now to Scotland and Wales. It follows, then, first that we believe devolution for both countries to be necessary now; and secondly that we believe legislative devolution to Wales to be as necessary as for Scotland.'

But the authors were disappointed that the government's Scotland and Wales Bill is no more than 'an unwilling concession to nationalist feeling', and they discerned signs of this in virtually all its clauses: 'It explains the complete refusal to give any financial powers to either Assembly, as well as the continued supervision that is provided for all Assembly Acts. Worst of all, it means that the Bill has not sprung from consideration of the principles which should govern an Assembly, but merely represents a political balance between what the government can get through Parliament and what is the minimum that will assuage Nationalist views.'

The report suggested five basic conditions for any satisfactory Assembly:

1. *The Assembly should be democratic, and should represent as nearly as possible the views of its electors.* The issue here concerns the merits of proportional representation over against the 'first-past-the-post' system. The Kilbrandon Commission recommended proportional representation, but the govern-

ment has refused to accept this. The authors of the BCC report were strongly in favour of proportional represent-ation on the grounds that, 'by bringing parliamentary representation more closely into line with votes cast it greatly strengthens minority parties, who under the present system have a long way to go before they appear in Par-liament at all'. They suggested that the objections to pro-portional representation often voiced by both Labour and Conservative supporters amount to no more than a euphe-mistic way of saying 'the present system favours us unfairly, and we are not going to let that advantage go'. And they concluded: 'We find the government's persistent refusal to accept any sort of proportional representation, which had led them to summon their forces against amendments in the Commons designed to insert it, most regrettable. If the Bill goes forward we would ask the House of Commons to think again. If the Commons will not do it, then we urge the House of Lords to put it in, and call on those who usually speak for the churches there to do their utmost to bring about its acceptance. If the present Bill is dropped, we see proportional representation as an essential feature in a new Bill.'

2. *The functions of the Assembly should be clearly defined and adequate.* If the Assemblies are to attract both the respect and the calibre of personnel they require, they must be in a position to have some impact on the direction of their countries' affairs. But under the present proposals all of Scotland's major industries—oil, steel, ships and fish—are to remain subject to Westminster control. Even in the field of housing, which is to be generally devolved, the West-minster parliament will retain control over private sector finance (for example, building societies) and rents and subsidies. 'The government has made no real attempt to devolve all the responsibility for any important field—because it is unwilling to allow any local taxation to go to the Assemblies.' This leads to the fear that both Assemblies, and particularly the Welsh Assembly with its more limited powers, may not attract the right people to serve in them. 'We regard it as important that the Assemblies should not

be regarded as one more scalp to be hung on the ageing County Councillor's belt. They must attract the professional politicians, the young, and those willing to seize the opportunities now open for creating new and more harmonious patterns of society.' And a third reason for giving the Assemblies real power and a real job to do is that this will help to maintain the unity of the United Kingdom. 'The United Kingdom is diverse—and Scotland and Wales present differences vis-à-vis England in many ways. One of the strongest arguments in favour of the Scotland and Wales Bill is that it recognizes this diversity and tries to find a place for it within those elements of the framework of life that are common to all subjects of the United Kingdom, and which are in tangible form the United Kingdom itself. Within that framework we believe that it should be for the Assemblies to determine as much as is consistent with the maintenance of that common life.'

3. *There should be clear and independent arbitration provisions in the case of conflict.* At the beginning of a creative development in government, it may seem regrettable that provision should have to be made for possible conflict. But devolution is about power, and it would be unrealistic not to recognize the possibility of conflicting interests appearing—first over the distribution of money, and secondly over political ideology and policy. The proposed arrangements for dealing with conflict leave power ultimately in the hands of the Westminster parliament and, though there is provision for reference to the Judicial Committee of the Privy Council before Royal Assent. the authors of the report would prefer arbitration provisions that would make such references less likely.

4. *The Assembly should have resources of its own in the form of taxation.* Contrary to what is commonly believed, government expenditure per head of the population has, throughout the 1970s, been substantially higher in Scotland and Wales than in England; and the BCC report suggested 'not only that this is right and necessary, but it is an unanswerable reason why the Union must be continued'. But, while some public expenditure must remain with the centre, the

authors of the report cannot accept what they describe as 'the anomalous position into which the government has pushed the Assemblies—to be able to spend money, but have no responsibility for raising it'. They regard this as unsatisfactory for two main reasons. First, because whoever is responsible for spending money should also be responsible for raising it, so that the amount of expenditure is subject to democratic control. Secondly, because the proposed arrangements are bound to lead to conflict between the Assemblies and Parliament. 'We regard it as necessary that the Assemblies should have some, at least, of the tools of economic management, some fiscal authority, in order that they can make a real contribution to the welfare of their countries.' On the question of North Sea oil as a potential source of national revenue, the report believed that any attempt to designate particular areas of extraction to Scotland and England would require artificial boundaries, lacking reality and without sustainable force in international law. 'It is clearly more desirable that such revenues as are going to be available from the oil under the North Sea should be distributed as and where they are most needed. We regret the materialistic tone that has been adopted in many discussions of this matter.'

5. *The Assembly should have formal representation in foreign affairs and international bodies.* Since the pressure for devolution contains powerful elements of nationalism, which will be expressed in the Assemblies, it is important that this should be leavened by some responsibility and representation in foreign affairs and international bodies. The institutions of the EEC dealing with such matters as coal, steel and fishing are obvious places for Welsh and Scottish representation, and it might be possible to have some cross-membership between the Assemblies and the European Parliament. 'We note that arrangements have already been made for a representative of the German Federal States, chosen by themselves, to attend [the Council of Ministers] as part of the German delegation and to hold a watching brief on behalf of the Federal States. We see no reason why similar arrangements should not be established for the Assemblies.'

The authors of the report concluded by indicating the obligation of the churches in respect of devolution, emphasizing that they have a duty to make the Assemblies work as best they can, if and when they are established, to support them and encourage them. Christians should be encouraged to take an active part in the Assemblies—that is, to stand for election to them. The churches themselves must regroup in a manner which relates to the Assemblies, taking advantage of the new opportunities for ecumenical work which this creates. 'In particular, we suggest that in both Scotland and Wales the churches, in consultation with each other, should designate a single liaison officer for each Assembly. He would carry accreditation from all the churches to the Assembly; Assembly members would be able to look to him for advice and help on the churches' points of view, and for first reactions to specific proposals; and he would also have a pastoral function vis-à-vis Assembly members and the Assembly's staff.' Above all, the churches have in the present situation, where mistrust and conflict over devolution is growing, and could in the future become much more serious, an important reconciling role: 'The churches must put aside any sectional tendency and work together to help people of different opinions and from different backgrounds to work together; to accept that there may be value in other people's proposals or views; and to agree on decisions that, while taking account of needs of individual areas, are yet fair to the country as a whole.'

Leadership Today

In its strong endorsement of this report, the BCC Assembly commended it for study. But there are signs that church members, in England at least, share in the general lack of concern about the issues involved, despite the vigour of the leadership provided here by the BCC and its three wise men. Yet paradoxically there is at the same time a cry for stronger leadership in both state and Church. Some of this may be attributed to a sense of frustration because of Britain's inability to cope with her most serious social and economic problems, and in the case of the Church to the general decline in church attendance and Christian commitment. If only another Winston Churchill or a William Temple could arise to lead the nation and the churches, if not into a new golden age at least into power and prosperity! The existence of such frustrations and aspirations provides the soil on which extremist, authoritarian movements in the political and religious spheres are now achieving a certain amount of growth.

But leadership of a highly personal or authoritarian kind is not easy to square with the wider distribution of power involved in a participatory democracy, and it is very difficult to exercise leadership—at least on a national scale—in a pluralist society where there are no common values or objectives. The problem was succinctly analysed by Principal Michael Taylor, of Northern Baptist College, in a paper submitted to the 'Britain Today and Tomorrow' project: 'It is not that all the leaders have disappeared. It is that the sense of movement, of going places, of purposeful enterprise, of reaching out towards the goal which alone makes leadership possible, is virtually non-existent. You cannot lead if you have nowhere to go.'

As a contribution to the project, a group of eight men and women from different religious traditions carried out a fair amount of work on the subject of leadership, extending over twelve months and involving a series of consultations with people from all parts of the country and from all walks of life. Their report, which included several personal contributions, emphasized a number of points about the nature of leadership in contemporary British society, and then moved on to discuss some of the issues now facing those who have the responsibility of exercising leadership.

On the nature of leadership itself, the Working Party emphasized six points.

1. *The leadership of a shared vision*. We need leadership in the form of a shared vision which acts as a motive in the present and an invitation from the future. We would hope for a renewed moral vision, which would transcend short-term,

selfish or purely national objectives. The basic element of such a vision has to be universal human community. In order that this vision can be shared by all people of good-will, it must be free of ideology and sectionalism. It must be sophisticated in so far as it is manifestly aware of the contemporary world, of history and human nature, but also simple enough to lodge in the memory and fire the imagination. It must be characterized by both a hopeful certainty that humanity is capable of idealism, justice and disinterested concern, and a realism about human capacity for their opposites.

2. *Law and order*. We cannot discuss leadership in isolation from its social setting. Leaders operate within a framework, which to a large extent determines the options for them. We would want to underline the importance of a context of order, both as an aim and a setting for leadership. 'Law and Order' need not have an oppressive, illiberal ring, because we believe that it describes a basic blessing and an essential precondition for human community. To bring order out of chaos is the purpose of the divine work of creation and creativity. The achievement and the maintenance of law and order is a fully dynamic process. It exists in proportion to the skill of the legislators, the responsiveness of those in authority and the co-operation put forward by members of society. It is therefore a vital question for leadership.

3. *Participation*. A key factor in the achievement of an ordered, purposeful society, which yet avoids a totalitarian style of government, must be the participation of its people in government and the acceptance of that participation by those who lead. But 'participation' is an umbrella term, describing everything from token processes of consultation to non-directive group decision making. It will not be the same thing in each of the layers of society in which we operate. But, because of the high and low potentialities of human nature, we feel that in principle participation must imply more than simple consultation and less than the comprehensive sharing of decisions. People are not participating in any real sense until they have some measure of co-responsibility and therefore a share of power. Those who

participate need to know that they are not playing games, that they have a stake in the outcome of their involvement and that they are integral to the process. The Church can encourage this process, not only through the participatory character of its own life, but by helping Christians to participate responsibly in social and political affairs. This can be done by training, by active support and nourishment, and by standing back and giving freedom to individuals to pursue a particular course. The Church should not only ask people to participate in private and church affairs; it should also equip them to work for the shared moral vision of our country. Only when this is a reality is it possible to say that another purpose of participation can be realized, that of limiting the power of the leaders, managers, legislators and rulers. At the same time we are aware that in practice participation is limited if the scale is too large, if communication is complicated, if professional expertise is involved and if the potential participators for some reason remain inactive. Therefore leaders become necessary to focus and channel decisions.

4. *Political leadership.* Political leaders are faced with the problem of finding a working relationship with, and functioning in, a constituency whose attitudes to authority are in transition. The dominant atmosphere is one of mistrust and denigration of those in leading positions. Some have had their faith shattered by the spectacular failure of a leader in high office; others have expected too much of their politicians and feel cheated when they cannot deliver. If this analysis is correct, then political leaders will want to give attention to the question of honesty, which might mean taking the people into their confidence, not only about hopes and fears, plans and actions, but also about the limitations within which decisions have to be made. All of which may undermine the popular conception of what, say, a Chancellor of the Exchequer is able to do, and lead to the rejection of the holder of this office. But perhaps this risk has got to be taken for the greater prize of a new relationship between government and people in a participatory democracy? The elements of this would be access to those in

power, their thoughts, plans and actions; a reciprocal openness between leaders and led; leadership always seeking to carry the people with it, and public opinion acting as a powerful limiting force as well as a climate within which legislation can be made.

5. *Community groups.* There is a growing number of community groups and these are in themselves an exercise of leadership, containing within them many significant experiments in styles of leadership. They also represent a challenge to the established, majority leadership. The most pressing need for these groups is some kind of recognition. If community groups are continually ignored and rejected, their only course is to take themselves out of the confines of society and attack it by any means of their own choosing. But if they are given a sign that their right to exist is accepted and that their cause, even though it may conflict with other interests, has its own integrity, then they are encouraged with the wider society in a responsible and accountable way. There is an obvious danger here of trying to domesticate and neutralize some powerful movements at the base of society, but it is none the less a valid principle to include minority groups within the community and conduct dialogue with them within the ring rather than over it. The churches, at both national and local levels, can take a lead in this, by stepping over their own boundaries to offer acceptance and support to the oppressed minorities in the community. They can also assist in the task of discriminating between minority groups which genuinely deserve legitimation and those which society ought to confront as a potentially evil and destructive force.

6. *Church leadership.* The Church is no longer a spokesman for the majority in Britain, but rather takes its place as one voice among many and one influence among many. But whether the Church is weak or powerful, leadership and authority have the same basis—a radical spirit of service. Spiritual authority is exercised only through the ministries of hearing, helping, bearing and proclaiming. Every other style of leadership in the Church represents some kind of accommodation to the way of the world. This under-

standing of Christian leadership applies also to the Church's variegated activity of 'giving a lead' to the nation; it is the offering of a moral vision, culled from what we have known, developed within the experience we are going through, and open to God's future.

What, then, are the growing points as a new style of leadership emerges?

The post-war years have seen the creation of more wealth in Britain, and with it a small measure of change in the proportional distribution among the population. But there has been little shift in the broad pattern: the wealthy keep their wealth, while the poor remain stuck. This represents a crisis for leadership, not least because in all sections of society there are expectations of a rising standard of living. Like the rest of the rich world, we can strive to fulfil our own expectations, using every political, economic and even military weapon in our considerable arsenal. But there are limits: sooner or later we must learn that the way we live now cannot go on. Leadership—industrial and political— is thus faced with some contradictory questions: How can we go on creating wealth? How can we, if we ought to, influence its distribution? But how can we get people to accept that their expectations cannot be fulfilled?

One of the extra elements in our economy, as in our politics, is the increasing internationalization of issues, problems and solutions. We did not get into our present situation, and we shall not get out of it, independently of the rest of the world. But awareness of the global context of life can have an unsettling effect, creating uncertainty about the identity, status and role of Britain in the world. Which may explain why identification with anything more than local reference groups has diminished: people feel the need to compensate for the vast scale of the map they now live on, by emphasizing their local unit.

There are certain parallels in the present state of the Church in Britain. The most recent initiative in the ecumenical movement, taken by the Churches' Unity Commission, proposes moving forward on a broad front, with the ultimate model in mind of a national church. But this is not the only movement going on: bilateral talks are going on, and there is a rash of local ecumenical life, taking many shapes and forms, which suggest a different mode of proceeding towards unity. Church leadership can see this breakup of the ecumenical movement either as a threat or as a challenge.

Equally major changes are taking place in the cultural climate. We are growing into a plural society, in race, religion and morality. This process gathered pace in the 1960s, when increasing affluence provided the impetus for a great release of self-expression—most visible in the arts and the media. Today the movement towards freedom is open-ended and has developed into a collection of sub-cultures, which occupy common ground in their rejection of authority in most shapes or forms. We are still trying to come to terms with a new popular morality which is one of the effects of these cultural changes.

The major challenge is pluralism itself. What is the nature of consensus in a pluralistic society? Since pluralism implies by its nature that all sections of society do not agree with each other about the nature of society, the tendency is for the idea of consent to be discounted by individuals and groups who accept only their own ground-rules. Hence the temptation to apply non-pluralistic solutions to this problem. This makes it all the more urgent to accept, welcome and work for the pluralistic society, engaging in the crucial task of seeking a minimum consent to form a framework for society. The questions for leadership revolve around the arrangements for a multi-cultural, multi-religious and multi-racial community.

Looking into the future, it may be that the debate will sharpen between those committed to pluralism and the devolvement of authority, and the various proponents of centralized authority and a monoform culture. But unless the extremists at either end of the political spectrum are allowed to gain power, this struggle is likely to continue in a see-saw fashion with no clear view emerging. Meanwhile it is likely that the present decline of hierarchical authority will continue. The power of the older institutions, with their particular style of authority relations, will continue to be whittled away. As cultural and economic pluralism increases, so power itself will follow the same pattern. As part of this power-pluralism there will emerge many more groupings in the middle range of society, between central government and the people, who will participate in government, and thus be committed to information-sharing and co-determination.

If we wish to resist trends towards anarchy or autocracy we must look for new models and modes of change; models which facilitate gradual development rather than revolution, and modes which encourage participation. An important factor here is the conscious appreciation of the fact that there are various groupings within the community, each with its own power and competing for equal freedom. We should reject what is known as the Zero Sum Theory, which states that there is only so much power available, and giving some of it to one means taking some from another. Power is not a cake that is carved up, but something much more fluid and dynamic. It is a potential which can be increasingly realized so that more is achieved. The way forward is to accept the interdependence of society—balancing equity and freedom: equity in terms of the sharing of resources, which are gained and owned by a group through the exercise of their power; and freedom to pursue ends which are often self-interested and potentially a source of conflict. Moreover it is important that power conflict should be seen as part of the struggle to fulfil human potential.

We also need to clarify our understanding of the way in which particular issues can be tackled, locating the appropriate level for each problem—international, national, regional, local or personal. In some cases small is beautiful, but in others big is vital for survival. By implication, a significant proportion of the population will be needed to participate, at least in local and regional decisions—and in more than a nominal way. Both individuals and groups will need a flexibility, and a capacity to develop in response to changing circumstances and the decline of institutional power.

In the present situation certain kinds of leadership are

possible. There is no one pattern because there are different levels and contexts in which leadership is exercised. We can highlight, however, certain elements required of leadership in a democratic, flexible, participant society.

(i) *Consultative*. Although there is no single form or style of consultation, a leader who is not open to the thoughts, feelings and wishes of his group is destroying the organic relationship between them.

(ii) *Accountable*. Leaders in any sector of life should be required by the constituency they serve to give account for the whole of their work.

(iii) *Representative*. A leader acts as a focus for the group and can represent it to those outside. He also interprets the outside world to the group. Ideally, the leader lives on the boundary of his group, aware of other groups and a wider context, and acting as a go-between.

(iv) *Honest*. Leadership is often rooted in mystique or an accepted myth, but this style becomes increasingly difficult in a pluralistic society, when the patterns of social cohesion become de-stabilized. In this situation honesty about hopes and plans and limitations is essential to acceptance and respect.

(v) *Persuasive*. A leader needs skill in communication, including the ability to take part in consultation, the capacity to reflect or crystallize the feelings of the group, and the knack of expressing the will of the group in word and action.

(vi) *Enabling*. A leader needs the ability to help release the group's full potential. This involves calling out of individuals their maximum personal contribution as well as helping to build the mechanisms by which the whole group can best operate.

(vii) *Resilient*. Leadership is an interaction between institutional roles and personality elements. Getting things done and keeping the group together are often, for instance, the incompatible goals of the leader, requiring the ability to live with the tensions and survive the pressures.

Those who are led must have access both to institutional power-holders and the means to exercise alternative leadership of their own. One cannot ask for responsibility without sharing power, and accepting the limitations and controls on one's own power. The responsibilities of those who are led towards their leaders include that of being a watchful check on them.

While it is impossible to generalize about authority and leadership as it is exercised in each denomination, there is always a potential for conflict between the practice of the Church and current thinking in society. Within the Church, Christians adhere in one form or another to a hierarchical system of authority and leadership, springing ultimately from God; within secular society it is taken for granted that there should be a right to question and to confront each other in honest disagreement, trying to find a greater truth through disagreements. Hence the tensions which often arise in the Church between the ordained minister and the laity, and which sometimes cause potential leaders among the laity to give up the struggle and remove themselves from the battle.

There are three groups in particular within the Church which have a potential for leadership but which present leadership is failing to accommodate—young people, women and blacks. What procedures do we have for recognizing the potential of the young and encouraging their participation in church leadership? Are we finding ways in which women can genuinely and willingly share in leadership? Are the objections to women in leadership of a fundamental Christian nature or simply the result of our complicity in the subjection of women? And concerning the black presence within our churches, why has no black leadership emerged which is comparable with that in the United States?

In facing these questions we are not asking how we can best fit in with present practice in society. Rather we are challenged to find ways in which we can act as a pattern of reconciliation and freedom for the world. We want the exercise of authority and the practice of leadership in the Church to be a parable which raises possibilities for society as a whole.

On this challenging note the Working Party ended its main report, and its analysis of the difficulties of exercising leadership in a pluralist society was not questioned by the church leaders attending the Swanwick Assembly. Given the scale of these difficulties, and the penalties attendant upon failure, it is perhaps a matter for surprise—and gratitude—that any man or woman should aspire to a position of leadership in society. Those who do so ought to be able to rely on the critical support of the Christian community. And at a time of change, uncertainty and pessimism in Britain, one of the most important contributions that any leader can make—at any level of society—is to help rebuild the sense of hope. Not a foolish optimism that refuses to face the difficulties, but a feeling of confidence derived from an honest examination of the problems and the possibilities, and the belief that it is within the capacity of the British people to cope with whatever challenges come their way. Without this confidence and hope—based on a wide vision of what individuals and society are capable of becoming— any proposals for serious social reform are doomed to failure.

9. EDUCATION:
THE DEBATE CONTINUES

The so-called Great Education Debate, initiated by Mr. Callaghan, as Prime Minister, in 1977, focused on major issues, and it is a matter for regret that there was in the end very little debate, and none of it very great. As far as the general public is concerned, there is undoubtedly anxiety about the changes which have been taking place in British schools over a comparatively short period and which are often alleged to have brought about a lowering of educational standards. There is also the commonly heard suggestion that the schools no longer make much effort to inculcate 'decent' standards of behaviour, based on traditional ethical norms, and that the schools themselves are communities of chaos and disorder. On the other hand, the educational system is being subjected to increasing criticism —voiced on at least one occasion by the Prime Minister himself—for remaining too traditional in its curricula and not equipping young people to work in those industrial enterprises whose output is crucial to Britain's economic recovery and who produce the wealth needed to support the social services—including education.

The Working Party appointed by the BCC to consider 'Education and Society' was, therefore, faced with a formidable task, and pointed out at the end of 1977 that its work was far from complete. None the less it contributed a fairly substantial interim report to the 'Britain Today and Tomorrow' project.

The Working Party decided at the outset to concentrate on schools, rather than try to deal with education in general, and to give its greatest attention to the secondary sector. The experience of secondary education, by pupils and parents, significantly affects their expectations of education in all the other sectors; and public concern and debate are largely concentrated on the secondary sector. As to method, the group explains: 'We tried out on one another the anxieties and uncertainties that we felt about secondary schooling, both as professional educationists and as concerned Christian parents with children of our own. We are aware of the potential conflicts of interest between professional educationists and concerned Christian parents. We tried, therefore, not so much to provide answers, as to raise questions which teachers and parents might fruitfully explore together.' They also commissioned a report on secondary education in Sweden, to provide a comparative study, and initiated a survey of the ideas and beliefs of young people, and their relationships with parents and teachers. The results of this survey have not been sufficiently analysed for any reliable conclusions to be drawn.

The Working Party found themselves sharing a number of basic convictions, the most important of which was the belief that in forming their views about education they needed consciously to take account of the Christian estimate of man. This estimate implies a positive view of the potentialities within every human being and raises a question about the extent to which the British educational system in general, and schools in particular, gives expression to so positive a conviction. 'We recognize that it is not possible for a compulsory institutional educational system to enable the development of the potentialities of all children in a society. Nevertheless, we wonder whether the British state educational system is not still too narrow in the range of potentialities that it is able to develop—especially in a society that has yet to devise a sufficient range of alternatives for those young people not helped by schools.'

The dilemma in which many middle-class parents feel themselves to be caught was also recognized. On the whole, in terms of future career prospects, their children appear to stand to gain most from a more academically orientated curriculum, and seem to be in danger of losing most from educational changes directed at encouraging new emphases in schools. But the group inclined to the view that any changes directed towards diversifying the curriculum will be of benefit to all, including the academically gifted. Other shared convictions included:

—Belief in an open society, recognizing the necessity for a wide interplay between varied gifts, talents and perceptions. A society enriched by the greatest variety of convictions and insights is most likely to contain the flexibility needed to enable it to adapt to the changing demands of a dynamic order of creation.

—Education is a lifelong learning process and its institutional expressions should be so structured as to recognize this more clearly.

—Some of the recent developments in education are unlikely to be universally reversed, in particular those developments under the general umbrella of 'progressive' at the primary and 'comprehensive' at the secondary levels. The British educational system will not generally return to learning by rote and a high degree of selection. It is therefore important that people should address themselves positively to making creative critique of the present realities.

—Recent developments in education have generally led in the right direction, but the principles on which they are based should be made to lead to a more effective education for everyone.

—Account should be taken of those elements in human personality which lead to selfishness and licence in individuals and over-rigid control in institutions. Human weakness is a factor always to be taken into account in discussions about education (as in everything else). Therefore what might be regarded as a creative development in one set of circumstances might have to be regarded as quite out of place in another.

With these shared convictions as a background, the group then addressed themselves to a number of specific questions.

Resentments in the Schools

Educational institutions, whether they like it or not, are involved in the business of transmitting values. The question, then, is whether these values are self-chosen or whether educational institutions are merely the unwilling victims of the dominant values of the culture in which they are set. All the evidence suggests that much of the present-day unrest about education largely reflects unrest about the way in which planning is effected in society generally. It is in its educational system that society attempts to give expression to those values which it regards as important and to those ideals that it sets before its citizens. For too many people the hopes and promises are empty—the dreams of planners who seem to have an inadequately developed sensitivity to the real needs of human beings. In fact, they are the dreams of people who probably care a great deal about the people for whom they are trying to create a better environment. The difficulties seem to arise because there is a too distant relationship between planners and the community. This causes resentment, and precisely because schools are experienced (by parents, teachers and pupils) as the manipulating forces of planning agencies they are felt to be concerned with the transmission of social values and with an implicit commitment to the institutions of society.

Commenting on this section of the report, the Chester Theological Group suggested that one way in which educational institutions have become the 'victim of values' is the stress on money. 'Money has been spent lavishly on an institution in which the primary value should be people.' Because children and adolescents themselves have more money, this has led to the need for more money to impress and satisfy them in their education. The Chester Group felt it was wrong to speak of educational institutions as being 'unwilling victims' of the dominant values of the culture in which they are set, (a) because educational institutions are automatically a reflection of the prevailing standards and values of society, and (b) because the word 'unwilling' seemed to imply that educationists are a detached profession capable of seeing some superior values from the rest of society. The gradual disappearance of Religious Education from the curriculum of many schools was instanced as an indication of the way in which the values of society are reflected in education.

Resentment about education is expressed in all kinds of schools, especially through high levels of truancy, violence towards teachers as well as other pupils, and through calculated vandalism. Those who direct their resentment at schools are not simply those who have opted out of society. Secondary schools are an institutional attempt to initiate young people into the conventions of their culture, and where they are successful in fulfilling this objective they are less likely to encounter violence and aggression from their pupils. It is not clear whether the problem is simply to do with efficiency in initiation or whether some of the values to which schools are committed are seriously out of harmony with the fulfilment of human potential.

Part of the function of schools is to initiate: learning to speak, to read, write and count, developing an awareness and appreciation for a cultural inheritance, understanding with sympathy and challenging where necessary the codes and conventions of society, developing gifts that can be used for the general benefit of the community. Why, then, do most schools appear to encounter opposition and resentment? Part of the explanation is that some of the standards against which pupils are judged are frequently inappropriate, for example, condemning teenage boys for having shoulder-length hair when the culture to which they feel they belong lauds such styles. Making judgements about pupils for failing in competitive processes might reveal more integrity if associated with a questioning of the institutions demanding the competitive process in the first place. Judgements made about people will always cause resentment if they are felt to be irrelevant or inappropriate.

But the schools have encountered difficulties for a number of reasons besides those that have to do primarily with values. The historically conditioned perception of what it was possible for British schools to be, implied that the secondary schools would for some time to come appear as formally ordered institutions where fairly rigid rules and conventions were incorporated into the régime. A too-hasty swing in any direction would have been counter-productive.

Even so, it was possible to exercise some degree of control and bring about some measure of change, and failures here compounded the basic problem. In many ways the odds were stacked against schools before they had even started: the resentment of older pupils who wished to leave but could not; the suspicion in which teachers were held by many parents; an inadequate salary structure during the 1960s placing pressure on teachers to move at frequent intervals in order to gain higher graded posts; a shortage of equipment; a high teacher/pupil ratio; and outdated buildings—all these factors contributed to making the task of the schools more difficult, and present-day uncertainties and re-organization have only added to the problems.

The Chester Group commented here that resentment of the traditional authority of old over young may always have been present in schools, but today the risks are less and so the resentment is expressed.

Many of the resentments directed at teachers by both parents and pupils reflect the parents' experiences of their own schooling a generation ago. This, in turn, often results in negative attitudes on the part of teachers towards parents. Schools would find their work a great deal easier if teachers and parents saw one another as equals in the educational process. Parents sometimes see teachers as people whose relationship with them appears condescending or dogmatic. Is there not a great deal which teachers themselves can do to improve their public image and, therefore, their effectiveness? How often are teachers able to allow parent-teacher associations to become arenas in which genuine discussion takes place about the educational aims of a school, rather than money-raising organizations for projects on which a school staff has set its sights? How easily are teachers able to chat informally with parents outside school premises?

Secondary schools still have to live down a great deal of historical commitment to a curriculum directed towards meeting the entry requirements of the universities. Education conceived in terms of a hierarchy of disciplines inevitably sees itself as primarily concerned with producing the labelled and categorized manpower for a society committed to that hierarchy of disciplines. Pressure in the same direction comes also from employers and parents, but it needs to be asserted ever more forcefully that much that in recent years has passed as a grammar school education was in fact educationally as well as academically mediocre. More discussion should hinge around an understanding of education as something enabling young people how (rather than what) to think, and how to handle their feelings.

Schools should strive to be places in which young people can develop qualities of relating, appreciating, responding and judging. The most important of them, *relating*, is a quality on which too little emphasis has been placed by those responsible for administering schools. The impossibility of a single teacher being able to relate adequately with 210 different adolescents during the course of a seven-period day is obvious. The consequences of a subject-based curriculum and a subject-trained teaching profession are that individual teachers spend an insufficient amount of time with pupils dealing with a wide range of subjects; hence the unlikelihood of establishing relationships which meet the emotional and social needs of developing adolescents. The emotional needs of teachers also need to be recognized, and there is evidence that teachers covering several subject areas do not feel intellectually frustrated and benefit from the possibility of more contact with the same pupils. Schools should be encouraged to include timetable periods in which pupils and teachers (and others) can meet informally.

A human being needs many skills to help him to deal with his environment. In addition to the basic social skills, he needs a range of other skills, like mending a fuse or painting a window frame; skills too easily devalued. He needs the self-esteem that comes with knowing that he can do some specific things rather well. He needs also to learn how to listen so that he can hear what other people are saying to him in the silences between their words. He needs to understand his own emotions and have some perception of why he behaved the way he did under certain circumstances.

The development of these skills in young people is an important part of what secondary schooling is about and it is doubtful whether sufficient opportunity exists at present for these aspects of education.

Appreciation of their inheritance is not easy to inspire in the young. But the task of the teacher would be eased if the pupil did not find himself impelled to feel that he needed to fight for the assertion of his own intrinsic worth. If schools, by their structure and relationships, were to make it more clear to young people that they are valued as people, the development of the quality of appreciation, both of history and of other people, would be considerably eased.

The quality of responding to need requires, in addition to a whole range of social and emotional skills, an honest recognition by the individual of what he has to offer. It is questionable whether schools can be concerned with the specific manpower needs of society. This might have been possible in primitive communities, but in complex cultures such as our own the range of talent needed is considerable. The educational system is more likely to provide society with a rich variety of manpower resources if it provides pupils in school with a rich range of options, all of which are regarded as having social and personal value.

One of the most important functions of the educational system is to help young people develop and exercise qualities of judgement. Considerable developments have taken place in this regard in the senior forms of secondary schools, encouraging young people to formulate their own views about the institutions of society as well as major moral questions challenging mankind today. But how far are educational institutions themselves sufficiently flexibly organized to respond positively to critical judgements on the part of pupils?

The Working Party's views on the curriculum were, however, severely criticized by the Chester Theological Group, which described some of their conclusions as 'naïve and ill-informed' and based on 'confused thinking about the end-product of the educational process'. The main criticism from Chester was that the curriculum had been regarded only as what happens in the classroom, whereas the whole life of the school community is to be seen as part of the curriculum in its broadest sense. There was also an undue stress on structures and an ignoring of the extent to which counselling is already being done in secondary schools. The Working Party's plea for a 'rich range of opportunities' might deceive pupils into expecting a rich range of 'job opportunities', and the report assumed the existence of an untapped source of dedicated teachers, whereas standards of dedication are falling among young teachers. The choices offered to pupils have greatly increased and there is now a great deal of consultation with pupils and parents. Finally, the report seemed to expect the schools to cater for the great range of adolescent needs—'there should be an acknowledgement of the place and value of the home, youth clubs and all other growing points and learning processes. Only so can there be a balanced view of education.'

Problems in Comprehensive Education

While much has been done to make secondary pupils feel that they matter as individuals—through house systems, tutor groups, year groups and so on—there remains the fundamental problem of the size of an educational institution. No matter what structural alterations are made within an institution, once a school grows beyond a certain size it is impossible to create a community in which more than a minimal number of people can feel significant. It seems that there is an optimum size beyond which it becomes extremely difficult, if not well-nigh impossible, for pupils to feel that the school is in a helpful way a community. And at this point the nature of the relationships within the institution, and between the members of the institution and the outside world, change dramatically. 'We had evidence of enormous energy being expended by open-minded and sensitive heads concerned to humanize institutions of inhuman size. We were left with the conviction that they were faced with an impossible task.'

How necessary are large institutions to ensuring the provision of a wide range of courses? Is it possible that the educational debate about courses understands them too much in terms of separate units, complete unto themselves? 'While we do not think it possible to stipulate precisely what the maximum size of secondary schools should be—it depends partly on the particular qualities of individual head teachers and teachers, and the perception of pupils in different localities—we incline to the view that about 700 is probably the limit. Clearly, in some cases the limit might be 1,000, while in others it could be as low as 500.'

The Chester Group had no quarrel with this analysis and opinion, but made the additional point that one of the most critical areas affected by the size of a school is staff and staff relationships. 'Experience suggests that staff relationships deteriorate with the increase in the size of schools. Great importance should be attached to teacher morale and therefore to relationships and management skills.' The Chester Group also suggested that special problems for religious education are caused by increasing the size of schools. Resentment at being functionally organized often expresses itself in apparent hostility to religious education. Moreover the large size of a school very seriously affects the teaching of religious education, because it removes any possibility of personal contact between the specialist and up to 500 pupils who may pass through his hands each week. Where, due to size, no assembly is possible for the school, worship suffers and there is no possibility of a meaningful relationship between head and school.

The Working Group confessed that the implications of its views on the size of schools were alarming, for they led to a fundamental questioning of the principle of comprehensive education. 'We started from the assumption that comprehensive education was right . . . But we are not convinced of the value of a comprehensive curriculum understood in terms of courses if the price is schools of a size that makes people within them feel that these institutions are inhumanly large.' It also seems to be the case that comprehensive schools, while attempting to provide comprehensive curricula, frequently fail to be socially comprehensive, especially when their catchment area is limited. Attempts in some localities to run a system comprehensive in name alongside a selective system is a cause for anxiety, and the question has to be raised: How comprehensive is the British educational system, anyway?

The Chester Group was apparently disinclined to grasp this particular nettle, emphasizing instead that 'bringing all secondary education into one organization does not overcome the need for selection and separation. Selection has to continue within the institution, and this means that for all the pupils separation remains obvious and persistently in view.' In some cases there is a valid place for 'the therapy of failure', though the increase in the number of specialists in counselling brings its own problems—not least the risk of creating more 'problems' to satisfy the new service.

The Working Party utterly rejected the notion that the school can be a vehicle for the imposition of alien values upon a community. At most, the school can provide an arena in which the values of the community are exposed to the values of a wider world. A far-sighted and visionary headmaster might find this frustrating, but in the interests of democracy he has to recognize that modifying his plans in the light of the community's wishes is a necessary part of the democratic process of society. There is no place now for an authoritarian head teacher; the need is for a head who sees the school as a place where the creative potential of teachers and pupils can be freed in order to flourish. Unfortunately, however, many far-sighted head teachers still encounter resentment among parents. This often arises from a failure to understand the attitudes and support mechanisms that sustain people. It is all too easy to lay out a blueprint of educational ideals without recognizing that for their fulfilment many of the cherished assumptions will have to be replaced. The need for the head teacher to relate sensitively to the local community demonstrates once again the vital importance of personal relationships in all aspects of education. In the long run the quality of relationships between people in the educational world is of the greatest importance—of greater importance than structures of organization and teaching methods.

The head teacher and staff frequently find themselves caught between the wishes of the community and the plans of their local authority. There is of course the need for a coherent and consistent educational system covering the whole country, and for some system of accountability, but there also needs to be much more local autonomy. Many heads of schools and colleges feel themselves pressurized against their professional judgement by an educational system in which the overriding decisions appear to be taken for reasons of political ideology and require a cumbersome bureaucracy for their application. Yet in the end the school belongs to the local community—and local authorities and central government need constantly to be reminded of this. If people could feel that the school in their midst was *their* school, whose facilities they could use—that it belonged to them, not they to it—there is the likelihood that the local community would support the work the teachers are trying to do.

The head teacher must of course stand accountable for the way in which his school is functioning, but what criteria are to form the basis for judgement of success or failure? It is a matter for concern that so many judgements about schools are made on the grounds of so-called educational efficiency, which is closely related to examination success rates. Most parents' expectations of education are to do with the acquisition of knowledge, which can be recognized by the award of a diploma or certificate. These expectations are reinforced by potential employers who demand that candidates for jobs should present certificates of academic attainment, irrespective of the relevance of the knowledge so measured to the work to be undertaken. The pressure on head teachers to 'deliver the goods' in measurable terms inhibits the imaginative development of education in areas where results are not as yet measurable, i.e. in terms of the development of community relationships.

The whole matter of awards needs wider discussion. If

education is concerned with giving encouragement, is it possible to relate awards to individual effort rather than to external standards? Many youth leaders and community and social workers who are in close touch with teenagers are critical of the educational system as being over-concerned with the labelling of people. This labelling inevitably results in many being regarded—and regarding themselves —as failures. All of which demonstrates the relative inflexibility of the educational system, and the need for the educational options open to young people to be continually widened.

Here the Free Schools seem to offer certain advantages: they provide an element of choice, they widen the options, they provide an unstructured approach, they involve the participants in planning and they use the resources of the community. On the other hand, they are dealing with only a small number of pupils outside the maintained system, they are having little effect on the maintained system and they are failing to realize some of the potential of the participants. None the less, the Free Schools represent a movement whose wider development should be encouraged.

The Working Party considered briefly the notion that 'educational vouchers' should be handed out for people to use as they themselves wished. While recognizing education as a lifelong process to which, in its institutionalized expression, any who wished could turn at any time in their life, the Working Party came to the conclusion that a voucher system was not necessary to make this possible. 'What is needed is, on the one hand, an extension of adult education facilities, and on the other a willingness to allow young people not to go to school if they do not wish to do so.' In the latter case, however, children would need to be protected from the less responsible attitudes of some parents who might abuse any abolition of compulsion.

The Working Party's handling of the 'voucher' issue provoked Professor Walter James, in an assessor's comment on their report, to raise the question of the absence of an explicit critical framework. This lack, he believed, made it difficult for others to judge whether the Working Party had a reliable map to guide them, gave the impression that it was uncertain about the levels of analysis appropriate for specific issues, and left the further impression that it 'could be rounding up the small-fry of the educational underworld whilst letting the master-minds go free'.

Applying his criticism to the question of vouchers, Professor James wrote:

The group is right to recognize that the values transmitted through the education system are affected by structures, and that structures owe some of their characteristics to their resource allocative functions. Resource allocation needs therefore to be scrutinized, but any evaluation of vouchers needs to consider at least their effects on, (a) freedom of choice, (b) equality of opportunity, (c) equality, (d) efficiency, (e) diversity, (f) accountability and responsiveness, (g) the level of resources devoted to education. The task for Christian assessment would then be to consider:
(a) whether the situation calls for any of these factors to be valued more than others, even at the risk of disadvantaging some of the others, e.g. to pursue *diversity*, even at the expense of progress to *equality of opportunity*;
(b) and if so, whether vouchers are the best available alternative for achieving these ends, e.g. would Alan Day's proposal in his note of reservation to the Report of the Layfield Committee, *Local Government Finance*, that a distinction be made between *national* public goods and *local* public goods, be a better way to achieve diversity?

Church Schools and a Churches' Council

The Working Party suggested that a number of sharp questions about church schools now need to be considered by Christians. Is it true that church schools are divisive in some communities, e.g. parts of Liverpool and Northern Ireland, and, if so, would it be of help to them if the dual system were to be abolished nationally? Should the provision of aided schools in England and Wales generally be influenced by the needs of those communities where such schools are thought by some to create problems? Do aided schools cream off Christian teachers from the maintained system when, as some believe, this is precisely where Christian teachers need to be? Is it a realistic understanding of Christian caring, or a misguided notion of Christian mission in the world, that the churches should provide schools for the education of their own members? Is there much that can be regarded as particularly Christian about most aided schools functioning within the framework of a state educational system? Are aided schools generally more likely to be in the vanguard or the rearguard of educational and social development? Is there substance to the charge, frequently levelled against church schools, that they often appear to be doing an inferior job, while parents are queuing to get their children into them because they offer an education which, though backward, is regarded as acceptably so when provided by the churches? Is there justification in the charge that, as the churches are preoccupied with the values and conventions of earlier ages, so church schools seem to attempt to embody these same attitudes?

Attempting to answer some of these questions themselves, the Working Party began with the assertion that schools which understand their *raison d'être* in terms of the inculcation of particular sets of attitudes in young people are socially divisive and to be discouraged. Aided schools should be regarded as Christian schools attempting to serve the community as a whole. The peculiar contribution of the Christian community to the world is that it is a community of vision. And, since the real justification for church schools is that they be distinctive, their distinctiveness should show itself in a style of operation appropriate to that of a community of vision, embarked upon a journey and rooted in hope that has reality for its members. The Working Party said:

We are critical of those aided secondary schools which appear to be socially selective, more concerned than the general run of secondary schools with providing a traditionally subject-orientated curriculum, and over-dominated by traditional authoritarian and undemocratic structures, which may have been appropriate in an age of more settled national assumptions but which are inappropriate in an era when society as a whole is involved in a search for values that will sustain a dynamic and plural culture.

We take the view that it is proper for the churches to attempt a Christian critique of education in society and that the existence of the dual system provides the churches with an opportunity to give through the educational service tangible expression of some of the ideals they wish to set before society. We wish, therefore, that aided schools would provide for all in the community (whether Christian or not) educational communities motivated by an overriding concern for the development of creative relationships through which all involved are enabled to grow as persons. We wish that aided schools (and colleges) were places of sensitive adventurous experimentation, providing the widest possible range of options for the personal development of the least privileged members of the community in as socially comprehensive a context as it is possible to create.

The churches with the largest institutional stake in education in Britain are the Church of England and the Roman Catholic Church, but, while these two churches are the legal guardians of their aided schools, these schools do in a sense belong to the total Christian community. One implication of this is that the two churches should, in the administration of their educational institutions, be responsive to the wishes of the total Christian community. This led the Working Party to propose the establishment of a Churches' Council on Education, with a threefold function—

1. Heightening the level of awareness among Christians in general of the issues at stake in the educational debate.
2. Representing the views of the Christian community at large to those churches having an institutional stake in education.
3. Representing Christian opinion on education to the secular world.

The Working Party also visualized the existence of a wide spread of locally-based Christian groups 'addressing themselves particularly to the educational needs of their own localities as well as those of the nation as a whole'.

The report concludes with an affirmation of the Working Party's conviction that the churches have a considerable contribution to make to the current debate about education in Britain, and also a clear responsibility to join in the debate:

We are of the view that a proper understanding of Christian mission implies that the churches should deploy the resources of the Christian community for the health of society as a whole. The churches have historically been at their most significant, either when they took upon themselves to provide needed services which the community lacked, or when they provided similar services to those already available in the community but in a distinctive way which made up some of the omissions (as the churches regarded them) in the secular provisions. The whole thrust of our report is that the churches should address themselves to these matters specifically in the field of education. The churches have an enormous investment of plant in schools and colleges. This investment should be seen as providing the opportunity of serving the community, rather than as something which needs to be defended against erosion. But the utilization of these resources in this way requires initiative and imagination. The churches possess a peculiar freedom imaginatively to respond to the educational needs of human beings in the contemporary world. Our hope is that they will act on that freedom with vision and realism.

At the Swanwick Assembly the spokesman for the Working Party made a special point of stressing that their report was to be regarded only as an interim statement. There is more work to be done, though no indication was given as to the direction that might be followed. Various matters certainly need the attention of the churches. One of these concerns the content and quality of the teacher training provided by the Colleges of Education. During the last few years those involved in the work of these colleges have faced great uncertainty, and experienced not a little anxiety, because of widespread closures and amalgamations. When the history of education in Britain during the period 1950–75 comes to be written, the handling of the Colleges of Education by successive governments will be seen, even more clearly than it appears today, as a scandal of the first magnitude. The building of many new colleges, some of which were declared to be surplus to requirements almost as soon as they were completed, involved the wasteful expenditure of hundreds of millions of pounds and appears to have been determined by a combination of false assumptions and aims. But the present concern must be for the proper equipping of the coming generations of teachers for the educational tasks they will be expected to perform. No improvements in curricula, organization and buildings will compensate for ill-equipped teachers, and current evidence suggests that the quality of their training is very uneven.

Another matter on which the Christian voice needs to be heard concerns the place of the educational system in the political arena. It is one thing to have different types of schools in different areas to meet different needs; it is quite another to have an entire system turned topsy-turvy because there has been a change of government. Comprehensive education has aroused a good deal of controversy—not all of it well informed or entirely disinterested—and it is now providing ammunition for politicians fighting for power. There is clear evidence that, in some places at least, the present organization of comprehensive schools stands in need of modification. But, above all else, secondary education in Britain needs a period of stability, during which mistakes can be rectified and new approaches thoroughly tested. It is far too early to make a final judgement on a system which holds great promise and is generally regarded as the right approach by professional educationists.

Also crossing into political territory are questions concerning Britain's Public Schools. The Working Party declared itself to be 'critical of those aided secondary schools which appear to be socially selective . . . which may have been appropriate in an age of more settled national assumptions but which are inappropriate in an era when society as a whole is involved in a search for values that will sustain a dynamic and plural culture'. It seems fair to assume that Public Schools fall into this category inasmuch as their pupils are drawn almost exclusively from privileged families, able to meet the expensive fees, and are offered not only privileged educational facilities but also lifelong membership of the most privileged sector of society. Some of the member churches of the British Council of Churches are deeply involved, in various ways, in the Public Schools and it would therefore be appropriate for their contribution to the Britain of today and tomorrow to be thoroughly evaluated—not simply in relation to their educational role but also in relation to their compatibility with many of the proposals for social reform contained in other parts of this report.

10. CULTURE AND COUNTER-CULTURE

Many of the issues raised in the education debate are closely related to the changes taking place in British society at large—changes in life style, changes in values, changes in expectations, changes of such a magnitude that together they constitute a profound disturbance in the pattern of culture itself. Those who are themselves involved in such a disturbance are not always the best-equipped to analyse what is taking place and to propose appropriate responses. None the less the 'Britain Today and Tomorrow' project included a section on 'Culture, Morality and Styles of Life', and thus encouraged a number of people to tackle some of the issues. Not surprisingly, no consensus emerged—neither did much in the way of coherent thought. But an effort was made, and a group convened by the Mothers' Union produced a report on 'The Family—Culture and Morality', which ran to 103 paragraphs.

The Family under Pressure

Having noted that society still demands from the family extremely high standards of care for its members, this report discussed certain major changes which have occurred in the pattern of family life during the past thirty years:

Marriage is increasingly seen as a partnership, and the relationship of the couple is of prime importance. As a result of this, it is considered by many people to be wrong to allow a marriage which is in any way unsatisfactory or unhappy to continue. Marriage is readily entered into, but is only expected to last as long as it is considered a success. More and more are choosing to live together without legal formalities.

There has been a great change in the choice of marriage partners. Owing to the weakening of class barriers, the mobility of young people and the multi-racial nature of our society, people are less likely to marry anyone from among their own family friends or neighbours. The average age of marriage has declined steadily since the beginning of the century. The young people of minority ethnic communities often become victims of a tug-of-war between the marriage customs of their own culture and those of modern Britain. Young people are also exposed to many conflicting ideas and attitudes to marriage and sexual behaviour, and among the many discussions the value of a permanent relationship is seldom considered. There may be several reasons for this. We have been led to expect an immediacy and authenticity in the marriage relationship, while we may not have been made aware or have been unwilling to accept the need for the maintenance that is required to keep the relationship in good repair. There is now a more gradually accepted expectation of equality of fulfilment, both sexually and socially, for man and woman. When frustration of these sometimes inflated expectations becomes intolerable, the relationship breaks. In a materialistic society relationships are sometimes submerged by the physical weight of the environment. Poor housing, stressful or poorly paid employment, or the arrival of too large a family too soon can put the most stable of relationships 'at risk'.

In all, Britain is having to live with the experience of marriage breakdown to the extent that in 1974 there were some 305,000 first marriages (for both parties) registered, and some 132,000 petitions for divorce filed—and the figures for other recent years are scarcely less alarming.

The increasing number of marital breakdowns and re-marriages brings considerable changes to the patterns of family life. Relationships become complicated and entangled. Children have to adapt to many different pressures, ways of behaviour and standards of living. Many families at different periods have only one parent to fulfil the roles of two.

Allied to the pattern of marriage is the increased openness

and permissiveness concerning sexual relations. Contraception has removed the most practical reason for chastity. Both Christians and others have, from the beginning of this century, become aware that sexuality is of value in itself, and is not only a means of continuing the population. Outside the churches there are theories that it is important to have fully sexual relationships from an early age; that it is important to become experienced in sexual activity before marriage, and that a couple need to discover whether they are physically suited. The general effect on young people is to make them think that sex is exciting, and an experience they should be allowed to enjoy. This very rapid change of attitude means that young people and their parents often have very different ideas as to what is acceptable behaviour. One consequence of this is that many older children do not have any constructive and understanding advice from their parents as they become mature.

The size of families has decreased in recent years and this has had an effect on all members. The large families, normal at the beginning of this century, provided opportunities for their members to learn to relate, from their earliest days, to different kinds of people. With only one or two brothers or sisters, a child may have little pre-school experience of competition or co-operation.

There are also fewer people in the extended family to support the young family in its difficult early stages. At the same time, a higher life-expectancy means that there are a large number of very old people needing care. These either have to live with, and possibly become a burden to, the younger family, or be looked after elsewhere and feel cast off.

The incidence of violence in families seems to be increasing. New laws and new methods are being devised to cope with the growing number of battered wives and babies. The violence is seldom premeditated, but is generally a sudden loss of control, which is often the result of the stressful nature of modern living. The percentage of illegitimate births has increased; this is due as much to society's tolerance of children being born to single women as to promiscuity. But now that so much emphasis is laid on planned families, some people feel it is morally right to terminate an unplanned pregnancy, both inside and outside marriage.

Until relatively recently, the roles played by the different members of the family were clear-cut and distinct. But the modern world no longer accepts the dominance of woman by man, so marriage is a partnership, and this democracy usually extends to the children of a reasonable age. This can be a very satisfying situation, provided the members of the family are sufficiently mature to accept these more demanding roles. Anarchy, destructive of personal relationships, can exist when everyone thinks they have a right to their own way.

Discipline is often found difficult to impose in the new family pattern, and the liberation and education of woman has resulted in uncertainty as to whether she is most usefully employed in looking after her children, or in working in the community. In many cases she does both, but whether she works outside her home or not, she may be perplexed as to whether she has made the right choice. A more fundamental change, even if only temporary, occurs when, owing to the greater earning power of the woman, or to the man's unemployment, the husband cares for the home and the wife goes out to work.

When the boundaries of class or race are crossed by marriage, children are sometimes subjected to conflicting patterns of behaviour and values from many different sources. Higher standards and further education often leave parents feeling estranged from their children. Some young people become increasingly separated from their parents by the current youth culture. The present growth of unemployment has come as a great shock to some of them and has turned their known world upside down.

The young people of minority ethnic communities face a dilemma which at times is most traumatic. Those who were born in this country have only one major cultural reference point, but their parents often try to impose other standards of cultural behaviour in the home. Thus they are presented with conflicting loyalties, and for survival most of them take refuge in the cultural identifications of their parents' country of origin, even though they have no real understanding of, or affinity with, the cultural values to which they then aspire.

The rapid growth of Britain's population in the present century is now leading to a situation in which there will be a far greater proportion of the population, both old and young, dependent upon those working people who provide for them. On the other hand, the most recently available figures suggest a considerable drop in the birth-rate which, if this were to continue, could even lead to a declining population.

Britain today is a multi-racial and multi-cultural society, and these aspects of life are manifested in many different cultures, customs, traditions and religions. The adverse social conditions under which peoples of all races live in inner-city areas often lead to tensions, hatred, fear and the division of communities—racially or religiously. These divisions threaten the very fabric of a multi-racial and multi-cultural society. On the other hand, if harmony is created between the races in these islands, then we shall be faced with more racially mixed marriages, with all the problems and benefits these will bring.

The effects on family life of the Welfare State have been many and varied. Its comprehensive provisions have led to a loss of power for the family, and a regard for the welfare services as a thing apart—an anonymous 'they' who will provide—though it is indubitable that many families have been able to surmount disaster solely as a result of the Welfare State's existence.

It is now very seldom that people continue to live in the same place all their lives. A man's work may take him and his family all over the country and away from the people they know. Local Authority housing schemes often move families away from the village or area they know. Young families have been uprooted from their accustomed neighbours and sent to far-away housing estates. Apart from causing loneliness and isolation, these moves mean that families and individuals are not always certain as to the behaviour expected of them. As a result of constant moves, some people are reluctant to put down roots and settle. In its determination that every family shall have a house of its own, the state has generally acted without giving much thought to the other needs of the family, with the result that a family becomes an impersonal unit, a number on a list, living in a place with no traditions, suspicious of and suspected by the families on either side.

Although the legislation which was introduced immediately after the Second World War was intended to ensure that the state provided for the basic needs of all those who were unable to care for themselves, it is now being recognized that the state cannot hope to meet all needs and that society must take responsibility for its own members. Hence the growing interest in 'community care' and in the use of volunteers in an increasing range of situations. On the other hand, the development of the child-care services has tended to surround mothers with experts—the midwife, the health visitor, the school doctor, her children's teachers— who are intended to help her, but may in fact make her feel of no importance or little worth in the care of her children.

Britain has become a country of vast enterprises, huge cities, hypermarkets, high-rise flats and vast factories. This enables people to enjoy many products and facilities that would not otherwise be available to them. But 'big' has meant that people have been replaced by machines; in many families, both father and mother work at impersonal jobs and their children can only look forward to a similar future. The hidden costs (the stress, the anxiety, the swallowing up of resources, the neglect of the inner cities) to the community of these vast enterprises are seldom counted.

The growth of the mass media means that people can no longer live in isolation. Much of this enlarges people's vision and imagination, but the glamorous life styles and the homes that are shown on television, especially in advertisements, can lead to disillusionment and a determination to achieve luxury. Small children find it difficult to distinguish between fact and fiction, and there is a suspicion, not completely confirmed, that the increase of violence in society is due to the constant violence shown on the TV screen. It is probably more true that those who have become violent through other influences learn new methods of violence from TV. The existence of TV has brought a considerable change to family life. In some ways it has drawn families together through enjoying the same entertainment in each other's company. In others it has driven the family away from normal communication by its continual presence. In all events, it is invaluable to inactive old people and invalids and provides an additional channel of education.

In order that industry should thrive, most things are now made needing replacement. The acme of the affluent society is always to possess the latest model and to wear the latest fashion. It is no longer a matter of pride to have preserved possessions which can be handed on to the future. This concentration on the new has lessened the importance of the past, and has an effect on relationships—my husband no longer suits me, my wife's interests are no longer mine, friendships are ended and not renewed. The rapid changes in our patterns of living tend to create a sense of paranoia in those who cannot cope with change, and have not been helped to value their previous experiences in relation to their current situations.

Britain hopes to provide social justice for all and the emphasis on self-realization means that people refuse to put up with disadvantages which were previously taken for granted, nor is society happy that they should. The law is compiled by society, but not all the members of our complex society agree that the law should be as it is. Consequently, certain sections feel that there is no disgrace in offending against certain parts of it—motoring offences, drug-taking, etc. We are also a society with strong and conflicting ideals, and groups who believe in one ideal see no wrong in offending in order to frustrate a group who work against their ideal.

The value of being honest or reliable often seems to have weakened to the point of disappearance. It does not seem wrong, to many, to cheat or steal from the vast concerns—

the factory or the supermarket—for they are totally impersonal and cannot be seen as representing people whom it would be unloving to damage. Many forms of dishonesty are current today, and one of the reasons for this may be the uncertainty of current social pressures. Many of the perpetrators have little sense of being morally wrong, and there are of course numerous unrecognized and subconscious factors that affect a person's choice of action. In general, it may be said that what is seen by each individual as personally satisfying will depend, to a large extent, on the example of his family during his formative years, and the relative importance which his parents and other influential adults attach to moral principles, and to the immediate gratification of self-centred desires.

Hopes for the Family

After this extensive analysis of the effect on family life of many of the changes which have taken place—and continue —in modern society, the Mothers' Union Group examined 'Family Life in a Biblical Perspective' and, in the light of a necessarily brief exposition of the teaching of Jesus on the subject, outlined what it believed to be a Christian evaluation of the present and hope for the future.

If we are looking at the needs of others first, we see that love implies a real discipline as opposed to licence. Society needs a respect for law, otherwise there will be no society. But laws will always be challenged and there will always be those who feel that obedience to certain laws is against their fundamental beliefs. A good society must see that young people are educated to understand the reasons for the need for maintenance of and obedience to law. Therefore society should be ready and able to change laws with the changing needs of its people.

Although we live in a democracy, the impersonality of our large institutions has become oppressive. Those which are designed to assist the community can become more bureaucratic than caring. Those which are at the heart of our commercial life often exploit in the process of succeeding. Problems of distributive justice remain. Some people have adequate houses, others have none; some have well-paid jobs, others—particularly the young and the black—have none. If social morality appears to be at odds with personal morality, then the standards of social honesty will also suffer. Our laws are framed by those who live in society as it is. It is therefore crucial for the Church to be involved both in influencing public opinion and in formulating the law. If it is not, then the values which underpin our beliefs will fail to affect the law as it develops.

It is difficult to see how the present mobility of families can be lessened in our modern economic world; the Common Market is going to make it greater. People must go where there is work, so employers of men who have moved long distances to work for them should take some responsibility for their workers' families.

The fact that the Development Corporations of some new towns are trying to persuade older people to join their younger families shows that some authorities have realized that it needs three generations to make a community out of a new town. The breaking up of families through slum clearance in our large cities, and the isolated living which has resulted from high-rise flats, is now generally recognized as disastrous. It is to be hoped that in future all committees responsible for planning new housing will consider first and foremost the essential but differing needs of each member of the family necessary to prevent frustration and to achieve good neighbourliness, rather than vistas of architectural styles.

Inevitably, as our society becomes more complex, the state will continue to co-operate in fulfilling the functions of the family. There are also likely to be more casualties of the system, and the state needs to consider how far it is possible to assist people in coping with the changing patterns of society. This requires consideration of new sorts of support systems: advice services, legal aid, day services for children where both parents need to work, self-help groups. However, the state cannot hope to meet all needs, and this is being recognized more and more with the use of volunteers. Attempts to provide community care for people who would formerly have been in hospital or other institutions are part of a similar concern, and Christians need to be involved in this.

If we believe that every individual, male or female, has the right to be accepted as a person with talents which can be developed and used, then it makes sense for a married couple to consider what they each have to offer to their relationship with each other and to their children. Often the traditional roles will be the ones that do make effective use of the talents available, but this will not always be so. Public policy needs to be flexible enough to respond to infinitely varied needs, to ensure that the people concerned are able to solve their own difficulties.

As the cultures of the different communities in our society become intertwined, it may become more difficult to make choices, there may be less clarity about what constitutes a right answer to problems. Reactions to change also vary. We need to develop a critical objectivity which enables us to make choices which preserve the best of the old, whilst accepting the good of the new. We need to give careful thought to those values which are ultimate and immutable, separating out those which are appropriate for a particular age. The Church has an important role in influencing public policy and it is crucial that this should continue, but sometimes it has been defensive and reactionary rather than open to new ideas and theories about God's world.

In a democracy it is important to recognize the links between authority, responsibility and power. Power should be given to those who have the integrity and skills to use it, and not simply to those who happen to stand for the party or programme in favour. There needs therefore to be careful education to ensure that people are aware of the power they have in distributing authority, and so that they may learn how to influence decision-making, to identify needs and to see that they are met. The growth in self-help groups for everything from bulk shopping to the provision of play-groups is an example of this.

If the individual or family is not to suffer unduly, public and Church policy must reflect an appreciation of the damage caused by prejudice, hatred, selfishness, greed and ignorance. Economic and social improvements need to be striven for, and the Church must move towards a stronger position in leadership. In all this, the relevant agencies must be aware of the ethnic identities, cultural conflicts and changing social values of all the people, for these have dramatic impacts upon personal relationships.

The facts of what is happening to marriage require a consideration of the whole question of permanence. There is first a Christian insight that the marriage relationship mirrors the permanent and abiding nature of God's relationship with us. There is also evidence of the need for permanence in the man-woman relationship as a condition of growth and maturation. Yet while we may not be able to 'celebrate' divorce (though we are slowly learning to 'celebrate' re-marriage after it), there must be a refusal to accept its stigma as a matter of routine. Opinion is divided as to whether recent divorce legislation has done a disservice to the concept of marriage, but there is certainly a need for the churches to make available greater resources of money and manpower for marriage education—both before and after marriage.

All things being equal, every child needs to have his mother at home when he is small, and society should ensure that no mother has to work for economic reasons alone. Many women, however, feel frustrated when forced to stay at home, or wish to continue in their careers. In these cases, it is probably in the best interests of both mother and child to see that suitable care is provided for the latter. The following suggestions would help to encourage women to stay at home as long as possible: (a) To raise the level of Child Benefit, or possibly introduce a special benefit for those mothers who stay at home until their child is five; (b) To educate people to know about the needs of young children, which would also increase the status of young mothers; (c) To see that there is more part-time work available at suitable times for women with older children;

239

(d) To encourage employers to show special concern to those of their employees who have small children at home; (e) To provide more courses for re-training women who want to return to employment after a period at home, especially training which can be done from home; (f) For professions to give help to their women members to enable them to keep up with changes.

The various suggestions now being made for such things as a Minister for the Family or an interdepartmental committee on the family should be given full consideration. Some arrangement needs to be found whereby the needs of the family as a whole will be considered when any changes in legislation are being discussed.

In many places the churches are providing support for bored, exhausted and lonely mothers, and crèches for small children. But more thought and discussion needs to be initiated on the dilemma created by the fact that children need their mothers at home, yet many mothers think it right to go out to work. The Church should demonstrate its belief both in the importance of the role of women as mothers of families, and in the basic equality of woman with man.

More Radical Questions

This careful report by the Mothers' Union group was clearly, and necessarily, based on certain assumptions about the nature of society and the place of the family within it. It seems not unfair to suggest that had the group been working a decade earlier its sensitivity to the changes taking place in society would probably have been less marked, and its report less open to new ideas. This fact is in itself evidence of the significant changes now taking place in Britain's culture, morality and styles of life. And the degree to which assumptions control conclusions, even among Christians, in these areas of the nation's development was neatly demonstrated by a contrasting contribution to the 'Britain Today and Tomorrow' project made by the Sheffield Urban Theology Unit as a result of a three-day consultation on this part of the project. Under the heading 'Sexual and Interpersonal Patterns of Behaviour', the report of this consultation said:

We are conscious of the assumed or stated 'standards' of our parents which some of us accepted at the beginning of our adult lives, i.e. around 18 years of age. These included highly controlled sexual contact except in deep relationships; no sexual intercourse before marriage; faithfulness in marriage. The importance attached to these standards in different families varied considerably and it seems they emerged more from reactions to events in other families than in specific instruction or prohibition.

We have all noted quite considerable changes in these patterns reflected both in our attitudes to the behaviour of others and, to a greater or lesser extent, in our own behaviour. These changes do not seem to us the result of the passing of a traditional culture, pluralism, affluence, the speed of change—large concepts which can only remove the discussion to a less immediate and less personal realm. What has actually happened is that quite small but specific experiences have called into question and modified our point of view. For example, one of us remembers vividly the effect of friendship with a couple who were sleeping together before (and indeed without particular commitment to) marriage. The acceptance of this couple at a level of friendship, and the respect engendered by that friendship, made it impossible simply to reject or condemn this behaviour. Or again, one of us, when moving to a strange town with her boyfriend, found it practical and sensible to take two rooms together and subsequently to live together. Both felt committed to each other, but not ready to get married, and the main stresses of the decision did not involve the couple but the expected reactions of parents. This year of living together is considered by both to have been, and to be, a very positive experience.

It is very difficult to assess the wider influences which promoted or affirmed these changes, but we acknowledge the importance, for example, of the financial and educational possibility of leaving the parental home, especially of moving a considerable distance away.

In terms of the 'Britain Today and Tomorrow' project, we were and are aware of breaking 'rules' as we have received them, but we do not see our new patterns of behaviour as in any way wrong, nor would we accept the pejorative label 'permissive' to describe them. We stress the sense of commitment, responsibility, caring and love involved. The levels at which these qualities are understood or expressed will of course vary according to cultural, educational and perhaps religious background. Thus, though we do not wish to speak of freedom, we do not thereby accept that our patterns have been replaced by no patterns, but rather by new patterns which for us seem to have more significance in that we have evolved them through our own experience. We do not regard these new patterns as determinative, either for ourselves or for others, as we have to say that new relationships or experiences may bring about new insight into the nature of love.

If we have any desire to evangelize, it is very much at the level of talking about the nature of love and not about new rules. In the same way, the bringing up of children means teaching them to value themselves and others; this will be reflected in their patterns of behaviour much more than imposed rules which invite rebellion.

The Sheffield Urban Theology Unit's challenge in the area of 'Possessions, Money and Property' took the form of eleven pointed questions, with brief explanatory notes, which may be considered significant as highlighting some of the fundamental issues in this section of the project, and as indicating areas in which a great deal of hard thinking remains to be done.

1. *Why is the question of possessions, money and property an essential question?*

   The fact that we are humans with needs that require objects and belongings, e.g. books and musical instruments.

   —The increasing consumerism in the West is reaching limits where it can no longer be sustained.

   —The need for worldwide redistribution of food and wealth is seen to be more urgent.

   —The call of Jesus to 'sit light' regarding possessions, and not be ruled by them.

2. *How much is our identity defined by our possessions?*

   Some things become incorporated as part of ourselves, e.g. books or records, through which we have grown and developed.

   —We express our personality and aspirations, who we are and who we would like to be, by surrounding ourselves with chosen things, e.g. clothes, means of transport, furniture.

—In our meritocracy the worth of a person is measured by his or her income and wealth.

3. *Are we bound to particular styles of consumption by the context in which we live?*

Professional city life demands smart dress, car owning, baby-sitting costs, maybe a 'presentable' name for business purposes.
—Force is exerted by the group to which we belong to conform to certain standards or styles of dress to maintain our position within it.
—Group identity is expressed by the same mark, e.g. tribal tattoos, regional accents, and how we use property for this purpose.

4. *When does the owning of possessions become acquisitiveness?*

Extreme examples are (a) buying a Rembrandt to keep in the bank and accrue money value, (b) having only one coat to keep warm and dry.
—What are our criteria for judging the middle ground where most of us live?

5. *How far do we depend on society to provide for us in future needs?*

Our Welfare State aims to cover a wide area of need, and increasing demands are made on it. When is individual enterprise stifled? We assume enterprise is not necessarily restricted to notions of personal gain.
—Questions about budgeting arise—individual, household, community, local authority, national government.
—When does thrift become hoarding? When does spontaneous spending become wastefulness?

6. *How far does society and our position restrict us from pursuing our ideal decisions?*

Inherited wealth is decided by law whatever the opinion of the recipient.
—People have to go on working in jobs which they may not agree with on principle, just to be able to pay their mortgages, hire purchase instalments, etc.

7. *How do we find our limits to basic needs?*

Bear in mind the inclusion of all the components of human wealth—food, shelter, warmth—and distinguish these from those needs created by society, by advertising pressure, social status-seeking, etc.

8. *What would be a more convivial use of ownership and property?*

    ('Convivial' in Illich's sense of all things being available for use in a humanly-fulfilling way)
    Social ownership of all housing?
    —Interdependence is today threatened by anonymity and selfish values. Would co-operation work better on a smaller scale, yet somehow relating to worldwide concerns?

9. *Are there ways of finding alternatives to living under the constraint imposed by society?*

    On becoming aware of the imposed values of one group, it may be necessary to move into another of the groups of society to live an authentic human life.
    —Can we learn from other countries, now developing but avoiding our problems of excess? Set up small-scale sharing schemes, e.g. community houses, food co-operatives, which work and show that we do not believe in the inevitability of conforming?

10. *'Opt out is cop out?'—a question of responsibility*

    Renting accommodation does not avoid property ownership —just that someone else owns it; likewise squatting. Working for socialized ownership by all in agreement faces the problem.
    —Change is necessary for underprivileged people, and it will involve everyone.

11. *Is all this a disgruntled middle-class reaction?*

    The middle classes see working people able to buy more and 'succeed', exercising social mobility. So those who have always had plenty of money either want to live without now or to spend their lives getting even more and keeping ahead.

The Sheffield Unit was, naturally enough, unable to offer even tentative answers to these large questions, but its broad position is indicated by the form of the questions and a brief statement on 'Culture and Race':

The acceptance that different cultures exist beside one another presupposes that none of them should oppress, dominate or exploit others—as is happening now. Changes are needed towards more sharing, mutual understanding and responsibility for each other. Chances for peaceful changes are very small. We expect that changes will create disturbances, especially for people within ruling cultures and strip them of their privileges. We feel that it is necessary to take a stand with those who are at the bottom, but we realize the difficulties as most of the members of our group belong to a culture of privileges at the cost of others.

The Homeless Mind

If further evidence were needed of the complexity of this section of the project, and different ways of approaching it, this was offered in the form of a series of essays written by a number of distinguished writers, some of them Christians, others not, in response to an important, but difficult, book *The Homeless Mind*, by Peter and Brigitte Berger and Hansfried Kellner (Pelican Books, 1974). These essays were intended to form a book in themselves, but were introduced into the 'Britain Today and Tomorrow' project to help the British churches face and discuss the issues at what was described as 'an appropriate depth'.

For the benefit of those who had not read *The Homeless Mind* or who had been mystified by its highly technical language, a convenient summary was provided by Elizabeth Templeton, of New College, Edinburgh, in an assessment of the responses:

The thesis is that 'modernization', a two-pronged development of technology and bureaucracy, has alienated man and rendered him significantly homeless. He finds himself, as a cog in the industrial machine, for instance, replaceable, reduced to a mechanical role, measurable and anonymous. This affects his consciousness, which is now that of a 'componential self'. Similarly, for bureaucracy, he exists as a file, not as an individual 'in the flesh'. Whereas, in earlier ages, the whole man moved in an integrated society, taking his whole self, so to speak, into his work or his social transactions, he now spends major areas of his time 'abstracted' into his social or productive roles, and the integrated self is relegated to the private sphere. This means that in the public world, he suffers from a deepening condition of 'homelessness', since in the secularized, pluralist, 'outside world' no unifying horizon of meaning can be found. This constitutes his alienation.

The theme is elaborated by accounts of the process of modernization in the Third World, and the diagnosis confirmed by a reading of various 'counter-cultures' in the West and anti-modernization movements in the developing world as a quest to keep or recover 'a home'. Throughout, the authors emphasize that the processes described are not simply a matter of external environments, but of internalized consciousness, which shift as the world is re-structured, and in turn re-structure it.

John Wilson, writing as a philosopher, makes no attempt to deny the data on which *The Homeless Mind* is based, but dismisses the broad thesis of the authors as yet another example of the leftist collectivism to which he believes sociologists are specially prone. He suggests that whenever Christianity has 'taken a line' on society as a whole, or even upon some large-scale and therefore inevitably complex swathe of social behaviour, 'it has always been naïve and very often ridiculously misguided'. He instances the 'line' taken on Darwin, Freud and Marx, and, since fashions change, traces the process to what he believes to be the churches' subservience today to the liberal or *avant-garde* establishment. 'It is', he adds, 'extremely important that Christians, instead of trying to solve all the problems of this sublunary world at a blow, should confine themselves—as, at this stage, we should all confine ourselves—to a programme which is not premature and fantasy-based. They must be clear just *what* these necessary truths and insights are which are incorporated in their religion (often in myths and parables), and *why* they are necessary for all men: and they must be able to make these clear, in non-partisan and non-doctrinaire language, to all men. They must *not* be swayed by fashion or fantasy into emphasizing some of these truths and insights and forgetting about (or trying to disown) others. It seems to me fairly obvious that most of these truths are not, or not directly, concerned with "society" at all. They are concerned with the individual, the inner man: and the general message, which is perhaps truistic enough, is that to save one's own or other people's souls involves far more than anything that "society" can do. It is a matter of individuals acquiring virtue and grace, in the teeth of opposition from themselves (not just from "the system"), which will alone provide a non-fragile basis for any society.'

In marked contrast to John Wilson's criticism of *The Homeless Mind* and the social concerns of the contemporary Church, Professor Ninian Smart accepts the general thesis of the book and pleads for a new pluralist and tolerant liberalism—social democracy with a human face—which he believes to be the most humane system available under which human beings may flourish.

'One source of pride for a forward-looking politics in Britain is that it could be "a light to the Gentiles",' he says. 'However, this must always be coupled with a strong drive towards the economic equalization of the world, in some new key, for traditional forms of aid very often work ill because of the structure, consciousness and power distribution in the recipient society.' As for the churches' involvement in all this, Ninian Smart writes:

It seems to me that the Christian faith is highly relevant to men's 'homelessness', because in important ways it deals with participation, with belonging. Thus sacramentally the Christian taps the power of the Creator, transcending worldly power through Christ's passion, and taps history divinely informed through participation in the gritty life of Christ. And he participates both in the glory and the pain as woven into the mysterious fabric of the world in which he has been for good or ill projected. Thus his faith goes beyond both the naked ego which *The Homeless Mind* sees as the privatized condition of modern man and the powers and principalities of the political and social order. But we are in a pluralistic condition. My very interpretation of Christian faith is only one, my, option among all the others. It is no coincidence that in the plural, rather rootless world of today, there are great attractions in unintellectual and uncritical devotionalism (Hare Krishna and Jesus People), fundamentalist Christianity, authoritarian togetherness (Unification Church), left sectarianism (Trotskyites, and points East), the National Front, etc. Nor is it surprising at a more individualistic level that the naked ego is pursued through Yoga and Buddhism, with raids into Sufism. We are now in the spiritual supermarket, and it is in its way no bad thing. Why not experiment with the spirit, as we experiment with everything else, if we are creative and free? Creativity must tolerate madness, extravagance, and many new pearls are waiting to be found in the limpid waters of a newly transparent planet.

Professor André Dumas, of Paris, also found *The Homeless Mind* stimulating, and in his essay expressed special appreciation of the concept of religion as ensuring basic continuity and a familiarity of vital points of reference. 'It provides inner stability amidst outer change.' This reveals the 'limitations of liberation theologies, whose one-sidedness is often all too similar to the one-sidedness of modern progress and which can easily become almost as frustrating.' This French scholar explains:

Liberation theologies have gone wrong when they have isolated the element of exodus, the breaking up of oppressive institutions, and have forgotten that this is but the prelude to the entry into Canaan, to the coming together in the integrating structures of a new society ... Yet I go on to wonder under what conditions re-integration can preserve the benefits of liberation: how are we to find a home for the human spirit that is frustrated by modernity without giving up the vital gains of that modernity—individual human rights, technological reliability, large-scale organization, and above all the secularization of society that can ensure both a multiplicity of choice and the freedom to choose one's own convictions?

There remains the basic and ultimate question: how are we to find a home in an efficient but meaningless universe? Insecurity has replaced progress as the symbol of technological society. This insecurity points to both the temptation of nihilism and the search for a sure word. Nihilism is the loss of heaven and of earth. The world is a home, more than a mere habitation, more than food and more than the piecing together of any artificial set of symbols. We live in a time of insecurity and must be grateful to the sociologists for requiring of theologians that they speak up, in order to see if theology can prove itself not so much a habitation left over from yesterday but a living home for today.

Critical Solidarity

Clearly a great deal of work remains to be done before the British churches can begin to speak with any authority about the cultural changes taking place about them and in which their members are inescapably involved. The position is complicated by the fact that until comparatively recently the Christian faith was one of the dominant factors in British culture, and its institutional expressions were near the centre of the established social order. And, even as this crumbles, much vestigial religious belief remains. It is quite inaccurate to describe Britain as 'de-Christianized', and wherever some form of identifiable community life remains the churches are normally an important constituent within it.

Yet the British churches dare not ignore the cultural changes, which appear to be gathering pace; neither can they expect to be unaffected by them. First, however, it is important to establish where the churches stand in relation to human culture and, since the Christian faith is based on what its adherents believe to be a divine disclosure, it can be said unequivocally that the Christian Church can never identify itself completely with the culture of a particular people or nation—even when it has played a decisive part in the shaping of that culture. Because humanity is prone to sin and is always under judgement, the Church—if it is to remain an instrument of the divine will in the world—can never abandon its critical role in society. Indeed, in some forms of society, the Church may itself embody a kind of counter-culture.

But the Church can only exercise its critical, prophetic function from within society and alongside the prevailing culture. The centrality of the Incarnation for Christian faith precludes criticism from the wings. Here there may be something to be learned from the origins of the Christian Church, which was born in the heart of Jewish culture and even to this day shares a common heritage with the Jewish people, but which exercised a critical role within Jewish culture, and later exercised a similar function in relation to Graeco-Roman culture. The danger arises when—normally through neglect of its own interior life—the Church loses its critical faculty and is duly engulfed by the prevailing culture. Then comes the need for a new generation of prophets to recall the Church to its foundation faith and to its proper service of human society.

Since the present situation in Britain is in many ways quite singular, it may be misleading to look elsewhere for assistance—especially in the direction of North America where apparent cultural similarities are exceedingly deceptive. But Britain shares a common culture with Western Europe, and there are interesting parallels, as well as marked differences, between modern Britain and the German Democratic Republic where secularization has made massive inroads into a culture once dominated by Protestantism, and within which the Lutheran churches were once closely integrated in the life of society.

Here numerically weak Christian communities are now called to witness under a totalitarian régime which has for more than a quarter of a century been building a new social order based on Marxism and seeking to indoctrinate the people with Marxist values. And the leadership of the Protestant churches has responded, not by denouncing or rejecting the post-Hitler régime, but by evaluating its social policies and offering open support and co-operation where these policies have appeared to be constructive and humane. Yet, at the same time, the churches have retained their freedom to criticize dehumanizing policies and their criticisms have had greater force because they have sprung from identification with the movement taking place within the social order. 'Critical solidarity' is the phrase the German churches use to describe their position, and something of this kind might well be the appropriate stance for the British churches in a time of social and cultural change.

11. FOR GOD'S SAKE SAY SOMETHING

The aims of the 'Britain Today and Tomorrow' project are to help British Christians, and any others who care to join them, to understand what is happening to the British people at the present time, to spell out some of the choices open to them at what appears to be a critical point in their history, and to trace the implications of these choices for public policy and church life. In other words, the project is an exercise in Christian social responsibility and may be seen as the latest in a line of similar, though differently organized, exercises which have been an important feature of church life in Britain during the last fifty years.

Throughout this half-century it has been the task of the Christian prophet to call the churches to a deeper concern for the life of society and to urge theologians and preachers to apply their religious insights to the political, economic and social issues which have dominated the lives of peoples and nations during an era of unprecedented change. It may still be argued, and the difficulties encountered in mounting the 'Britain Today and Tomorrow' project lend substance to the case, that the churches have still some way to travel before they begin to grapple seriously with the major problems of the modern world. The agendas of ecclesiastical assemblies, local and national, still suggest that the primary interest of church communities is with their own domestic affairs, and that the life of the wider world is of only peripheral concern.

Even so, sufficient work has been undertaken in the field of Christian social responsibility to lead to the charge being levelled against the churches that they have forsaken their 'real' task of preaching the Gospel and converting souls, and embraced liberal political ideologies, concerned only with feeding bodies. The fact that there is no credible basis for this charge does not, however, mean that it can be ignored, and this for two reasons. First, because it is necessary to show that there is no dichotomy between evangelism and social responsibility. Social responsibility can be a form of evangelism and may well be the most effective one. Where Christians take seriously their share of responsibility for our common life this is itself a telling way of confessing Christ and witnessing to faith. But, having asserted this, there remains the necessity for offering an explanation of the basis of Christian social action, and a growing awareness that the traditional content of Christian affirmation is no longer an effective means of communicating what Christians believe and what motivates their actions.

Hence the growing concern of the British Council of Churches—itself a reflection of a world-wide Christian concern—to hold together the twin responsibilities of evangelism and social action, word and deed, and in the case of the 'Britain Today and Tomorrow' project the serious attempt to ensure that the various subjects under investigation were brought beneath the light of the Christian revelation. As part of this concern the working parties were provided with professional theological assistance, and a group of theological consultants provided a substantial and important paper on the task of proclaiming the Gospel in Britain today and tomorrow. The fact that the outline and discussion of this paper appears at the end of this report of the project is in no sense a judgement on its relative importance, nor should it be interpreted as appearing here as an 'inspired afterthought'. Indeed, it is a moot point as to whether it ought not to have appeared first in the sequence of subjects covered by this book. But the emphasis of the consultants on the contextual character of preaching and evangelism seemed to demand that their contribution should appear last—and possibly be strengthened by its position. The decision was influenced also by the existence of a good deal of reflective theology in other chapters of the book.

Evangelism Inside the Situation

The theologians' report begins by explaining that they

intend to use the word 'evangelism' to refer to the Church's attempts to put the Gospel into words and to talk about its faith. A serious criticism of the report, made later by one of its assessors, is that no attention is given to non-verbal means of communicating the Gospel, through symbols such as church buildings and worship, but the consultants might fairly reply that they lacked the time and expertise to deal adequately with this aspect of evangelism, and would be glad to see it fully considered in the next stage of the project. Nothing in their report would preclude this.

Two reasons are given for regarding evangelism as a central task of the Church. First, it gives expression to the distinctiveness of the Church, which lies not in its social policies, however essential it may be to have them, but in the Lord it serves and, because of him, in the Gospel it preaches and the faith it proclaims. Second, evangelism can and should be pursued in the interests of truth. Fully aware that any account of things is partial and therefore debatable, preaching should be the attempt to make clear to ourselves and our contemporaries the truth about our human condition under God as revealed to us through Christ, so that we can at least respond to reality and not to illusions or half-truths or lies.

Regarding words like 'preaching', 'preachers' and 'sermons', the consultants are anxious to avoid misunderstandings arising from the traditional pictures evoked by their use. 'Preaching the Gospel is not restricted to rather formal sermons in churches. Indeed on our understanding, most "sermons" that are preached will be brief, informal remarks in arguments and conversations. Neither is preaching restricted to isolated professionals. Just as the Church is made up of all sorts of people scattered throughout society, belonging to all sorts of groups within all kinds of institutions, so the preaching of the Gospel, taking many different forms, is carried out more often than not by those varied people in those scattered places. Their need is not for professionals to relieve them of the task and do it for them (they could not) but for adequate support in what is essentially their task of being witnesses to their faith.'

Equally, those who undertake preaching in the form of addresses on public occasions or sermons in the liturgy cannot do their job in isolation from the rest of the people of God. 'They speak out of the corporate life they share with their fellow Christians, with its common traditions, shared attitudes and insights, and mutual support. And they depend upon their fellow Christians for much of the substance of what they are going to say. They can only speak out of the wisdom and experience of those who have wrestled with the concrete realities and issues they encounter in all the places in which they are set.'

The news which Christians have to announce, for all its awareness of the darker side of human experience, is fundamentally good news. The Gospel remains more or less the same because it is primarily news about the heartening reality of Jesus Christ—his birth, ministry, death and resurrection—made accessible through the written records of the New Testament. But it is not always the same because there can be sharp differences of opinion about the character and significance of Jesus. The one Lord has from the beginning been seen and understood by different people in different ways.

Again, the Gospel remains more or less the same because it deals with abiding truths about human life in God's world. These truths find expression in the teachings of the Church—its creeds and confessions. But the Gospel is not always the same because not all Christians believe in exactly the same abiding realities and, even where they do, their understanding and expression of them varies and develops in the light of fresh insights and new ways of thinking. The Gospel also has to do with here and now, with particular sets of circumstances rather than generalities, and the differences and discontinuities between one situation and another make it difficult to say the same things about them all.

Faced with these particularities, the Gospel is to be seen not so much as the same existing good news which has only to be announced whatever the occasion, but rather as something which varies from one setting to another and has to be discovered within each of them. Put differently, if there is one Gospel for all mankind because there is one God revealed in one Lord Jesus Christ, there are also many gospels because that same Christ-like God does different things at different times. The good news for Britain today is not the same as the good news for Latin America or South Africa today or for Britain as it was, say, a hundred years ago.

This understanding of the character of the Gospel was firmly challenged by Derek Williams, editor of the evangelical magazine *Third Way*, who wrote in his assessment:

None would dispute the fact that every generation of Christians faces the task of translating the Gospel into terms appropriate to its context, but that is not to say that the essential message of evangelism is itself radically different in content (even if different in terminology) in different places and at different times. I feel it is a great pity, when the Lausanne Covenant, WCC Nairobi 1975, and the papal *Evangelii Nuntiandi* (1975)—and very recently the Church of England Board for Mission and Unity report—all agree that the evangelistic message 'concerns the announcement of God's Kingdom and love through Jesus Christ, the offer of grace and forgiveness of sins, the invitation to repentance and faith in him' (WCC, Nairobi, 1.57), that this document (which has as one of its aims the unity of Christian traditions in a common purpose) almost completely ignores this 'core of the Gospel'.

But the BCC's consultants foresaw that disagreement would arise at this point and suggested that, while such a disagreement could hardly be papered over, it need not amount to sterile opposition. 'We ourselves understand the more permanent and changing elements in the Gospel to be interdependent and interrelated. Most attempts at evangelism will contain elements of them all, whilst emphasizing one more than another. None should be neglected and it is not our intention to do so. We are simply directing most of our attention here to the good news which has to be discovered within particular situations, such as Britain in today's world, and to the manner in which that discovery can be made.'

At this point two questions were raised by another assessor, Gilleasbuig Macmillan, a Scottish theologian, who wrote: 'While I find it impossible to quarrel with the general perspective of the report, I wonder if it leaves two crucial questions unresolved: first, Is the desire to discover the good news for, and out of, every situation a possible escape from the scandal of particularity? and, second, Is it right to proceed with the enquiry without asking what the word "God" means, and whether a major translation of religious language is required (not only on apologetic grounds, but, if language has context, from the need for integrity in metaphysics as in social action)? The report's use of "God's world", for example, leads me to wonder if more reflection on language is needed.'

The consultants did not discuss the language question but concentrated on the relationship between the words and deeds of the Christian evangelist. 'What the evangelist says must be all of a piece with what the evangelist is and does as an individual, and as one who is bound up with Christian institutions.'

This integrity is of the utmost importance if the message is to carry any credibility. We can be under no illusions about the difficulty of gaining a hearing for the Gospel at the present time, let alone persuading our contemporaries to believe it. The difficulty is insurmountable if there is no evidence that we actually mean what we say. This is not to demand that all Christians and all their institutions must exemplify the standards—moral or otherwise—set for them by the vision of Christ before they can claim any right to speak. They do not point men to themselves and to any goodness in their own lives, but to the basic goodness which gives hope to all life. What is required is not perfection but that the faith we proclaim should be none other than the faith by which we live, or to put it the other way round: that we act as if we believe what we say to be true. Our words, if they are to carry any weight, can be no more and none other than the attempt to articulate that perception of reality which genuinely informs and inspires our life. We may not live up to it but we do live by it; and in evangelism we simply confess it.

There is another reason why this integrity is so important. Only if we live by the message can we demonstrate the meaning of what we say. Our words are best defined not by more words, but by deeds. The Gospel message itself will be mainly in the indicative mood. It is an attempt to speak about how things really are in the light of Christ. But it will need to press on from there into the imperative mood and spell out the implications of the reality. A message about hope, for example, may only begin to explain itself and demonstrate its meaning as it is set within committed actions which set out to enhance life and change our society whatever the odds. Of course, people disagree about the precise implications of the message and what it means, and no single set of commitments can take into itself and embody all those realities to which the Gospel bears witness; but if the Gospel apparently carries no implications for those who announce it, and its meaning cannot be spelt out, then men are not only left wondering what it means but will suspect that it means nothing. If after our evangelism everything remains the same as before, then maybe nothing has been said. What is said must go hand in hand with the task of trying to work out and implement the changes Christians would like to see in the world to make it at least a more likely vehicle for not totally distorting the Kingdom of God.

Situation Evangelism

The consultants' insistence that integrity in evangelism requires deep involvement with the everyday realities of life leads them to propound four reasons why they believe that involvement is also necessary for the discovery of what the Gospel really is.

There is always the task of translation. Although the evangelist may be drawing his message from those aspects of the Gospel which are more or less unchanging, it must still be cast in the living language of the day. Traditional vocabularies may need to be set aside in favour of new ways of communicating old truths.

What we may think of as the abiding message of Christianity is itself the product of an endless series of discoveries. The given facts are that Jesus of Nazareth exercised his ministry in Galilee and Judaea, was crucified under Pontius Pilate and was raised from the dead. But the meaning of those events was worked out by the earliest Christians and has been reworked again and again ever since. In doing so, believers have inevitably drawn on their own ways of thinking and experiencing the world at the time, and the results have varied accordingly. This sort of variety is already present within the New Testament. As a result, we are not merely left with the task of translation or of repeating what others have said. The evangelist must try to appreciate the factors which have already shaped the message which he now inherits. He must take them into account when he seeks for the truth to which the message, in that particular form, bears witness. He must then reshape and recast it in the thought-patterns which he shares with his hearers.

In addition to the closely related tasks of translating and reshaping the Gospel, there is the task of concretizing it. The message is not about life in general but about the dark and intractable, redemptive, creative and ultimately hopeful realities within this slice of life in particular. The evangelist must be specific. He has to speak about the world which is now in front of him, acutely aware that he will be one of a number of often conflicting voices, none of which can be wholly right. This is akin to the prophetic task of not only foretelling the future but of attempting a true account of the present out of which the future will grow. For example, the evangelist may speak of the coming to Britain of substantial numbers of people of other races, cultures and religions in recent years as a gift of God to the British, offering to a people who have often been cut off on their island a chance to grow into world citizenship, and to a people whose wealth and conquests have let them too often feel superior to others, an opportunity to live alongside those others in mutual respect and dialogue.

The Gospel has to some extent to be discovered from within the situation itself. Here we believe that God is still at work and may be heard speaking to his people. What he has to say may open our eyes to what has not been seen or understood before. Sometimes fresh truth may take us by surprise. More often it will dawn only as the seeming result of careful attention, contemplation and a believing curiosity. Always however there remains the possibility that the situation itself will provoke us to insight and faith.

There are many reasons, then, for insisting that evangelism is an 'inside' job. Involvement cannot stop at the level of intellectual enquiry but, so far as possible, extend to active commitment. Both clergy and laity are equally well placed to be involved, though in each case their involvement is inevitably limited. One is inside one area of experience, another another, which means that in most cases if they are to have any hope of taking adequate account of the context they will stand in very great need of one another. As Christians complement and supplement each other in involvement and detachment, evangelism—even if the speaking falls to an individual—becomes very much a community enterprise. Unfortunately, the traditions of the Church often militate against anything very fruitful coming of Christian involvement in the life of the world. There is presence in the world but no engagement with the world—partly because many of our habitual ways of thinking tend to separate off Christianity into a religious or private sphere of personal preference, and partly because the Church as an institution organized into parishes and local congregations finds it almost impossible to relate in a lively fashion to many areas of contemporary life.

Christ in Context

Crucial though the context or immediate situation may be to the discovery and effective preaching of the Gospel, the evangelist must not be confined to it and needs the resources which can be brought to it, just as much as those he discovers within it. Otherwise he will not see the situation in its true perspective; the onlooker is as important as the inhabitant.

An obvious reason why we cannot be totally absorbed with the context is that, while it is an important source of faith, the primary source for Christians is Jesus Christ. Although it makes sense to many to say that he is known and encountered in the present, sometimes starkly in the poor and oppressed, it is not here but in a quite different set of circumstances, when Pontius Pilate was governor of Judaea, that he is most clearly seen. If he is to be seen again today, it is to those events and all that bears witness to them that we must look. We also need to know what has been made of Christ by many different people, in widely differing circumstances throughout the long history of the Christian community, if our account of the truth is not to be limited to what the idiosyncrasies of the moment make it possible to believe. Finally, it is not enough to pay attention only to the context, since if we do we may find that it does not just contribute to our message but comes near to dictating what the message is to be. There is a narrow but deep division between the Gospel which is truly contextual and the message which is not a gospel because it is dominated by the context.

What then must be brought to any particular situation if the good news about it is ever to be discovered? First, the heartening news about the reality of Jesus Christ, the most revealing Word about all that has life. Second, the faith we confess not just about this situation but about the abiding realities of all situations involving man in God's world. And it is impossible to draw on these two resources without drawing on the rich treasures of the catholic Church, gratefully and critically. These treasures include the Church's history and its people, its liturgies and traditions, its doctrines and creeds; and among them the Scriptures are of special importance as the key witness to Christ and to the responses to him made by some of the earliest Christians.

Given the available resources, how is the message to be

discovered and prepared? What are some of the disciplined procedures we should attempt to follow?

We shall use all the means at our disposal to study the context, including those who observe the scene from within and without. We shall take note of the professional interpreters and the less professional inhabitants. We shall be interested not only in what people say but in how they feel. We shall ask ourselves what is implicit as well as explicit in what they are saying. We shall take seriously all points of view as having something to tell us about the whole. We shall take no point of view too seriously as being wholly correct. And we shall be aware of the need to make up our minds about what to accept and select out of all that we are told, and of our tendency to want to believe and select some things rather than others. We shall try to be clear about the most significant features of the context which call for comment. It is difficult to imagine how any sermon which takes seriously the context can be preached without some form of conversation between the preacher and his hearers, in which the preacher does far more listening than talking— for example, reading the newspapers and constantly meeting and talking and being with the people involved.

The faith to be spread cannot in the end be any other than the evangelist's own faith: the faith he is able to confess, the Gospel he has heard and received, the truth about the abiding realities of human life in God's world by which he actually lives. But he will need ways by which the possible fullness of that faith can be set before him, and his partial or mistaken grasp of it can be challenged, corrected and completed. Paying attention will not therefore be just a matter of taking notice of his own faith but of setting it alongside the earliest expressions of faith in the Bible, the repeated formulations of it in the creeds and confessions and doctrines of the Church, and the faith of his contemporaries in the local and universal Christian community. He will remember that, although it is often expressed in rather compressed and abstract ways, the faith that comes to him from the past is no less the result of a struggle to make sense of the actualities of experience in the light of

Christ than is his own. That can be said equally of the classic Christologies of the early centuries, for example, as it can of the Reformation doctrine of justification by faith. He may ask of all of them what the truth about life must be if those people in those circumstances spoke about it as they did.

In paying attention to the faith, the evangelist will not unnaturally ask which of its themes and insights seem particularly relevant to the context he now has in mind. Selection is inevitable but it will be done with a measure of awareness of the underlying interrelatedness of all its parts so that any interpretation of a particular situation can only be really adequate when they are all taken into account. He will also try to reckon with his reluctance to attend to those parts which seem difficult or too relevant for comfort.

Having selected, he will try to be clear as to just what is the reality to which this article of faith bears witness (remembering that one way to define it is to ask what practical difference it could make). Then come the all-important questions: 'If I am prepared to believe that that is the truth about the on-going human situation, can I believe it to be the truth about this particular situation, and —if so—how can it be restated in these very particular terms?' The evangelist will be well aware that at this point he may find himself in serious difficulties, most notably for example when he asks whether his faith in a Christ-like providence will survive in the context of un-remitting sorrow and suffering. At such times the context offers a sharp and critical challenge to the Gospel as well as being challenged and illuminated by it. Such is the constant interchange between faith and experience, 'text' and context.

The Lord we preach must ultimately be the Lord in whom we ourselves believe; the vision that wins our allegiance; the truth as it is focused for us in what we understand to be the reality of Jesus of Nazareth. But we can only hold on to that if our account of it is set alongside many other accounts, from the epistles and gospels of the New Testament to the portraits of Jesus exhibited within the life of the Church, and those understandings of Christ-likeness which are implicit in all that the Church has said and done throughout all the ages. All of them show a tendency to make Jesus in someone else's image, and we can only hope to be delivered from the distortions of our own account of the matter by constant dialogue with the distorted accounts of others.

Contemplation will therefore mean as careful a search for the historical Jesus as we are capable of mounting—studying the gospels and comparing our own conclusions with those of our fellow Christians. It will not however be limited to an intellectual exercise or to reading the New Testament or to hard-headed arguments and discussions. Contemplation will also involve that prayerful reflection which is ready to open the whole of oneself to the vision of God as encountered in Christ.

The object of our contemplation is we believe the final word about the true nature of reality. The word is spoken in the manner of Christ's coming and staying amongst us, in his living and dying and rising from the dead. As the final word it remains sovereign over all other words that attempt to articulate the truth about human experience in general or in particular. It is even capable of being at odds with the very words which claim to represent it most faithfully. It is a built-in critical principle. No particular message can ever be identified with it completely. Once equated with the Gospel which is Christ such a message becomes a 'no-gospel' which has ceased to call him Lord.

For these and other reasons, we shall not expect to move in any single or over-confident way from what we understand to be the reality of Jesus to what we say about our world. There are few, if any, straightforward deductions to be made. We may prefer to regard him not as the answer to the questions we ask about the truth of this and that, but as the question that can still be put to all our provisional answers. We must ask of what we come to believe about any concrete set of circumstances, whether such an account of things is compatible with the reality we see in Christ. It may after struggling be sufficiently so to rest our case for the time being; but there is a sense in which the answer will always remain 'No'. As a result of the discipline of contemplation, we shall not expect to rest our case but to have it continually re-opened; not to settle down with our opinions, but to have them repeatedly and creatively disturbed.

The disciplines of studying the context, paying attention to the faith and contemplating the Lord, Jesus Christ, do not of course add up to a mechanical route, by which the preacher can move without let or hindrance from wondering about what he should say to the text of the sermon he will eventually preach. They do represent ways by which the raw material for preaching is produced. The sermon has still to be designed and put together. It will remain a matter of judgement or insight or inspiration, or all three, as to what—out of all the material—can be used at any one time because it most needs saying or is the most appropriate thing to say. And it will remain a matter of skilful and sensitive communication as to how best the material can be ordered, expressed and explained.

The Quality of the Church and of its Message

All that has been said about preparing the 'sermon' presupposes the opportunity for deliberate and careful study and reflection by the preacher. But most evangelism is informal and spontaneous, carried out in unexpected moments or in unstructured and intimate conversations. What preparation is possible in these circumstances?

The theological consultants answered this question by saying that in the end they were less concerned with the preparation of a sermon than with the formation of a preacher; less with the conscious procedures by which a particular message is thought out and eventually put together, and more by the on-going process which forms a person in such a way that when the moment arrives to speak he may have some hope of doing so with a measure of success and profound simplicity because of what he has now become. His words appear to be spontaneous, his insight intuitive; he shares something of the mind of Christ, but that is only because of what has nourished his growth over a long period of time. In a similar way, the conscience which experiences an immediate ability to discern right and wrong is the product of a lengthy education of which we are scarcely aware.

How then are preachers to be formed, rather than sermons prepared? How are *all* the Lord's people, not merely the ordained ministers, to be evangelists? What is the nature of the context, not in and about which the message is proclaimed, but in and by which the proclaimer is formed? These questions turn us back to the nature of the Christian community itself as the most obvious place of Christian formation. On the basis of our earlier arguments about how the Gospel is discerned and re-discovered we should expect the community to be perpetually marked by a number of characteristics.

There will be an unremitting engagement with secular realities—small-scale and large, personal and institutional. To live in the Church is not to escape them. They should be an inescapable feature of the Church's life. The determination to make them so has serious implications for the shape and locality of the Church, the items on its agenda, and the partnership between the clergy and the rest of the people of God.

Membership of any Christian community must be a way of growing ever more fully aware of the catholicity of Christianity so that the believer, simply by being there, may assimilate more and more of its riches. These riches—biblical, historical and ecumenical—are not so much items to be remembered and referred to when one is wondering what to say next. They are part and parcel of a cast of mind. This inheritance will be made available chiefly through the adequacy of worship, but also through imaginative Christian education, including the deliberate widening of experience, maybe by travel and first-hand contacts, and by the practice of contemplative prayer. Passing on this inheritance may well be the special responsibility of those ordained to represent the great Church to its local manifestations. Only where such an inheritance is available and continuously drawn upon can Christians hope to see the vision of Christ and grow into those patterns of believing which are the essential ingredients of their evangelism.

The Christian community will be characterized by a concern for integrity. It will not allow the actualities of life—domestic, industrial, political or whatever—to fall apart from the resources of the Christian tradition. All of them deal with the same reality. The Church will know why they must constantly interact with one another, and it will ensure that they do. Concerned for integrity, the Christian community will be equally wary of allowing its reflective life to be isolated from its committed actions, or the faith it confesses to be anything less than a serious working hypothesis for its experiment with life—both in terms of its own institutions and outside of them. Such integrity can only result from a high degree of support and pastoral care, mutually offered and received by all the members of the body. It is difficult to see how this can be achieved without plenty of opportunities for small-group experiences, which allow for encounter and conversation both among people of similar background or outlook and among those of a very different cast of mind. There will also need to be genuine interdependence and interaction between the ordained members of the Church and the rest of the people of God which does not deny them their separate contributions.

Our ability to discern what it is we have to say and the quality of our evangelism can be no higher than the quality of the Church's life. But, granted there are words to speak and that we can gain a hearing, what motivates the evangelistic task and what do we hope to achieve?

The answers are many and varied and do not necessarily exclude one another. Some are uncomplicated: we preach out of a sense of obedience and love for our Lord, or because the news we have heard is too good not to share. Evangelism is the spontaneous overspill of our discipleship —'Here I stand, I can do no other'. Some answers are more dubious. The proper attempt to win men by our preaching in order to build up the Church for mission and service i easily distorted and confused with the desire to win them in order to aggrandize the Church and the evangelist—a desire which is understandable but incompatible with the vision of the crucified Christ. Some answers seem best left in the form of a question: What could count for success when we look for growing human maturity but do not expect any person to attain to the full stature of Christ, or the Kingdom to come in all its fullness, within the limits of space and time? What could count for success where the most perceptive words, sharper than any two-edged sword, may lead many to stop their ears and even drive the evangelist on to a cross?

There remains, however, deeply ingrained in the Christian tradition, the hope of changing the face of the earth, converting it, redeeming it, moving it on to its true end, creating out of it the new humanity, raising it from the dead. God has entered into a covenant with his people for the completion of this missionary task. The evangelist does not look for immediate results, though he does not despise the authentic signs that God keeps his promises; and he does not deceive himself that the outcome depends solely on himself, though he takes seriously his own contribution. The conviction which sustains him is that truth is the surest agent of change, the bearer of its own creative power. It may often be embodied in the deeds and lives of individuals, communities and institutions much more effectively than in his words. But where the evangelist attempts to speak it with integrity and in love so that men perceive reality as being other than what they had understood it to be; where eyes are opened to see things for what they are; where people are enabled to understand themselves and their world in an altogether different and better light, then the old ways of living and doing become inappropriate.

Repentance may follow. Change may take place. Precisely how and when is not the evangelist's responsibility—even if it belongs to a normal human relationship to suggest what form it might take. Such changes where visible may be as varied as the persons, communities and situations involved. Their full repercussions are not immediately apparent. They are certainly not inevitable because the bearers of the news are not always easy to believe and, in any case, some having heard them will prefer darkness to light. Nevertheless, the evangelist, in public and in private sets out to announce the truth that he consciously seeks and 'intuitively' knows—a Gospel that is troublesome but fundamentally heartening—out of the conviction that given time, all the time in the world, that truth will set men and women free to become the children of God.

A pluralist message and a pluralist Church for a pluralist society! This is a simple summary of the results so far of the 'Britain Today and Tomorrow' project. From one point of view it may appear to be a disastrous recipe for disintegration in an ever-shrinking world where the need for the renewal of human solidarity and unity has never been greater. Yet for those who have taken part in this first stage of the project pluralism is a sign of hope—a sign that the one God has many different ways of dealing with his people, and that there are many different routes to that freedom, happiness and fulfilment which is God's will for all who are made in his own image and likeness.

Movement along these routes is, however, a matter of deeds, rather than of words. The cry of the world to the churches of Britain and elsewhere is not, 'For God's sake *say* something'. It is, 'For God's sake *do* something'. And what is to be done is made plain in Martin Conway's modern amplification of the Beatitudes from the Sermon on the Mount:

Happy are those who know that they are spiritually poor
—who are aware that they don't have ready answers to the big questions and are prepared to keep looking;
Happy are those who mourn
—who know that there are millions who are suffering physical or social deprivation and who ensure that policies are framed primarily to benefit them;
Happy are those who are humble
—who don't see themselves as superior to others but give

each person and each people an equal standing;

Happy are those whose greatest desire is to do what God requires
—who are prepared to walk by forgiveness, and change their minds and ways, who look to the longer term and to the interests of all;

Happy are those who are merciful to others
—who don't see others as a market to be exploited but as partners from whom to learn;

Happy are the pure in heart
—who by concentrating on God's larger purposes are freed from the worries and jealousies of immediate quarrels and conflicts;

Happy are those who work for peace
—who make justice and fulfilment for all their steady concern;

Happy are those who are persecuted because they do what God requires
—who are prepared to be awkward and unpopular among their peers and to let their own nation come off second-best if that can serve the long-term good of all.

INDEX

LIST OF THE PARTICIPANTS
IN THE PROJECT

It is impossible to list all who participated. Many groups of people throughout the country contributed directly or indirectly to the project, and work done independently of the project by several bodies within the churches and within the British Council of Churches came to be reflected in it. The names of all those involved in these ways are either unknown or too numerous to mention. For these practical reasons and at the risk of glaring omissions, the list which follows is confined to the members of the central groups which were responsible for organizing and refining the work and for writing the reports on the major themes. To these are added the principal participants in a series of 'hearings' at the special Assembly in the autumn of 1977, in which these reports were scrutinized and reviewed. Members of staff of the British Council of Churches participated in the project in various capacities in one or more of the groups; they are listed separately.

1. Britain in a World Setting

Groups

Most of the reports were the work of individual authors working with a group of consultants, who gave general advice, but did not take responsibility for the final form of the paper. Amongst those involved were:

The Rev. Boris Anderson
Canon John Arnold
Sydney Bailey
The Rev. Simon Barrington-Ward
The Rev. Arnold Bellwood
The Rev. Donald Black
The Rt. Hon. the Lord Elton
Mr. Peregrine Fellowes
Father Sergei Hackel
Mr. Hugh Hanning
The Rev. David Harding

The Rev. John Hastings
The Rev. W. J. Milligan
The Rev. Paul Oestreicher
The Rev. John Reardon
The Rev. Edward Rogers
Mr. Michael Rose
Canon Peter Schneider
Canon H. R. Sydenham
Members of the Council on Christian Approaches to Defence and
Disarmament

Hearing
Dr. Paul Abrecht
The Very Rev. Alan Webster (also in Hearing on World Justice
and British Economic Priorities)
The Rev. Robert Whyte

2. *World Justice and British Economic Priorities*

Group
Dr. Jeremy Bray, M.P.
Canon David Edwards
Mr. Reginald Green
Mr. Alfred Latham-Koenig
Dr. James Mark
Mr. Richard Miles
Mr. Owen Nankivell
Miss Mildred Nevile
Dr. Colin Pritchard
The Rev. John Reardon
Dr. Radha Sinha
Mrs. Phyllis Starkey
Miss Pauline Webb

Hearing
Mr. Richard Bingle
Mr. Francis Cripps
Dr. Harry de Lange

3. Law, Freedom, Justice and Equality

A composite report was prepared on the basis of work done by several bodies within the British Council of Churches and by the Christian Frontier Council, which offered to follow up its earlier work on the theme of equality. Main participants, apart from British Council of Churches staff, were:

(a) from the Christian Frontier Council:

Mr. Alistair Forrester-Paton

Mr. Mark Gibbs

(b) from the BCC's Police in the Community Committee:

Mr. James Anderton

Mr. Giles Ecclestone

Hearing

The Rev. Colin Buchanan

Mr. Raymond Clarke (also in Hearing on Employment and Unemployment)

The Rev. Eric Forshaw

Miss Marion Sindell

4. Employment and Unemployment

Group

The Rev. John Atherton

The Rev. Paul Brett

Canon Peter Challen

Mr. Con Harty

Miss Margaret Kane

The Rev. David Muston

Mr. Michael Smart

Mr. Stanley Tolson

Miss Mary Towy Evans

Canon Bill Wright

Hearing

Mr. John Garnett

Mr. John Hughes

The Rev. Alan Tanner

Professor George Wedell

5. Creating Community

Group
Mr. John Bennington
Miss Dorothy Edwards
The Rev. Ronald Ferguson
The Rev. Andrew Hake
Dr. Robert Holman
Canon David Jenkins
Sister Mary McAleese
The Very Rev. Edward Patey
Mrs. Muriel Smith
Mr. Gerry Williams

Hearing
Professor Graham Ashworth
Mr. Clyde Binfield
The Rev. Harry Salmon
Miss Mary Towy Evans (also in Hearing on Education and Society)

6. Violence, Non-Violence and Social Change

Group
The Rev. Paul Ballard
The Rev. Robert Brown
The Rev. John Johansen-Berg
The Rev. Peter Matheson
The Rev. John Reardon

Hearing
The Rev. Donald Black
Sir Frank Cooper
Professor Adam Curle
The Rev. Professor James Whyte (also in Hearing on Good News for Britain Today and Tomorrow)

7. Power and Powerlessness

Group
Canon John Austin Baker
The Rev. Robin Bennett
Mr. Raymond Clarke
Professor John Ferguson
The Rev. Malcolm Goldsmith
The Rev. Robert Reiss
Mr. Garth Waite

Hearing
Mr. Giles Ecclestone
Professor Robert Moore
Mr. Alfred Stocks
Mr. Brian Worth (also in Hearing on Leadership)

8. Leadership
The Free Church Federal Council provided finance and secretarial help for this piece of work.

Group
The Rev. Michael Atkinson
Miss Mary Bray
The Rev. Robin Bennett
The Rev. Roger Greeves
The Rev. George Mann
The Rev. Edward Rogers
Mr. Michael Smith
The Rev. Michael Taylor

Hearing
Mrs. Anne Hepburn
Dr. K. B. Everard

9. Education and Society

Group
Mr. Harry Ashmall
Mr. John Barnett

Mrs. Elnora Ferguson
The Rev. John Johansen-Berg
The Rev. John Sutcliffe

Hearing
Professor Walter James
The Rev. John Richardson
Mr. Edward Semper

10. Culture, Morality and Styles of Life: The Family – Culture and Morality

The Mothers' Union undertook this piece of work.

Group
Mrs. Anne Hopkinson
Dr. A. F. Baldwin
Mr. Neil Barnes
Mrs. E. A. Birch
Mr. R. Brunswick
Mrs. J. A. Farnill
Mrs. C. M. Hallett
Miss R. Haworth
The Rev. Gerard Irvine
Mrs. A. Jahan
Mr. D. V. John
Miss H. V. Jones
Mr. G. J. T. Landreth
Mrs. A. B. Long
Mrs. Rachel Nugee
Mrs. G. L. S. Pike
Mr. Jonathan Ray
Miss Jennifer Ruddick
The Rev. David Wainwright
Mrs. M. J. Walker
Mrs. Mary Wilson

'The Homeless Mind'

Contributors
Professor André Dumas
Dr. Una Kroll

Professor Rosemary Ruether
Professor Ninian Smart
Professor John Weightman
Dr. John Wilson

Hearing
Mrs. Frances Charles
Mrs. Maidie Hart
The Rev. Leonard Moss
The Rev. Trevor Rowe
The Rev. Alberic Stacpoole
Mrs. Elizabeth Templeton

11. Good News for Britain Today and Tomorrow

Group
The Rev. Paul Ballard
Canon John Austin Baker
Miss Margaret Kane
The Rev. Arthur Meirion Roberts
The Rev. Michael Taylor

Hearing
The Rev. Gilleasbuig Macmillan
The Rev. Philip Morgan
Canon Eric Saxon
Mr. Derek Williams

12. A 'task force' took responsibility for stimulating local partici-
pation in the project and developed models for relating reflection
to action. Its members included:
The Rev. Donald Black
Miss Joan Bloodworth
Canon Stephen Burnett
Mr. Kevin Muir
The Rev. David Peel
Sister Jean Robinson
The Rev. John Reardon

Groups within the British Council of Churches, which were not formally
part of the project but which contributed in effect to it, and to

which reference is made in the text of the book, included the Directorate of Economic Studies and its regional groups, the Working Party on Britain as a Multi-Racial Society, an *ad hoc* group concerned with nuclear energy questions, an editorial group on inequality, as well as the Boards and Units of the standing Divisions of the Council concerned with community affairs, international affairs, ecumenical affairs, world mission and Christian Aid.

Staff of the British Council of Churches with special responsibilities within the project were:

The Rev. Andrew Morton (Project Co-ordinator)
The Rev. Tony Addy
Miss Ruth Anstey
Mr. Martin Bax
The Rev. Sebastian Charles
Miss Gwen Cashmore
Mr. Martin Conway
The Rev. Michael Doe
The Rev. Brian Duckworth
Miss Pamela Gruber
The Rev. Elliott Kendall
The Rev. Philip Lee-Woolf
The Rev. Harry Morton
The Rev. John Nicholson
The Rev. Krister Ottosson
Miss Jean Owen
The Rev. James Wilkie

The participation of these staff members was dependent on the support of the total executive and secretarial staff of the Council.